WITHDRAWN

AESTHETIC HEADACHES

LELAND S. PERSON, JR.

Aesthetic Headaches

WOMEN AND A MASCULINE

POETICS IN POE, MELVILLE,

AND HAWTHORNE

THE UNIVERSITY OF GEORGIA PRESS

ATHENS AND LONDON

Designed by Richard Hendel
Set in Mergenthaler Galliard
The paper in this book meets the guidelines for
permanence and durability of the Committee on
Production Guidelines for Book Longevity of the
Council on Library Resources.

Printed in the United States of America
92 91 90 89 88   5 4 3 2 1

Library of Congress Cataloging in Publication Data

Person, Leland S.
   Aesthetic headaches: women and a masculine poetics in Poe,
Melville, and Hawthorne / Leland S. Person, Jr.
     p. cm.
   Bibliography: p.
   Includes index.
   ISBN 0-8203-0985-0 (alk. paper)
   1. American fiction—19th century—History and criticism.
2. American fiction—Men authors—History and criticism. 3. Women
in literature. 4. Sex role in literature. 5. Poe, Edgar Allan,
1809–1849—Characters—Women. 6. Melville, Herman, 1819–1891—
Characters—Women. 7. Hawthorne, Nathaniel, 1804–1864—Characters—
Women. I. Title.
PS374.W6P47 1988   87-12536
813'.3'09352042—dc19   CIP

British Library Cataloging in Publication Data available

for Connie, Lynnan, and Michael

This, then, is the reason why woman has a double and deceptive visage: she is all that man desires and all that he does not attain. . . . He projects upon her what he desires and what he fears, what he loves and what he hates. And if it is so difficult to say anything specific about her, that is because man seeks the whole of himself in her and because she is All. She is All, that is, on the plane of the inessential; she is all the Other. And, as the other, she is other than herself, other than what is expected of her. Being all, she is never quite this *which she should be; she is everlasting deception, the very deception of that existence which is never successfully attained nor fully reconciled with the totality of existents.*

Simone de Beauvoir, *The Second Sex*

Woman, in the picture language of mythology, represents the totality of what can be known. The hero is the one who comes to know. As he progresses in the slow initiation which is life, the form of the goddess undergoes for him a series of trans-figurations: she can never be greater than himself, though she can always promise more than he is capable of comprehending. She lures, she guides, she bids him burst his fetters. And if he can match her import, the two, the knower and the known, will be released from every limitation. Woman is the guide to the sublime acme of sensuous adventure. By deficient eyes she is reduced to inferior states; by the evil eye of ignorance she is spellbound to banality and ugliness. But she is redeemed by the eyes of understanding. The hero who can take her as she is, without undue commotion but with the kindness and assurance she requires, is potentially the king, the incarnate god, of her created world.

Joseph Campbell, *The Hero with a Thousand Faces*

CONTENTS

ACKNOWLEDGMENTS

Parts of chapters 5 and 7 originally appeared in *American Literature* and *Studies in American Fiction* respectively; I wish to thank the editors of those journals for their permission to use some of that material here in a revised form. Although I may be charged (or credited) with doing here what I observe Poe, Melville, and Hawthorne doing in their fiction—feminizing my discourse by incorporating (or appropriating) a feminist perspective—I want to acknowledge a special debt to Annette Kolodny and Nina Baym, whose readings of male-authored texts have obviously influenced and informed my own. *Aesthetic Headaches* has been fathered as well. I especially want to thank Reginald L. Cook, for setting a standard of thoroughness and integrity I am still trying to reach; Alan H. Rose, for showing me how to read literary texts in his own original way; Terence Martin, for showing me by his own example how to write; and Frederick Kirchhoff, for encouraging me to write and revise and, most of all, finish. Indiana University-Purdue University at Fort Wayne provided me with a sabbatical leave during the fall of 1984, enabling me to write the bulk of the manuscript. I wish to thank Cheryl Truesdell and especially April Allen-Devine for being the next best thing to a library.

CHAPTER ONE

The Feminization of a Masculine Poetics

On a brilliant day in May, in the year 1868, a gen-
tleman was reclining at his ease on the great circular
divan which at that period occupied the centre of the
Salon Carré, in the Museum of the Louvre. This com-
modious ottoman has since been removed, to the extreme
regret of all weak-kneed lovers of the fine arts; but the
gentleman in question had taken serene possession of its
softest spot, and, with his head thrown back and his legs
outstretched, was staring at Murillo's beautiful moon-
borne Madonna in profound enjoyment of his pos-
ture. . . . He had looked out all the pictures to which an
asterisk was affixed in those formidable pages of fine print
in his Bädeker; his attention had been strained and his
eyes dazzled, and he had sat down with an aesthetic
headache.

Henry James, *The American*

The "aesthetic headache" that Christopher
Newman suffers at the beginning of Henry
James's *The American* seemed to me an appropriate figure for a phenomenon I shall ex-
amine in the fiction of Edgar Allan Poe, Herman Melville, and Nathaniel Hawthorne: the problem that male authors and characters
experience as, their attention "strained" and their eyes "dazzled," they
attempt to respond to women associated in one form or another with

art. This study began, in fact, when I noticed how frequently these three authors characterize women through artistic imagery and how often they depict male-female relationships in aesthetic terms. Women are regularly compared to statues, paintings, or other art objects; male artists often struggle with problems of representing women in various media; women characters are frequently portrayed as artists or as sources of artistic vision. In general, it seemed to me that these writers used women characters to dramatize and explore problems in their creation and experience of art. Not only did they sense a similarity between male relationships to women and relationships (as creators or observers) to works of art; they also used female characters to test the limits of aesthetic form, to represent the conflict they felt between objectifying and open forms. Their works reflect a tension between identification with women whose creative energy resists easy formalization and the containment of such women in artistic forms that subject creative energy to the artist's control—often to the detriment of the work as a whole.

Certainly the subject of women in American literature has been extensively treated in recent years, most often in typological studies that assign discrete and usually rather limited meanings to female characters. Many critics, notably Leslie Fiedler and Joel Porte, have analyzed the familiar motif of the Fair Maiden and Dark Lady, while others, such as William Wasserstrom and John Eakin, have examined more specialized character types such as the American or New England girl. In *The Faces of Eve,* Judith Fryer expanded the categories for nineteenth-century heroines to include Temptresses, American Princesses, Great Mothers, and New Women. All of these studies tend to identify Woman, positively or negatively, as an *Other* with whom male characters must come to terms. To Fiedler, the Dark Lady is a "surrogate for all the Otherness against which an Anglo-Saxon world attempts to define itself," while to Porte she represents the "darkest secret of human sexuality."[1] Wasserstrom argues that in genteel literature American girls were "designed to represent the whole range of attitudes and ideals, achievements and failures, that defined civilization in the United States." Eakin's characterization of the New England girl is very similar: "Woman functioned as an all-purpose symbol of the ideals of the culture, the official repository of its acknowledged moral code, and she appears accordingly as a redemptive figure in the fiction of the era."[2] Fryer's classification is only a little more complex. Her Temptresses and

American Princesses, for instance, are acknowledged elaborations of the Dark Lady-Fair Maiden dichotomy, although she does focus on the development of these character types from simplicity to complexity.[3]

Although all of these studies offer important insights into the use of character types, they tend to ascribe a single meaning to a particular character type. To assume that such meaning inheres in character—fixed and static—from the beginning to the end of a novel does a disservice to many authors. More important, such typological criticism of female characters is rooted in a reductive, oppositional, essentially phallocentric concept of male writing, which emphasizes male authority and dominance over female characters and, through them, female readers. Such a view of male writing ignores the potential complexity of a masculine poetics—for example, the possibility that male writers use female character types in order to challenge or even subvert their objectifying power. According to this prevailing view of male writing, women characters are reduced to allegorical or symbolic "others"—"mirrors for men," in Cynthia Griffin Wolff's terms—whose truth inheres not in their "ability to capture feminine experience of women's life-problems," but in their "capacity for revealing masculine dilemmas and postulating fantasized solutions to them."[4] As Judith Fetterley argues in *The Resisting Reader,* male writers not only define experience in male terms but also represent women as scapegoats or enemies, "others" from whom men often violently dissociate themselves.[5] Joyce Warren attributes such negative attitudes toward women to the pervasive influence of American individualism. "Like the legendary Narcissus," she maintains, "the American individualist focused on his own image to such an extent that he could grant little reality to others," and in privileging an "inflated image of the male figure, his image of women is proportionately diminished."[6]

For these critics, female characters (as well as the female reader, who is encouraged to identify with them and thus against herself) are reduced in male-authored texts to positive or negative signs of male values. Narcissistic mirrors reflecting male concerns, such characters are robbed of their complexity and their personhood, subordinated to the authoritarian rule of the phallus. As Jane Gallop puts it, "The rule of the Phallus is the reign of the One, of Unicity," and men who are "arrested" in that phase are "obsessively trying to tame otherness in a mirror-image of sameness."[7] Male writers, in other words, want not only to control the texts they create but also to exercise a patriarchal authority over the female characters they embed in those texts. Indeed, for many feminist critics, the exercise of such authority is the sine qua non of a masculine poetics; describing women means inscribing patriarchal power. As Sandra Gilbert and Susan Gubar argue in *The Madwoman in the Attic,* traditionally "the text's author is a father, a progenitor, an aesthetic patriarch whose pen is an instrument of generative power like his penis." This "author-father is owner of his text and of his reader's attention," as well as the "owner/possessor of the subjects of his text, that is to say of those figures, scenes, and events—those brain children—he has both incarnated in black and white and 'bound' in cloth or leather."[8] As Gubar herself contends, the longstanding patriarchal or phallocentric model of creativity has reduced the female to the status of the male's "passive creation—a secondary object lacking autonomy, endowed with often contradictory meaning but denied intentionality." She is, in short, an art object: "she is the ivory carving or mud replica, an icon or doll, but she is not the sculptor."[9]

The depiction of women as art objects, which is a prominent feature of many works we shall examine, obviously suggests the myth of Pygmalion and Galatea. Not surprisingly, at least one critic has discovered that myth behind several American novels (including *The Blithedale Romance*) and has argued that they, too, reflect the exercise of patriarchal authority over women. "The reiteration of this myth in literature," maintains Judith Montgomery, "must be ascribed to its successful fusion of two basic impulses in man: creation and possession—here, the creation of the beautiful object and possession of that object by himself alone."[10] Montgomery, in other words, views Pygmalion as a version of Narcissus, projecting himself and his self-centered ideals upon a female object, thereby reducing her to a reflection of him.

It is not my intention in this study to offer an extended apology for male writers or to argue that they have simply been misinterpreted or misunderstood by feminist critics. There can be little question that all three writers considered here depict marked ambivalence toward many of their female characters, or that women in their texts are commonly associated with danger and destructiveness. Furthermore, from a feminist point of view, the stories they tell about women almost always end in failure and very often involve the woman's death (*e.g.,* Ligeia, Madeline Usher, Isabel Glendinning, Beatrice Rappaccini, Zenobia). Without trying to mitigate the designs of such narratives or their effect on female readers, I wish to argue that current views of male writing, particularly those that have been inferred from the depiction of female characters in works by men, have not done justice to the complexity of a masculine poetics. Although there is certainly evidence of phallo-centrism in the fiction, these three writers do not take an exclusively phallic view of male identity or creativity. Even a cursory look at their fiction serves to distinguish it from what Leslie Fiedler has called the "male novel"—sadomasochistic, demipornographic, exploiting sex and aggression.[11] And, while these male writers may still be essentially narcissistic—self-centered and masculine—it is simplistic to maintain that, in their creation of female characters, they are therefore mis-ogynistic, obsessed with possession and dominance. Narcissism does not preclude a desire to explore a variety of relations between a privi-leged male self and a female other—even a desire to surrender power to women. If women are still to some extent mirrors for men, in other words, they are not simply passive reflectors. Indeed, these male writ-ers commonly invest their female characters with extraordinary creative power that resists objectification in art: statues come to life, the figures in paintings seem to leave the canvas and dissolve their frames, or the objectifying language of art proves inadequate to express the meaning of women's characters. In effect, such female characters respond to men out of their "otherness," offering a new vision—a reflection of themselves—that men may imitate.

Although Nina Baym has made a case for Hawthorne as a feminist or protofeminist writer, none of these three writers was very interested in examining the social and political status of women. Each writer was interested in gender and gender-related issues, but more often from a psychological than from a social or political point of view. By con-sistently representing the failure of male efforts to objectify women, for example, these three writers came at least implicitly to many of the same conclusions as modern feminist critics about the dangers (to men and women alike) of exercising power over women. An objectified image of woman, like an excessively structured text or a rigid male self, they realized, is clearly limiting and limited, stifled in its potential for change and growth and in its exercise of creative power. Interestingly, these male writers anticipate some of R. D. Laing's conclusions about what he calls "petrification" and "depersonalization"—the tendency to objectify others, "to turn someone else into stone, by 'petrifying' him," to negate "the other person's autonomy," and to regard him "as a thing."[12] Such an individual, Laing says, "is trying to be omnipotent by enclosing within his own being, without recourse to a creative relationship with others, modes of relationship that require the effective presence to him of other people and of the outer world." But Laing also notes the "tragic paradox" of such defensive strategies, the counterproductive, even self-destructive effects of defending the self by objectifying or petrifying others. The "more the self is defended in this way, the more it is destroyed," he points out; the destruction is "caused by the inner defensive manœuvres themselves" (77). Thus, to deaden or petrify the other is to deaden and depersonalize the self—to treat the self as an alien object.

Many of the works we shall examine feature the sort of self-destructive defensiveness that Laing notes. In projecting women into art objects in order to contain their creative energy, male characters repress those aspects of their own minds—especially their own creative power—with which women are identified; they thus run the risk of committing themselves to a creative process that is not only destructive of women but self-destructive as well. Most important, these male writers seem aware of the problem. The objectification of women which feminist critics have decried, in other words, should be understood as an extreme that male authors themselves recognized to be destructive both to the male self and to a masculine poetics. They are consistent in equating the objectification of women with personal and artistic failure.

Not only do these writers demonstrate that objectification is seldom successful or desirable; more positively, they explore the possibility of discovering creative power through communication with an other—woman and/or text—by cooperation and receptivity to the other's presence and the other's discourse. By focusing on the moments when women cease to be male creations or mirrors for men, moments when male characters are most dazzled by women's vitality and creative power, they hold out the hope that, through relationship, they can share in women's creative power. The tendency among these writers, in other words, is to deconstruct conventional masculinity, which manifests itself in objectifying power over women, in order to achieve a "feminized" creative self, which comes into being through the surrender of power *to* women. Rather than objectifying women, these writers "subjectify" them. Instead of creating Galatea in order to satisfy a need for possessive power, the American Pygmalion wants

Galatea to create herself and, in the process, to create him—to create her creator.

The "feminization" of creativity, then, manifests itself in the fiction both negatively and positively: negatively, in such works as "Ligeia" and "The Fall of the House of Usher," where female characters simply resist objectification without achieving significant, self-expressive power; positively, in such works as *Pierre, The Blithedale Romance,* and *The Marble Faun,* where female characters are artists in their own right and represent an alternative, female poetics. As I have noted, in fact, rather than conforming their female characters to type as a means of controlling them and thereby enhancing their own sense of power, these authors use female characters to test and challenge the limits of verbal, imagistic, and literary form—and thereby the limits of male authority. They commonly invest such characters with qualities or impulses that are either resistant to form or sponsor new forms. Identified with the creative vitality of the work as a whole, often granted the power to generate the text itself, women characters regularly "dazzle" the male imagination (to borrow a term from James and from Roland Barthes), virtually transcending the representational power of language and image. As Barthes says in *A Lover's Discourse,* "I cannot classify the other, for the other is, precisely, Unique, the singular Image which has miraculously come to correspond to the specialty of my desire. The other is the figure of my truth, and cannot be imprisoned in any stereotype (which is the truth of others)."[13]

In exploring the possibility of a "feminized" masculine poetics, male writers were implicitly challenging cultural norms. Inarguably, the dominant ideology of maleness in nineteenth-century America was the Jacksonian cult of masculinity and its emphasis on action, energy, rugged individualism, and aggressive self-reliance. Andrew Jackson himself, according to David Pugh, represented "this nation's first official prototype of the manliness ethos."[14] The Jacksonian mystique exaggerated ideological and psychological conflicts in American culture and, in particular, polarized American thinking along gender lines. As John William Ward put it, American men increasingly divided life into "two parts, one the province of the home, the other that of the practical world."[15] Identifying themselves more and more with the practical world, men gradually came to define themselves and their masculinity in opposition to women. "For men to define and to assert their masculinity," says Pugh, "they had to seek its opposite so that it could be rejected or avoided as inferior." This meant women or, "more precisely, femininity" (61). Men wanted to "prove themselves worthy of society's rewards and superior to the effeminate gentility and high culture they despised" (40). In becoming "simply an adjunct to the home," Ward argues, the American male identified himself with a "function in which virtue, appreciation of the arts, or leisure time had no organic part" (193).

Even within the home, the manliness ethos encouraged men to exercise increasing authority. Working outside the home gave men new status and "special authority" because they "performed those mysterious activities that maintained the entire household"; consequently, they became "more distant, less nurturant."[16] In their sexual relationships as well, men were advised to be assertive and "avoid the slightest hint of femininity" and to follow an "archaic male ethos—one in which physical vigor, and particularly aggressive sexual behavior was a central component."[17] Nancy Chodorow, in fact, considers such antifeminism a central component of the attainment of masculine gender identity. In his "attempt to gain an elusive masculine identification," she says, a boy "often comes to define this masculinity largely in negative terms, as that which is not feminine or involved with women." The effects are twofold: the repression of "whatever he takes to be feminine inside himself," and the denigration of "whatever he considers to be feminine in the outside world."[18]

Given the identification of masculinity with vigorous, self-reliant activity both inside and outside the home, it must have been difficult indeed for male writers to reconcile their profession with their masculinity. After all, Nina Baym points out, writing in nineteenth-century America was clearly "established as a woman's profession, and reading as a woman's avocation." Being a writer, therefore, according to the dichotomous terms of the masculinity cult, meant being what John Cawelti calls an "emasculate gentleman."[19] Ironically, then, the male writer faced the very problem that Gilbert and Gubar describe for women who attempted the pen: being a writer in a culture which identified authorship with the other gender. To solve this problem, it seems to me, these male writers tried to accommodate the feminine in their fictional works and in themselves, not by exercising power over women, but by identifying the creative vitality of the works with the women embedded in them. If to be a writer was to be a woman, to surrender the text to powerful women was to identify with woman's creative power, to become creatively empowered in the feminine.

In this regard it is important to recognize that, despite its dominance, the Jacksonian mystique did not offer the only model for masculine behavior in nineteenth-century America. Counterpointing the cult of masculinity, for example, was the ideal of the Christian gentleman—an ideal of selflessness, courtesy, even passivity. The "essence of gentlemanliness," according to Edwin H. Cady, "is to learn to 'postpone' ourselves for the well-being of others, to protect others from ourselves."[20] In his relationships with women in particular, the Christian gentleman was an "athlete of continence, not coitus, continuously testing his manliness in the fire of self-denial. This paradigmatic figure eschewed excess in all things and, most important, allowed his wife to dictate the nature of their sexual interaction" (Rosenberg, 139).[21] Rosenberg points out that nineteenth-century American men were trapped between the relatively "feminine" ethos of the Christian gentleman and the archaic male ethos of the masculinity cult (150), but the ideal gentleman really combined traditionally masculine and feminine characteristics. In certain respects, he represented an ideal of feminized masculinity. Cady, moreover, associates each of the three writers in this study with Christian gentility. He sees "fragments of gentlemanly notions" in Poe and notes that Melville and Hawthorne both use ideas of gentlemanly conduct in their writing (Cady, 30–31).

It would be a mistake to press the analogy too far, of course, for in several respects the values of Christian gentility were incompatible with the romantic aesthetic espoused by Poe, Melville, and Hawthorne. While Christian gentility stressed the subordination of passion to reason, a central tenet of romanticism was the surrender of rational control over the creative process, the emergence of another passionate, essentially nonrational, creative self. In surrendering themselves and their texts to women, moreover, these male writers clearly hoped to evoke that sort of passionate female other rather than the sort of ideally chaste maiden that a true Christian gentleman would have preferred. The paradigm of the Christian gentleman is still useful as an analogy, however, because the masculine poetics that can be inferred from the fiction of Poe, Melville, and Hawthorne does not reflect an aggressive, objectifying male ethos but a certain passivity—the creative surrender to an other. Despite complaints about "scribbling women," psycho-

logically and aesthetically these writers tried to work out a compro-
mise, a strategy of accommodation, with the feminine.

Even though women necessarily remain "other" in their fiction and
in the experiences of their male characters, each writer depicts a variety
of relationships between male self and female other. And each, it seems
to me, offers evidence to support Laing's concept of complementarity
in human relationships: that we identify ourselves, not in opposition
to others, but in relation to others. "All 'identities' require an other,"
Laing says, "some other in and through a relationship with whom self-
identity is actualized."22 By further identifying women characters with
art—as artists or works of art that come alive within the text—the male
writer discovers an additional complementarity: an object-relation in
which both women and the work of art function as others, a relationship through which the male's self-identity as man and artist is
actualized. This process becomes understandably critical when the text
incorporates female characters and relationships between men and
women, for such relationships mirror the relationship between the author and the text. The woman within the work becomes identified with
and creates the work; she is an other who generates a text.

By surrendering creative authority over his work-in-progress to a
female character within it, the male writer becomes an observer-reader
of another's writing. He enjoys a similar relationship with both character and text. The text becomes a woman; the woman becomes a text.
Identified with each other, each is self-creative and independent of the
male writer's authority. The idea of an object-relation between author
and text (and between author and character) can be illuminated by
examining the work of Anton Ehrenzweig and Roland Barthes, because both stress an essentially nonauthoritarian, nonphallocentric relationship of the artist to the work of art—an identification of the self
with the otherness of the work and a surrender of control over the
creative or reading process.

Although Ehrenzweig focuses mainly on graphic arts in *The Hidden
Order of Art,* his theory of creativity is also applicable to literature. The
greatest level of creativity, he argues, is achieved when the artist relaxes
rational, intentional control over the creative process. He thus emphasizes an "open" visual relationship between the artist-observer and the
work of art: "syncretistic" rather than analytical vision, and an ability
to accept seemingly formless images. "In any kind of creative work,"
he says, "a point is reached where our power of free choice comes to an

end. The work assumes a life of its own, which offers its creator only the alternative of accepting or rejecting it. A mysterious 'presence' reveals itself, which gives the work a living personality of its own."23 As a primary other of male experience, women incorporated into the work of art are logical symbols for the work itself—that is, for the work's own otherness. This is doubly true in the case of those literary works in which women are identified with art objects and with a creative, self-generating principle within the work. That is, in such works, women, as well as the art objects with which they are often identified, do assume a life of their own; a mysterious presence does reveal itself within the work, most often embodied in the character of a woman.

Ehrenzweig explores an important connection between creativity and object-relations in general—that is, a similarity between an artist's relationships with other people and his relationship to the work of art. Most important, he sees a direct connection between creativity and the artist's ability to achieve productive object relationships. "Any work of art functions like another person, having independent life of its own," he says. "An excessive wish to control it prevents the development of a passive watchfulness towards the work in progress that is needed for scanning half consciously its still scattered and fragmented structure" (102). The potential result of such "passive watchfulness," Ehrenzweig says, is communication, or "conversation," between the artist and his work: "The medium, by frustrating the artist's purely conscious intentions, allows him to contact more submerged parts of his own personality and draw them up for conscious contemplation. While the artist struggles with his medium, unknown to himself he wrestles with his unconscious personality revealed by the work of art. Taking back from the work of art on a conscious level is perhaps the most fruitful and painful result of creativity" (57).

Although Ehrenzweig does not deal specifically with works of art that contain or represent other human beings or human relationships, it seems logical to suppose that such works offer exceptional examples of the phenomenon he cites. If the work of art by itself can be experienced as if it were an independent being, this should be doubly true when it actually represents another human being. By the same token, what better way is there to represent the independence of the work of art than in the independence of a fictional character who in some sense takes responsibility for inspiring and/or creating the work? The relationship between the artist and another human being is essentially the

same as that between the artist and the work of art. The best relationship in both cases will be a "conversation-like intercourse" (189)
between the artist and the other, a conversation free of the sort of "ego
rigidity" (84) by which others become mere projections subject to the
artist's authority.

That Ehrenzweig's theory of creativity should be paralleled by the
fiction is not too surprising; similar concepts of the mind and of
creativity were prevalent in nineteenth-century romanticism. In his account of the beginnings of a dynamic psychiatry, for example, Henri F.
Ellenberger notes the rise of spiritism and hypnotism in America between 1840 and 1850, a period obviously critical in the literary careers of
Poe, Hawthorne, and Melville. Hypnotism, he observes, "provided
a first model of the human mind as a double ego, a conscious but
restricted ego that the individual believes to be the only one, and a
subconscious, much wider ego, unknown to the conscious one, but
endowed with unknown perceptive and creative powers. The phenomenon of inspiration could be explained as a more or less intermit-
tent outburst into the conscious mind of psychic material, which had
been stored in the subconscious mind."[24] I shall have more to say
about each author's conception of the creative process; at this point it
is enough to say that each of them posited an essentially dualistic theory of the mind and creativity. For Hawthorne, being creative meant
having a "haunted mind," surrendering rational control of the creative
process to forces within himself—an experience very similar to the loss
of narrative control that Poe represents in his fiction. For Melville, as
Mardi and *Pierre* suggest, the most creative state of mind was experienced as possession, as being inhabited by a stranger who writes. As
Ellenberger notes, this analogy was common during the nineteenth
century: the phenomenon of inspiration was "often compared to that
of a second personality, which slowly develops underground and suddenly emerges for a while; hence the feeling of having the work dic-
tated by some kind of unknown being" (169).[25]

Of course, postulation of a psychic dualism in which the creative self
is identified with subconscious forces is consonant with traditional
contrasts between romance and novel, symbolism and allegory. As
Michael Davitt Bell has recently pointed out, nineteenth-century writers such as Poe, Melville, and Hawthorne accepted a "radically dualistic" definition of romance, whose "root meaning" was "fiction as

opposed to fact, deviant imagination as opposed to normative actuality, subversive delusion as opposed to sober truth." Bell argues that for personal, artistic, and social reasons, all five of the writers he examines (Brown, Irving, Poe, Hawthorne, and Melville) chose "deviant careers" to validate a "sense of alienation" from their culture.[26] Writing romances meant openly defying basic assumptions of nineteenth-century culture—Puritan doctrines, Scottish Common Sense philosophy, aesthetic theories of "rational mimesis." "In its heart, as our romancers learned well from their culture, fiction was irresponsible and dangerous, threatening to psychological, social, moral, even formal literary order." Writers such as Poe, Hawthorne, and Melville in particular "embraced the neurotic dualism of romance—the tension between language and impulse, form and suggestion, repression and expression" (Bell, 31, 129). Bell does not examine the question of whether the writers he analyzes might also have deviated from conventional notions of masculinity, but he does suggest that they rebelled against various constraints of form, embracing open forms that allowed considerable freedom of imagination. To say that these American writers sacrificed their social, political, and even aesthetic relations, however, is not to say that they sacrificed relation per se. The fiction demonstrates, to the contrary, that from an essentially psychological point of view these writers were fascinated by the possibilities of male-female relations. They often equated imaginative freedom with female characters and with "abnormal" male-female relationships, and they certainly seemed to recognize that their masculinity, as well as the creative power it generated, had to be dependent upon and tested by productive relations with others. Thus, they depicted female characters whose characters and meaning are beyond words, who provoke impulsive visions, who suggest meaning without definite form, who express meanings that cannot be repressed or that exist just beyond the threshold of conscious awareness.

Given the tendency among critics to emphasize male writers' power over women, their reduction of women to manageable types—in short, their conscription of women to the service of patriarchal authority and the sociopolitical status quo—it is certainly ironic that the subversive or deviant tendencies of nineteenth-century male writers should so closely resemble the resisting and subversive goals of contemporary feminist writers and critics. Indeed, I accept Catharine

Stimpson's caveat that, while male writers "may speak of, for, to and from the feminine," they cannot "speak, except fictively, of, for, to, and from the female"; however, it is interesting that the qualities in male fiction which I have noted bear striking similarities to those most prized by feminist critics in women's writing.[27] The creation of female characters who challenge male perception and resist type, whose images for men remain fluid rather than static, seems remarkably similar to the sort of fluidity which Luce Irigaray, for example, advocates in and seems to restrict to women's writing. "How can I speak you, who remain in a flux that never congeals or solidifies?" she asks. Whereas male writers, in Irigary's view, circumscribe women in their writing by reducing them to words, women are more likely in her view to discover a language of their own, a plural or multiple style that accommodates their indeterminacy: "We know the contours of our bodies well enough to appreciate fluidity. Our density can do without the sharp edges of rigidity. We are not attracted to dead bodies."[28] The male writing we shall examine, however, belies the notion that indeterminacy or resistance to the "sharp edges of rigidity" in characterizing women is an exclusively female concern. Male writers, too, appreciate the fluidity of character. Even Poe, attracted as he was to the death of beautiful women, was consistently fascinated by the vitality of women who refused to remain dead.

Much male writing also seems to anticipate Jane Gallop's advice to women to avoid "precision" in their writing in order to unsettle the "economy of the One": "Equivocations, allusions, etc. are all flirtatious; they induce the interlocutor to listen, to encounter, to interpret, but defer the moment of assimilation back into a familiar model."[29] The tendency among these male writers to subvert traditional literary forms, to depict women who cannot be codified or even understood in conventional language, inscribes a similar desire to flirt with conventional models. It bears an interesting resemblance to what Mary Jacobus regards as a salient feature of women's writing: "The transgression of literary boundaries—moments when structures are shaken, when language refuses to lie down meekly, or the marginal is brought into sudden focus, or intelligibility itself refused—reveal not only the conditions of possibility within which women's writing exists, but what it would be like to revolutionise them. In the same way, the moment of desire (the moment when the writer most clearly installs herself in her writing) becomes a refusal of mastery, an opting for openness and possibility, which can in itself make women's writing a challenge to the literary structures it must necessarily inhabit."[30] In their efforts to escape inherited conventions of British writing, of course, American writers of the nineteenth century were embarked upon an effort not too dissimilar from that confronting modern feminists. They, too, wanted to revolutionize the conditions of writing, and that meant opening up possibilities of literary form. What Jacobus characterizes as a female writer's "refusal of mastery" certainly would have been understood by Hawthorne and Melville. They, too, recognized that discovering an authentic voice meant challenging the literary structures their works must necessarily inhabit. In short, in their attempts to feminize their fiction by incorporating strong female characters, these writers help support the contentions of feminists such as Peggy Kamuf and Hélène Cixous that writing *like* or *as* a woman is something that can be achieved by men as well as by women.[31]

It is not surprising in this regard that works of fiction designed to challenge the limitations of artistic form should embody their subversive energy in female characters who challenge the social and moral order. Hester Prynne, Zenobia, Miriam Schaefer, Isabel Glendinning—all, to varying degrees, violate conventional morality and behavior patterns. Poe's female characters, so far removed from the social order and from normative moral standards, are nonetheless associated psychologically with bizarre states of mind and relationships: necrophilia, madness, incest. The socially and often sexually revolutionary energy embodied in many of these female characters is sublimated in the aesthetic form of the works. Such works thereby seem very similar to what Roland Barthes calls the "text of bliss": the "text that imposes a state of loss, the text that discomforts . . . , unsettles the reader's historical, cultural, psychological assumptions, the consistency of his tastes, values, memories, brings to a crisis his relation with language."[32] But, as we shall see, at the same time that they carry the potential for subverting formal order, these narratives illustrate the struggle between subversive energy and its repression or containment by social and artistic form.

Barthes uses similar terms to describe what he calls the "writerly" text; much like Ehrenzweig, he suggests a connection between human relationships and the object-relation of reader and text. Like the "other" who "dazzles" the lover's imagination and challenges his discourse, the writerly text is the result of a refusal to structure the text excessively and a willingness to remain open to its meanings. "The writerly text is a perpetual present," Barthes says, "upon which no *consequent* language (which would inevitably make it past) can be superimposed; the writerly text is *ourselves writing* before the infinite play of the world . . . is traversed, intersected, stopped, plasticized by some singular system (Ideology, Genus, Criticism) which reduces the plurality of entrances, the opening of networks, the infinity of languages."[33] Something analogous to this "writerly" experience occurs in many cases where male characters confront and attempt to "read" women associated with art (and thus with the text as a whole). The aesthetic experience of that encounter is of "himself writing"—of formlessness and infinity—of the text writing itself. Hawthorne expresses such an experience in moments of heightened creativity and, over the course of several works, in the power of "writing" and resisting the imposition of a deterministic form which he attributes to his female characters. Poe does so in the mysterious depths of his female characters' eyes and in their strange voices that speak many languages, as well as in their remarkable power to return from the dead. Melville's Hautia and Isabel "speak" of experiences that transcend the power of words. Woman after woman "refuses" to be structured excessively or to be "intersected" by "some singular system." Insisting upon their plurality, such female characters disrupt and even subvert male efforts to enclose them in verbal or iconographic forms. As Barthes says, "The lover's discourse is usually a smooth envelope which encases the Image, a very gentle glove around the loved being. It is a devout, orthodox discourse. When the Image alters, the envelope of devotion rips apart; a shock capsizes my own language."[34]

Although each of these writers expresses some anxiety in his characterization of women, although each of them uses female character types and depicts women objectified by men, their portraits are not two-dimensional, nor is their writing simply a medium for asserting authority or exercising domination. If anything, it seems to me, they suggest a deep reluctance to objectify women. Many of their works represent sincere efforts to explore the complex dynamics of male-female relationships. Their portraits of women are dynamic, conflictive, and represent a struggle toward open—writerly—relationships to women and toward open literary forms. Even as representations, projections, or mirrors for men—even as others—images of women in the works of these three writers are more complex and their behavior more dynamic than is ordinarily acknowledged. And in their most compelling roles, accorded the power to instruct the text, women characters simply do not conform to conventional types. Although they are inevitably *other* for men, they retain extraordinary creative power; they represent others who generate texts and empower the men who create them.

Whether or not we accept the rather enthusiastic conclusion of Joseph Campbell that the hero who can accept a woman "*as she is*" is potentially a king, an "incarnate god *of her created world*" (italics added), American literature does suggest that men's imaginative vitality depends, in art, upon achieving open, mature object-relations with women. It explores the possibility, in other words, that the artist/man who can resolve the "tragic paradox" within his own imagination, who can create and accept an elastic, "writerly" aesthetic form for his image of woman, shall free himself of "aesthetic headaches."

Taken to extremes, feminist and masculinist readings of literature can have the unfortunate effect of segregating male and female readers (and their texts) into opposed camps. Such readings encourage and seem to derive from some kind of essentialism that can perpetuate the differences that gender criticism typically attacks. I have heard some women colleagues, for example, boast of eliminating male writers from their classrooms and thus of creating a "different" canon. Instead of taking the trouble to resist the designs of male writing, the argument goes, women should simply ignore it altogether—at least until it ceases to be male or masculine (for some, an impossibility). As Hélène Cixous says, "I write woman: woman must write woman. And man, man; it's up to him to say where his masculinity and femininity are at: this will concern us once men have opened their eyes and seen themselves clearly."[36] That the reader's gender is of crucial importance to his or her interpretation of literature has been a central tenet of feminist criticism. In challenging all readers to become competent readers of female texts, on the other hand, Annette Kolodny implicitly challenges women to do the same for male texts. Kolodny has no desire to alienate men and women readers from each other's writing. Quite the contrary. As she says, if feminist critics "insist on discovering something we can clearly label as a 'feminine mode,' then we are honor-bound, also, to delineate its counterpart, the 'masculine mode.'" Although she points out that no one "has yet dared such a summation" of men's writing, in fact she resists the very idea of such "modes," believing that the richness and variety of men's and women's writing makes summation too confining.[37] I am not daring such a summation either, nor trying to reclaim male authors and their writing for male critics. My context of inquiry is obviously masculine—I suppose this study could be called "Some Notes on Defining a Masculine Poetics"—but I hope it is informed by an awareness of feminist concerns. Certainly many of the questions I have asked of these male authors and their texts, especially of the way women behave in those texts, have been prompted by feminist criticisms.

At the same time, I recognize that legitimate questions can be raised about what stance I expect the feminist reader to take either toward this critical work or toward the works it examines. My goal is not to suggest that male readers should resist the arguably misandrous designs of feminist critics, or to preempt the feminist reader from addressing the "masculine mode" of men's writing. While I would like to think of this study as an exercise in what Kolodny calls "pluralism," I am aware that a plea for pluralism can be viewed as a strategy for defusing or co-opting the power of feminist "difference."[38] I am not naïve enough to believe in an objective or gender-neutral literary criticism; however, I do hope that *Aesthetic Headaches* is a step in the direction of what Kolodny might call "Some Notes on Defining a 'Fully Humane' Literary Criticism."[39]

CHAPTER TWO

Poe's Fiction

Women and the Subversion
of Masculine Form

everal critics have noted that for Edgar Allan
Poe the best woman seemed to be a dead
woman.[1] In alleging, in "The Philosophy of
Composition," that the death of a beautiful
woman was, "unquestionably, the most poetical topic in the world,"
Poe suggested that women's deaths were somehow integral to his art.
"Killing women into art" (in Gilbert and Gubar's terms) became almost a prerequisite for the highest form of creativity. Joseph Moldenhauer argues, in fact, that Poe's protagonist-artists " 'murder' their beloved and lovely women, who already resemble works of art, in order
to further their perfection as *objets de virtu*." These symbolic murders,
Moldenhauer reasons, reflect Poe's effort to transcend life in its "cus-
tomary categories—time, space, matter, the body, sex, birth, motion,
variety, change" (294, 297). A glance at Poe's best-known stories about
women ("Morella," "Berenice," "Ligeia") seems to support the notion that his women are little more than wraith-like characters—reve-
nants, haunting and continually metamorphosing spirits, anatomized
ideals—who are mirrors for men.[2]

Whether they are idealized before or after death, Poe's female characters are identified with the masculine poetics at the center of his
writing. The ideal toward which Poe's heroes strive, most critics agree,
is a heightened rationality, the omniscient and omnipotent power of
reason. As Richard Wilbur puts it, Poe "identified poetic imagination
with the power to escape from the material and the materialistic, to
exclude them from consciousness and so subjectively destroy them,"

and he continually sought to represent a "hypnagogic state," a "condition of semi-consciousness in which the closed eye beholds a continuous procession of vivid and constantly changing forms."[3] This impulse to escape the material world and the limits of a consciousness wedded to sensual perception helps explain Poe's depiction of women as ideal representations of Beauty or as symbols of the idealizing imagination itself. Relationships with real, complex women obviously threaten imaginative self-reliance. Real women cannot be adequately encountered with a "closed eye," while dead women or women who have been "killed into art" easily become narcissistic mirrors for men. In particular, as Simone de Beauvoir has argued, because men recognize their own mortality most tangibly in the changes women's bodies undergo, "the more the features and proportions of a woman seem contrived, the more she rejoices the heart of man because she seems to escape the vicissitudes of natural things."[4] In other words, the anatomization of women and the deification of selected body parts that can be observed in Poe's tales seem to reflect a desire to transcend mortal limitations, to realize ideal and idealizing states of mind, and to avoid the contingencies of relationship.

The prototypical woman in Poe's canon is Helen in the poem "To Helen" (1831). In a letter to Helen Whitman (October 1, 1848), Poe said that he had written the poem to the "first, purely ideal love of my soul—to the Helen Stannard [actually Jane Stannard] of whom I told you" (*Letters,* 2:385).[5] Jane Stannard was the mother of one of Poe's boyhood friends, but the poem, like the later stories, offers scant evidence of being inspired by any actual woman, and Poe's sending the same poem to Mrs. Whitman further reinforces the idea that the verse expresses an all-purpose ideal. In short, the poem illustrates the typical imaginative process by which women become art objects. Poe begins with the name "Helen," but immediately abstracts her most important quality—"beauty." After an analogy to "those Nicean barks of yore," he anatomizes Helen by reducing her to two qualities, her "hyacinth hair" and "classic face." Finally, he projects her into the form of a statue in a window-niche, where she becomes Psyche, the poet's soul and muse. For Poe, then, it would seem that the most beautiful woman was not only a dead woman but also an art object that he had created. The death of a beautiful woman or the idealization of a woman in art—in both cases the woman is reduced to a beautiful object.

Poe's letters to Helen Whitman, however, explore an alternative male-female relationship much less subject to imaginative design. Even though Poe idealizes Mrs. Whitman, he imagines the possibility of a creative relationship with her, even equating his creative powers with her response to his courtship. In the same letter in which he explains his inclusion of "To Helen," he admits that his love for this real Helen has caused his "power of words" to falter. While such an admission is characteristic of romantic letters, Poe's exploration of the relationship between verbal power and love for a woman has important implications. Initially lamenting his limited power to communicate what he feels in the "depths of [his] soul," he goes on at great length, struggling to express the connection he obviously senses between writing and relationship.

> But I—who so lately, in your presence, vaunted the "power of words"—of what avail are mere words to me now? *Could* I believe in the efficiency of prayers to the God of Heaven, I would indeed kneel—humbly kneel—at this the most earnest epoch of my life—kneel in entreaty for words—*but* for words that should disclose to you—that might enable me to lay bare to you my whole heart. All thoughts—all passions seem now merged in that one consuming desire—the mere wish to make you comprehend—to make you see *that* for which there is no human voice—the unutterable fervor of my love for you:—for so well do I know your poet-nature, oh Helen, Helen! that I feel sure if you could but look down *now* into the depths of my soul with your pure spiritual eyes you *could* not refuse to speak to me what, alas! you still resolutely have unspoken—you would *love* me if only for the greatness of my love. (*Letters*, 2:382–83)

In wanting Helen Whitman to read the depths of his soul, Poe feels confident that she will be inspired to "speak" her own love for him. He thus makes his "power of words" the means by which he can evoke love—spoken love—from a woman who is herself a poet. Yet at the same time he feels that he has lost that power of words and thus his power to evoke love and, rather pathetically, he is reduced to sending Helen Whitman an old poem that he had written to another woman.

Poe's relationship to Helen Whitman, as defined and expressed in his writing, offers an entry point to his fiction. Poe was a notoriously calculating letter writer, especially when soliciting money or some personal favor, but his love letters show him adopting a persona similar to those of his narrators in his stories about women. In both cases, he identifies the male's power of creativity with his potential relationship to women. In the same letter in which he sent Mrs. Whitman "To Helen" and generally bewailed his lost "power of words," Poe grants her the power as the reader of his words to confirm his identity as a writer. Rather than realizing a creative identity in the act of creation, Poe realizes himself through Helen Whitman's reading. "At length, when I thought you had time fully to forget me (if indeed you had ever really remembered) I sent you the anonymous lines in MS ["To Helen"]. I wrote them, first, through a pining, burning desire to communicate with you in *some* way—even if you remained in ignorance of your correspondent. The mere thought that *your* dear fingers would press—*your* sweet eyes dwell upon characters which *I* had penned—characters which had welled out upon the paper from the depths of so devout a love—filled my soul with a rapture which seemed *then* all sufficient for my human nature" (*Letters,* 2:386). Poe's sense of anonymity, of being forgotten or, worse, never known at all, causes him to replace the self with language, with "characters" that the self has created out of its love. Language becomes a mirror in which he can recognize himself.[6] But for that creative and self-creative process to occur, a woman seems essential—as both the source and reader of language. To complete the creative circuit, Helen Whitman must become the created and then creative principle that will bring the writing-loving self into being. She is still idealized as "the Helen of a thousand dreams—she whose visionary lips had so often lingered upon my own in the divine trance of passion" (*Letters,* 2:387)—but she is also an other (with her own "poet-nature") whose responsive presence will confirm male identity. Always sources of tension, relationships in Poe's fiction express a similar possibility: the creation of a creative male self.

While accurate to some degree, in other words, the predominant view of Poe as an idolater, even "murderer," of women offers only a partial portrait and does not explain the tendency in story after story, for example, of idealized women to metamorphose into their opposites—for the "most beautiful" to become the "most hideous," or for dead women to come back to life.[7] My thesis is that the centrifugal tendency in Poe's imagination, which encourages the idealization and deaths of women, is matched by a centripetal tendency, a powerful if anxious attraction to the creative possibilities of relationship. This tension in Poe's imagination, moreover, accounts for the dynamic behavior of women in his tales and, because women are identified with the narrative's creative momentum, for the form that those tales assume.

Despite his narrators' comparisons of women to art objects, Poe's heroines seldom remain in such a static form. Even as male characters work to transform women into aesthetic objects, female characters resist that effort; as a result, in nearly every tale a male character's attempt to create an aesthetic effigy of a female character ends conspicuously, terrifyingly, in failure. Implicitly in tales such as "Ligeia" and "The Fall of the House of Usher," explicitly in later tales such as "The Oval Portrait" and "The Spectacles," Poe criticizes the objectifying tendencies of his male characters. The mental impulse toward idealism and its preference for secondary qualities is checked and balanced by a tendency toward participation in the physical world and an indulgence of sensation—and by recognition of the need for relationship. The essentially aesthetic process by which women are freed from their fearsome, embodied existence remains antithetical to imaginative vitality and psychic health. Evasive and repressive, it causes a serious disturbance within the male imagination and the subversion of those reductive imaginative forms in which the male imagination would contain women.

In the typical Poe scenario, the image of woman resists such a transformation (which often requires her death) and haunts the narrator-protagonist in a more threatening form. Thus, as every reader of Poe's fiction knows, many of the tales involve some "return of the repressed" —a record of "progressive hallucination," to borrow a term from G. R. Thompson, in which an image of woman seemingly assumes an autonomous life of its own to the male imagination, changes into a frightening form, and causes the disintegration of mental stability.[8] Rowena assumes the form of the dead Ligeia, Morella's daughter assumes her mother's name and appearance, Egaeus repossesses the teeth of the entombed Berenice, and Madeline Usher returns from her tomb to accuse her brother of having killed her. In these stories and in others, the male who tries to deny or change a woman in her most challenging aspect is haunted by the image he has resisted and repressed. Poe is a "haunted man," observes Daniel Hoffman, "haunted by the recrudescence, in daydream or in dream, of the spectral love-object, imprinted on the proverbial film of the deepest reel in memory's stor-age-bank, neither life nor language can ever actually assuage."[9] Put another way, the male imagination refuses to accept a two-dimensional version of the creative forces it has projected into the abstracted form of a woman. Poe's static, formalized art objects, therefore, display an alarming and compelling tendency to come independently to life. The aesthetic implications of this phenomenon are important. In Nina Baym's terms, Poe's fiction offers the "most severe indictment of imag-inative self-reliance in the entire mid-century"; his protagonists' sym-bolic journeys away from reality and into their own minds usually end "with an imagination clearly pictured as a destroying prison."[10] Poe is not explicitly antiromantic; rather, he dramatizes the limitations of a radically idealistic vision. As G. R. Thompson puts it, "Poe almost uniquely in American literature possessed the power to touch the un-seen, unconscious life, to render forcefully certain dark psychological states, to suggest the demoniac in mankind and in nature—and yet at the same time to bring a cool rationality, an ironic skepticism, and even mockery to bear on all that he examines" (67). David Ketterer has gone further, emphasizing, in his analysis of the "arabesque" vision, Poe's efforts to "melt away the rigid pattern that is imposed by man's rea-son" and to dissolve the "lines that separate one thing from another" in order to "reveal the shifting and fluid state, the quicksand, which may allow a perception of ideal reality."[11] Ketterer, moreover, points out that Poe clearly identified his female characters with the arabesque.

That is, like the other writers we shall examine, Poe represented the power of the imagination in figures of women who resist the formaliz-ing tendencies of the mind—who dazzle the male imagination and become irreducible to type. It is important to emphasize, therefore, not so much Poe's failures to depict fully realized women—"real per-sons"—but the prototypical way in which, especially in "Ligeia" and "The Fall of the House of Usher," he attempted to liberate the creative power of women within his stories. Whether the women return in fact or simply in the minds of the narrators, their returns significantly affect the nature and form of the narrative. Not only do Ligeia and Madeline Usher return from the tomb, but their returns also interrupt the nar-ratives, adapting them to the requirements of their own imaginations while the narrators passively observe—often petrified in the process.

Indeed, Madeline's startling reappearance from her tomb at the end of "The Fall of the House of Usher" directly influences the form the narrative assumes. In Poe's parable of the imagination, Madeline is associated with the depths of the mind, with human mortality and the weaknesses of the flesh. Her disease, emaciation, and death, seemingly orchestrated by her brother, leave Roderick free to exist in his mental world of "pure abstractions" (2:405). It is this world that the narrator gradually comes to share, so it is doubly ironic that the tale he reads to Roderick at the end of the story (the "Mad Trist" of Sir Launcelot Canning) should be interrupted by the sounds of Madeline's escape from her tomb. Associated in Roderick's own poem, "The Haunted Palace," with irrational forces and vision, Madeline subverts the two male characters' attempt to escape into art (in the upper reaches of the house-mind of Usher). Most important, the sounds she makes intrude and are incorporated by the narrator into the narrative he is reading. In this sense Madeline appropriates the freedom to generate a text.

The reasons for this phenomenon, it seems to me, are reasonably clear. For Poe, women characters become symbols of certain irrational but potentially creative forces within the male psyche. But through the imaginative process by which those unconscious impulses become projected into a female form, the image of woman becomes devitalized or divided in two: a repressed "content" and an abstract aesthetic "form." Because such bifurcation carries a high price—the objectification of otherwise vital aspects of the woman's character and of the imaginative forces with which they are identified—what we see in the fiction is a dynamic image of woman, a kind of fluid double exposure in which the act of creating an aesthetic or objectified image of woman spontaneously evokes a subversive or "subjectified" double. From the beginning, in other words, that circumscriptive aesthetic form tends to decompose. Most commonly, a dead woman (a "dead" image of woman) is rejuvenated, returning to life before a dazzled male imagination with such force that she all but destroys the male character and seriously disturbs the form of his narrative.

Poe's first story in which a male-female relationship figures prominently, "The Assignation" (1834), or "The Visionary," illustrates the common motif of a woman who is likened to an art object. In G. R. Thompson's view, however, "The Assignation" is a "pretended Romantic tale of passion which actually lampoons the type" (126).[12] As such, it exemplifies Poe's ability to question even while depicting a male character's effort to imagine and then wed a disembodied female spirit. It is the story of Pygmalion and Galatea in reverse.

At the outset, both the Marchesa Aphrodite and her husband Mentoni are statues who come to life. The Marchesa, whose child the hero saves from drowning in the canal, stands immobile at the entrance of the Ducal Palace: "no motion in the statue-like form itself, stirred even the folds of that raiment of very vapor which hung around it as the heavy marble hangs around the Niobe" (2:153). To begin with, then, the image of Aphrodite is essentially lifeless, contained by the aesthetic form of a statue. When the hero proves successful in rescuing the child, however, Aphrodite "starts" into life: "The pallor of the marble countenance, the swelling of the marble bosom, the very purity of the marble feet, we behold suddenly flushed over with a tide of ungovernable crimson; and a slight shudder quivers about her delicate frame, as a gentle air at Napoli about the rich silver lilies in the grass" (2:154–55).

In the context of Poe's fiction, the Pygmalion theme has special significance, for Poe's male characters ordinarily prefer the woman-as-statue to the real thing. As Edward Pitcher has argued, however, Poe actually dramatizes opposed perspectives in "The Assignation." By contrasting the narrator's objectifying vision with the more visionary perspective of the artist he meets, Poe implicitly criticizes the objectifying tendency of the male imagination. "The narrator characteristically fixes images of people and things and stores them up like so many photographs in his album-memory. . . . He lives in a world perceived as so many mimetically rendered statues, paintings, and mental photographs—a world explored and known more by sense and sense-based understanding than by imagination or insight."[13] It is appropriate, therefore, that any promise of a relationship between the hero and the Marchesa is prevented by her marriage to the old, "Satyr-like" Mentoni, a figure clearly identified with human mortality and sexuality. Mentoni can also be considered a nightmarish alter ego for the narrator himself: the part of the self that must be repressed, even exorcised, if the desired, uncomplicated, and unthreatening image of woman is to be created.

The hero of "The Assignation" is a famous collector, and among his possessions is a portrait of the Marchesa which clearly represents her in just such an idealized form: "One small, fairy foot, alone visible, barely touched the earth; and, scarcely discernible in the brilliant atmosphere which seemed to encircle and enshrine her loveliness, floated a pair of the most delicately imagined wings" (2:164). Poe's other male character is an artist whose most important feature, an almost superhuman power of reason, is expressed as a remarkable configuration of evil, sexuality, and creativity, a serpentine power of vision. "Nor can I better define that peculiarity of spirit which seemed to place him so essentially apart from all other human beings," comments the narrator, "than by calling it a *habit* of intense and continual thought . . . interweaving itself with his very flashes of merriment—like adders which writhe from out the eyes of the grinning masks in the cornices around the temples of Persepolis" (2:161). Male sexuality is projected not only into images of evil (the adders) but into instruments of perception. Instead of serving as a medium of experience—of physical involvement with the female—the impulse to become involved is transformed into a desire for distance and a power to keep the male self "apart from all other human beings." Thought as snake-like writhings from the eyes—in that one image Poe has not only sublimated sexual energy in perception, but also intimated the danger to women inherent in the male imagination.

Appropriate to this penchant for abstraction, the stranger has established himself in a garret far removed from the world below. To dream, he tells the narrator, "has been the business of my life. I have therefore framed for myself, as you see, a bower of dreams" (2:165). As Richard Wilbur points out, such arabesque chambers "symbolize a triumphantly imaginative state of mind in which the dreamer is all but free of the so-called 'real' world" ("The House of Poe," 270). In this case, however, such withdrawal into the self and identification with omnipotent reason are clearly destructive to male and female alike. Not satisfied with contemplation of the Marchesa's image in the painting, the artist wishes to remove all barriers between his imagination and its object—to transform the woman herself into an image of woman. He plans a double suicide by poison in order that the relationship which has been socially enjoined on earth may be consummated spiritually in heaven. If the most beautiful woman is a dead woman, the best relationship with her must be in death; so the achievement of such an ideal relationship requires the male character's death, as well as the female's.

Although this kind of *Liebestod* is fairly common in Poe's fiction, the posthumous "assignation" between the stranger and Aphrodite seems uncharacteristically benign, involving none of the necrophiliac connotations of such stories as "Berenice" or "Ligeia." Aphrodite, the very goddess who animated Galatea, does not herself return to life in some more threatening form.

Poe's most famous stories about women ("Morella," "Berenice," and "Ligeia," all published in the late 1830s) offer almost clinical examples of the imaginative process by which women are transformed into objects of wish-fulfillment only to revenge themselves upon the men who have so transformed them. Each story follows a similar pattern: a woman dies and then returns in some form to haunt her husband. As Daniel Hoffman observes about "Ligeia," Poe commonly imagines a "condition of blessedness, its loss, the loser's search for its recurrence in another love-object, the intensification of that love into hatred for its substitute and longing for the lost love, and a final apotheosis in which the lost love seems to reappear."14 For my purposes, however, it is not merely that plot which is important, but the implications of such a plot about the workings of the male imagination and of a masculine poetics.

Each heroine, for example, is associated with extraordinary powers of learning and knowledge. Each of them is both a tempting and a fearsome projection of the imagination, embodying some hidden aspect of the male imagination. Ligeia, for instance, "came and departed as a shadow" (2:311), and the narrator cannot even remember their first meeting; he has transformed her into a figment of his imagination whose only identity coheres around certain abstract qualities evoked by her name. By that "sweet word alone—by Ligeia," he says, "I bring before mine eyes in fancy the image of her who is no more" (2:310–11). Similarly, the deceased Berenice has been memorialized by Egaeus's imagination; her idealized form is subject to instant recall from memory: "Berenice!—I call upon her name—Berenice!—and from the gray ruins of memory a thousand tumultuous recollections are startled at the sound!" (2:210). Egaeus, moreover, admits that his love for Berenice proceeds not from the heart but from the mind. From the beginning he has abstracted her into the formal essence of woman. "I had seen her," he confesses, "not as the living and breathing Berenice, but as the Berenice of a dream; not as a being of the earth, earthy, but as the abstraction of such a being; not as a thing to admire, but to analyze; not as an object of love, but as the theme of the most abstruse although desultory speculation" (2:214).

Specifically, by fixing his attention on her teeth, which he covets as ideas (*"des idées"*), the narrator dissociates Berenice from her diseased, embodied existence just as thoroughly as the hero of "The Assignation" ignores Aphrodite's physical reality (identified with Mentoni). As David Halliburton points out, "Alienation such as Egaeus' involves a double process: replacing a true object of desire or fear with a surrogate object, and changing the true object into a more manageable form." The motive, he argues, is to "defend consciousness from something it cannot face: the teeth preserve the numinous attributes of the original object (the living Berenice) while purging it of its flesh; the protagonist, by concentrating on them, is able to forget the phenomenon from which they are detached so as to recapture it in a disguised and acceptable form."[15] As the story makes clear, however (in the revelation that Egaeus has mutilated Berenice's body by pulling out all her teeth), even the teeth gradually assume a frightening and seemingly autonomous form. Even though Egaeus cannot remember removing them, the teeth (or their images) force themselves into his consciousness until, at the climax of the story, he is forced to recognize his actions. As ideas, or knowledge, the teeth objectify that aspect of Berenice which refuses to remain repressed.

Even more than Berenice, however, Ligeia most completely fulfills the parameters of Poe's archetypal story of male relationships to women. As much as any woman of the poems, she is the incarnation of ideal Beauty, the "radiance of an opium dream" (2:311). With her skin "rivalling the purest ivory" (2:312) and her "marble hand" (2:311), she seems more than anything an animated statue.[16] Her hair, for example, evokes a comparison with the "full force of the Homeric epithet, 'hyacinthine'"; her nose recalls the "graceful medallions of the Hebrews"; her chin reveals the "contour which the God Apollo revealed but in a dream, to Cleomenes, the son of the Athenian" (2:312). But it is Ligeia's eyes and the power of vision they represent that chiefly fascinate the narrator. Suggesting a depth "more profound than the well of Democritus" (2:313), they provoke a wild curiosity to plumb their secrets. At the same time, they suggest a vision just beyond the threshold of consciousness. The feeling of mystery which they evoke is similar, the narrator says, to "certain sounds from stringed instruments" or certain "passages from books": "how frequently, in my intense scrutiny of Ligeia's eyes, have I felt approaching the full knowledge of their expression—felt it approaching—yet not quite be mine—and so at length entirely depart!" (2:314).

The narrator's anatomization of Ligeia, description through artistic analogy, makes him a Pygmalion with words. He creates a perfect woman part by part. The rest of the story, on the other hand, can be viewed as the record of the tension which this act of creation generates, as Ligeia (or her image) resists the objectifying tendency to keep her a pure product of imagination and memory.

Poe was fascinated by the gap between words and things, signifiers and signifieds, and nowhere does he represent that "difference" more thoroughly than in "Ligeia," which offers an object lesson in the power (and finally the powerlessness) of male language to define and control a woman. Michael Davitt Bell notes that Poe's tales "abound" with examples of "linguistic impotence." The narrator of "Ligeia," he says, "prefers her name, her verbal sign, to the reality it signifies," because her name "seems finally meant to keep her dead and buried." When the name has the "opposite" effect of "raising her," on the other hand, the narrator's "verbal control is shattered."[17] G. R. Thompson goes further in his ironic reading of the tale to regard Ligeia not only as the "construct of the narrator's agitated Gothic mind," but also as his "'demon,' a device of his own 'self-torture,'" and thus as an "absurdist, if serious, parody of the ideal woman" (*Poe's Fiction*, 85). The tale can also be read from Ligeia's point of view (albeit mediated by the male narrator) as an account of her own struggle to stay alive and then come back to life in the face of the narrator's efforts to kill her and keep her dead—from his point of view, to keep her under control as an imaginative creation. Rebelling against the death-in-life of objectification and against the conventional substitution of Fair Lady for Dark, Ligeia insists upon having a dynamic presence in the narrator's life—and in his narrative—through a monumental act of will. More than a record of the narrator's hallucination, the tale can be read as a male-female struggle, a battle of wills between two characters and two competing literary forms, a battle of wills finally won by a woman.

Despite the tendency to objectify Ligeia as a composition of aesthetic attributes and associations, Poe also clearly suggests her irreducibility, the presence of an identity that cannot be objectified even in imagination. In this regard I think Joseph Garrison is essentially correct in reading the tale as an illustration of the narrator's "epistemological predicament" and in observing his failure to understand Ligeia (and himself) because he is "too rational, too intellectual." As the story proceeds, Garrison notes, the narrator becomes "less and less receptive" to the revelations his rhetoric would disclose; he "imposes confining rational norms upon his quest, and finds himself at the end of the story in a condition of unrelieved bewilderment."[18] In fact, as soon as the narrator's description-creation moves past Ligeia's physical characteristics to her character, his words rapidly lose their power. Pondering the expression of her eyes and the "something" that "lay far within the pupils" of his "beloved" (2:313), he actually looks past Ligeia, hardly seeing her at all. He focuses instead on the "sentiment" her eyes arouse in him. He finally dissociates Ligeia's eyes even from that sentiment because he catalogs the other objects and experiences that produce the same emotion: a rapidly growing vine, a moth or butterfly, a chrysalis, a stream of running water, the ocean, a falling meteor, the glances of old people, one or two stars, certain sounds from stringed instruments, and even passages from books (2:314). Almost comically indiscriminate, the narrator eclipses Ligeia's image—the self-expressive power of her eyes—with his own feelings. Her "expression," he would have us believe, is equivalent to *his* emotional response. Describing her, in other words, means inscribing himself.

The closer the narrator comes to Ligeia's self (and his description moves from the expression of her eyes, to her powerful will, to the "stern passion" that consumes her, to the "wild words" she utters [2:315]), the less confidence he has in the power of his language. The more she dominates him, the more he must rely on the sort of indeterminate language that Luce Irigary says characterizes women's style. Several times the narrator emphasizes his verbal impotence in the face of Ligeia's fierce struggle for life. "Words are impotent to convey any just idea of the fierceness of resistance with which she wrestled with the Shadow," he admits (2:317). In a marked reversal of power along gender lines, Ligeia's energy silences the male narrator. Confronted by her "wild longing," the "eager vehemence of [her] desire for life," he finds himself with "no power to portray—no utterance capable of expressing"—what he sees (2:317–18).

With Ligeia's death, the narrator abandons all pretense to mature relationship; whether or not he actually murders her, her death serves his purposes by enabling him to regain at least temporary imaginative control over her image. As Evan Carton puts it, "Only after [Ligeia] has been dispatched to memory and physically supplanted by the wholly serviceable Rowena can the narrator assert his own mastery."[19]

Admitting that his "memory flew back, (oh, with what intensity of regret!) to Ligeia, the beloved, the august, the beautiful, the entombed," for example, he "revelled in recollections of her purity, of her wisdom, of her lofty, her ethereal nature, of her passionate, her idolatrous love" (2:323). This image of Ligeia has been purged of its threat—and of its suggestive meaning—for as we have seen, abstracting a "real" woman into a more manageable and less complicated form results in her devitalization and death. The rest of the story graphically illustrates the hallucinatory imaginative process by which Rowena is transformed into the image of Ligeia, the process by which the resilient Ligeia intrudes into the narrator's consciousness and into his narrative.

The image of Ligeia which is finally superimposed upon Rowena is hardly the ethereal lady of "angelic aspect" the narrator has imagined. Indeed, he finds the artistic tables abruptly turned, for instead of conforming to the stereotype of a two-dimensional object, Ligeia possesses the power to petrify the narrator. He is "paralyzed" and "chilled" into "stone" by the "crowd of unutterable fancies connected with the air, the stature, the demeanor of the figure" which rush through his brain (2:329). This is not the incipiently passive and creative state of romantic desire, because instead of surrendering creative control to the image of Ligeia, the narrator has become self-enclosed and resistant to her dazzling presence. As the shrouded form unloosens the "ghastly cerements" which encase her head, "there streamed forth, into the rushing atmosphere of the chamber, huge masses of long and dishevelled hair; *it was blacker than the wings of the midnight!*" (2:330). And as he beholds the "full, and the black, and the wild eyes" of Ligeia (2:330), the narrator once again apparently fears the experience they portend, for he "shrieks" aloud. Instead of Ligeia's sponsoring or encouraging a new aesthetic form, the sort of "free form" of which Ehrenzweig speaks, the narrator breaks off his narrative at the moment of her greatest strength.

My reading of "Ligeia" complements those of G. R. Thompson and others who view the narrator as self-deluded and the object of at least some authorial irony. Indeed, whether the story is read as a supernatural account of Ligeia's resurrection or as a psychological account of the narrator's hallucination, Ligeia herself has a powerful creative presence in the text. Either as a symbol of the narrator's creative potential or as a creator in her own right, Ligeia resists objectification, death, and denial.

Poe's own identification of Ligeia with creative vitality becomes clearer in his revision of the story for the New York *New World* in February 1845. Not only did he add the poem "The Conqueror Worm," but he attributed the poem to her. He even notes that, just before her death and just after the narrator has admitted that he has "no power" to portray her desire for life, Ligeia makes him repeat the verses she has composed, as if she would have him read the poem into his imagination and accommodate her creative voice in his subjective narrative. When read as Ligeia's creation, "The Conqueror Worm" can be viewed as an embedded critical text which expresses her perception of her fate as a woman. To be sure, on one level the poem and the play that is its subject are about human mortality. The Conqueror Worm is Death, reducing all human life to "human gore." But from Ligeia's point of view the play "Man" can have a more pointed reference; pleading her case for eternal life to God, the Divine Father, she can also be complaining about her victimization at the hands of men. The imagery she chooses to express her sense of Man's fate, of course, has special significance to her experience as a woman and a wife. As Joel Porte puts it, "from Ligeia's point of view, the play is the tragedy 'Woman' and its hero the conquering male organ."[20] Conjoining death and sexuality in the figure of the Conqueror Worm, she complains of the male tendency to conquer and reduce women to objects.

Although Poe suggests the possibility of change in his narrator in the direction of a more open mind and a more open relationship to Ligeia, he does not show successful fulfillment of the possibility. To argue as Eric W. Carlson does, for example, that, with Ligeia's reappearance, the narrator is "reunited with the Ligeia depths in himself," is to ignore the narrator's terror and his abrupt termination of his narrative at a point when, conceding Ligeia's creative significance, he might be expected to achieve a fresh creative vision.[21] On the other hand, from Ligeia's point of view, and from Poe's to the extent that he identified with her, the end of the tale is a triumph. Having attempted to repress and then reform Ligeia, the narrator sees her returning to consciousness with redoubled fury and in a "dishevelled" condition that suggests resistance to any rigid form. Having attempted to project a benign image of Ligeia into the deceased form of Rowena, the narrator finds himself unable to control such a dehumanizing imaginative process. He is unable, finally, to create the harmless art object he desires, and he must end his narrative at the precise point when the powerful Ligeia subverts it and threatens to take it over.

"The Fall of the House of Usher" (1839) certainly represents Poe's most sophisticated subjective narrative. As numerous critics have argued, the story is a compelling account of an interior journey in which characters and setting operate as projections of a single narrative mind. Richard Wilbur, for example, identifies Roderick Usher as the narrator's "visionary soul" and sees the latter's narrative as a "journey into the depths of the self": "we must understand *'The Fall of the House of Usher'* as a dream of the narrator's, in which he leaves behind him the waking, physical world and journeys inward toward his *moi interieur,* toward his inner and spiritual self. That inner and spiritual self is Roderick Usher" ("The House of Poe," 265). While Joel Porte also identifies Roderick as the narrator's artistic double, he goes a step further by arguing that Roderick's "secret subject, with an obvious but unacknowledged borrowing from Byron, concerns what can be called the Manfred Syndrome: the artist brother's illicit and finally murderous passion for his twin-sister" (*The Romance in America,* 67).

Although both the narrator and Roderick have been extensively analyzed, Madeline's role in the "interior journey" and in Poe's parable of art has received much less attention. This is understandable, of course, because Madeline obviously plays a much smaller role in the story than, say, Ligeia played in hers. Nonetheless, because Poe's male protagonists (and first-person narrators) are so similar in "Ligeia" and "The Fall of the House of Usher," because he represents a very similar imaginative and psychological process (climaxed by the return of a repressed or deceased woman), it seems reasonable to associate Madeline with Ligeia, particularly in her identification with the depths of house and mind. For Eric Carlson, she represents the "moral energy" in the "split Usher self," while to Colin Martindale she is a malignant anima figure or "Terrible Mother";[22] but whether or not her "content" can be reduced to such terms, Madeline's character and role do suggest a third aspect of the single mind at the center of Poe's house-mind metaphor—a scarcely perceptible female form which haunts both male characters and is closely allied, I shall argue, with creativity. Because of what happens to Madeline, the story as a whole depicts an abortive interior journey which discovers (and finally evades) the creative potential of male-female relationship. "The Fall of the House of Usher" can thus be considered Poe's most dramatic account of the male's self-destructive repression of women.

In accepting Roderick's invitation to visit the house of Usher, the narrator enters a world of decadent art; although books and musical instruments proliferate in Usher's studio, they "failed to give any vitality to the scene" (2:401). That loss of vitality, moreover, can be linked to Roderick's declining relationship with Madeline. Indeed, Roderick has withdrawn within himself so far that he suffers from a "morbid acuteness of the senses" (2:403) and feels oppressed by all sense impressions. He cannot eat; "he could wear only garments of certain texture; the odors of all flowers were oppressive; his eyes were tortured by even a faint light; and there were but peculiar sounds, and these from stringed instruments, which did not inspire him with horror" (2:403). The tolerance of certain music—and that of the most tenuous kind—is revealing, for it indicates an artistic mind at odds with the material and temporal world. Anything which asserts the inextricable participation of the self and the artistic imagination with the physical world—anything that intimates the relationship between self and other—mitigates the artistic tendency to project a purely fantastical world out of the self. As Renata Wasserman observes, Roderick's state of mind suggests an "absolute refusal to enter into relations with the Other," and his art, which is "antirational" in both genesis and form, according to Charles Feidelson, "is terrifying in its escape from the canons of reason."[23] At the same time, of course, Roderick's invitation to the narrator suggests his desire to rediscover such relations—and to have the narrator serve as a medium for that rediscovery.

The most insistent material presence for the isolated Roderick is his sister Madeline, and he admits that his "peculiar gloom" has its origin in her "severe and long-continued illness" and "approaching dissolution" (2:403–4). Madeline's mysterious illness, a "gradual wasting away of the person" (2:404), corresponds to the tendency of Poe's male artists to destroy, emaciate, and disembody the female in order to formalize her image in art. Moreover, Roderick's relationship to Madeline is a symptom of his artistic deficiencies: a desire to create "pure abstractions" (2:405). "If ever mortal painted an idea," the narrator observes, "that mortal was Roderick Usher" (2:405). Symbolically, Madeline threatens such imaginative self-reliance. In her illness (which parallels her brother's), she is identified with human mortality and the limitations of the body. In his effort to escape mortal limitations, to live in a mental realm of pure abstractions free of sensual oppression, it is not surprising that Roderick should project his fears of the flesh on Madeline—that she should become another example of what Beauvoir considers man's palpable encounter with the "deteriorations of the flesh."

Such an alienated condition of soul and mind is dramatically expressed both in Roderick's miniature painting and in his poem, "The Haunted Palace." An example of Roderick's "phantasmagoric conceptions" (2:405), the painting of a tunnel that lies "at an exceeding depth below the surface of the earth" graphically represents his withdrawn and isolated self. "No outlet was observed in any portion of its vast extent, and no torch, or other artificial source of light was discernible; yet a flood of intense rays rolled throughout, and bathed the whole in a ghastly and inappropriate splendor" (2:405–6). The perfect representation of that locked chamber within the mind in which both the female and the inspiration (the "flood of intense rays") she represents are entombed, the painting also foreshadows Madeline's fate at the hands of her brother and his friend.

Roderick's poem, on the other hand, depicts a mind haunted by its own repressed imaginings. An allegory both of his mental state and of the predicament of the House of Usher, the poem corresponds to the painting in its image of a mind dominated by "monarch Thought" (2:406) which is able, at least temporarily, to create art. The first four stanzas, in fact, express a condition of aesthetic bliss in which "Spirits moving musically / To a lute's well-tunéd law" remain wholly under the control of the artist's reason. The creative faculty, moreover, is clearly characterized as feminine, and in this part of the poem the female principle appears thoroughly benign and uncomplicated, a projection of regally masculine thought and a mind

> Through which came flowing, flowing, flowing
>   And sparkling evermore,
> A troop of Echoes whose sweet duty
>   Was but to sing,

In voices of surpassing beauty,
    The wit and wisdom of their king.

(2:407)

The final two stanzas, on the other hand, complicate such a trouble-free mental state, as subterranean forces erupt into the palace of mind and art. The "evil things, in robes of sorrow" that besiege and over-throw the "monarch's high estate" (2:407) suggest that the artist has lost control of the creative process, which has been taken over by the unconscious. Although such a condition might promise the openness of the primary process, it is clearly viewed as dangerous in Poe's story, for it describes what will happen in the rest of the story, as the order of Roderick's and the narrator's minds is disrupted by the rejuvenated Madeline.

When Madeline abruptly dies, Roderick insists, in an obviously dis-placed ritual of repression (of the figure who most threatens his "pure abstractions"), that she be entombed for a fortnight in one of the vaults in the main building. As Carlson comments, "Madeline's illness and entombment, comparable to the illness and death of Ligeia, sym-bolize the suppression of the deeper self by the amoral and over-refined sensibility of her brother" ("Poe's Vision of Man," 17). In becoming a willing accomplice in Madeline's burial, moreover, the narrator allies himself with Roderick and with Madeline's repression. The location of Madeline's tomb "immediately beneath that portion of the building in which was [his] own sleeping apartment" (2:410) suggests that, like most of Poe's male characters, the narrator is destined to have a haunted sleep.

In the remainder of the story Poe emphasizes both the narrator's growing understanding of Roderick's relationship to Madeline and the meaning of both characters to his own experience. Indeed, for the rest of the story the relationship between the narrator and his host grows increasingly close—so close, according to G. R. Thompson, that the story can be read as the "progressive hallucination of the two pro-tagonists" (90).[24] Thus, as the narrator becomes aware, apparently for the first time, of the "striking similitude between the brother and sis-ter" (2:410), he begins to recognize the deleterious effect of Madeline's death on her brother. Just as Madeline's tomb, like the room in Roderick's painting, is "entirely without means of admission for light" (2:410), the narrator now observes that the "luminousness" of Roderick's eye had "utterly gone out" (2:411). That potential for illumination, in other words, has been buried in the mind, suggesting very explicitly the importance of the woman and of the unconscious with which she is identified for the artistic imagination. And even the narrator himself feels implicated in Roderick's benighted condition. "I felt creeping upon me, by slow yet certain degrees," he says, "the wild influences of his own fantastic yet impressive superstitions" (2:411).

The source of those superstitions, the "irrepressible tremor" (2:411) that both characters subsequently experience, is, of course, Madeline. Like other apparently deceased women in Poe's fiction, Madeline retains a powerful residual effect on the male imagination. Even as the two men screwed down the lid of her coffin, the narrator noted the "mockery of a faint blush upon the bosom and the face, and that suspiciously lingering smile upon the lip which is so terrible in death." (2:410). And soon afterwards, as the two men ascend into the upper reaches of the house, Roderick begins to feel haunted by Madeline's person. The entire landscape seems animated by "impetuous fury" (2:412), and while Madeline's cell emits no light, the land around the house now seems luminescent. The "under surfaces of the huge masses of agitated vapor, as well as all terrestrial objects immediately around us," the narrator comments, "were glowing in the unnatural light of a faintly luminous and distinctly visible gaseous exhalation which hung about and enshrouded the mansion" (2:412). Poe's choice of words is interesting in this description, for Roderick had depicted a "flood of intense rays" rolling through the subterranean chamber of his painting (and his mind), and he now perceives a landscape flooded by similar rays of light. The "illumination" extinguished from Roderick's eye and associated with the chamber in which Madeline is entombed seems to have erupted to "enshroud" house and mind alike. Indeed, the use of the word "enshroud" is especially suggestive, for when Madeline herself actually appears, she too is described as "lofty and enshrouded" (2:416).

Despite this agitation of the atmosphere, however, both male characters attempt to avoid the implications of events. The narrator, for example, tries to rationalize away the luminous vapor in a scientific explanation about "electrical phenomena" (2:413), but, most importantly, he suggests that he and Roderick assuage their fears by escaping into a world of romance—by reading a book about the "Mad Trist" of Sir Launcelot Canning. As elsewhere in Poe's fiction, art seems to offer an alternative to experience. Almost immediately, however, art and life become confused, and the deeper into the story they go, the stronger becomes its evocative and symbolizing power. Like Ligeia's eyes, the story suggests a meaning well beneath the surface of its form, until, finally, the creative unconscious, liberated in the abandonment of reason to the enchanting power of art, seems to evoke the figure of Madeline Usher. Art exerts such a powerful effect on the narrator's mind that its version of reality is reproduced in the world.

In keeping with the house-mind symbolism of the story, the "Mad Trist" details Ethelred's violent efforts to gain admittance to the dwelling of a hermit, but, given the two male characters' state of heightened awareness, the story acquires symbolic meaning in its recitation. As Ethelred tries to break down the hermit's door, the sound reverberates through the Usher mansion and becomes, to both male characters' imaginations, the sound of Madeline breaking out of her subterranean tomb. Joel Porte, among others, has recognized the suggestive ambiguity of the "Mad Trist" and its virtually autonomous effect on events. From Roderick's point of view, he argues, the "sexually tempting sister is the 'dragon' that has infested and corrupted the 'palace' of his soul." For Madeline, on the other hand, the "sexual dragon is her lustful and attacking brother" (68). Whatever the psychosexual symbolism of the dragon, the story makes clear that, to the minds of Roderick and the narrator, Ethelred is projected as Madeline, a woman as questing *male* knight seeking entrance into the sterile imagination of her hermit brother. That Madeline should be fictionalized as a man suggests, it seems to me, how completely Roderick has cut himself off from productive object-relations. Initially, as fraternal twins, Roderick and Madeline complement each other; here, in assuming a male guise, Madeline is much more a narcissistic mirror-image of her brother—as if in burying her, Roderick has meant to repress her sex, her womanhood. The narrator of "Ligeia" had substituted one woman for another and then watched passively—even petrified—as his effort proved unsuccessful. In "The Fall of the House of Usher," a more radical substitution is also a failure. In returning from the dead (whether in fact or in imagination), Madeline subverts male designs—her inscription or fictionalization as a man—and appears in her own person, ironically, to cause the death of the *male* twin who has repressed and unsexed her. When Ethelred falls upon the dragon, killing him with his mace, the tale forecasts Madeline's shocking entrance into her brother's room. Even though her form is "emaciated," her meaning for her brother's imagination retains considerable power.[25]

As it becomes increasingly subjective, the end of the tale seems (to the narrator) to be occurring within Roderick's mind. Roderick's eyes become "bent fixedly before him," "throughout his whole countenance there reigned a stony rigidity," and he seems entirely "unconscious" of the narrator's presence (2:415, 416). Roderick seems, in other words, much like the narrator of "Ligeia," to be a passive host for a violent internal struggle that proceeds largely against his will. The male artist, avatar of reason and the deliberate, abstracting imagination, having repressed the female figure who represents that otherness which is inimical to his theory of art, sits passively while a vengeful—a compensatory—image of woman, her robes stained with blood, forces itself upon him, so shocking him in the process that his house and mind disintegrate. And as in other Poe stories, the deaths of Madeline and Roderick, the mutually exclusive and twinned opposites fighting for control of the narrator's mind, signal a virtual death of the imagination, the dissolution of the single, composite mind represented in the story. As Thompson argues, the "sinking of the house into the reflecting pool dramatizes the sinking of the rational part of the mind, which has unsuccessfully attempted to maintain some contact with a stable structure of reality outside the self, into the nothingness that is without and within" (90).

For Poe, the best woman may very well have been a dead woman, but, as the endings of nearly every one of his stories make clear, the process within the male mind by which an image of woman is deadened inevitably results in the woman's revitalization. The state of heightened consciousness or pure rationality which seems to accompany the devitalization or disembodiment of women is violently disrupted by the very forces which have been sublimated or repressed. For nearly all of Poe's protagonists, in fact, the repression of all but the most benignly idealized image of woman consistently results in a violent shock to the creative imagination, as the woman in effect refuses to be repressed and so returns, often in a vengeful form, to assert her freedom from male domination and manipulation. And by robbing the woman of those elements in her being which he fears, by transforming her into an art object and thus containing her identity, the male character robs self and art alike of their vitality. Like Roderick Usher, he falls victim to the "terrors he had anticipated" (2:417), while an image of woman which had seemed to promise the fulfillment of a supernal and abstract beauty subverts masculine form and disrupts a male narrative.

Despite his desire for imaginative freedom, Poe seems to have recognized the inevitable implication of his mind and of his art in relationships with others. The stories we have examined certainly illustrate the danger of avoiding such relationships or attempting to reform others—particularly women—in the image of the self. Although none of the stories about women published after 1839 compares in complexity with "Ligeia" or "The Fall of the House of Usher," Poe did continue to explore the issues that those stories had raised. In fact, in "The Oval Portrait" (1842) and "The Spectacles" (1844) he much more explicitly criticizes the male attitudes he had treated largely by implication in earlier tales. In "The Spectacles," for example, he illustrates the dangers of projecting women into radically opposed "characters," while in "The Oval Portrait" he explores the difficulties of representing women in art without threatening their integrity. Both tales support the conclusion that the male imagination can be deadly, particularly when it turns its attention to women.

"The Oval Portrait" can certainly be considered the prototypical treatment of the Pygmalion myth in American fiction; it anticipates Hawthorne's "The Birth-mark" and *The Marble Faun,* as well as Melville's *Pierre.* At the same time, however, like those later fictions, instead of simply fulfilling male desires for creation and possession— dominance over women—Poe's tale illustrates the cost to male and female alike of the male artist's penchant for objectifying a woman's character in art.

Having been wounded in some unidentified battle, the narrator of "The Oval Portrait" lodges one night in a chateau in the Apennines, where, in a state of "incipient delirium" (2:663), he is attracted to a series of paintings. When he originally published the tale as "Life in Death" (*Graham's* magazine, April 1842), Poe created this highly subjective vision by having the narrator take opium; in the revision, he attributes it to the protagonist's wound and to the quality of the painting itself, thus making the tale much more an account of the relation between an artist-observer and a largely independent, female art object.26 Initially acting the role of objective observer and critic, the narrator gradually becomes drawn into the act of viewing until he suffers a lapse of will and self-control, a loss of self in art.

By emphasizing the subjectivity of what follows, Poe is able to explore as explicitly as possible the imaginative process of male responses to women, and by making his narrator an observer and only a secondhand participant, he is able to achieve a greater perspective on this process than he had in the earlier tales. When the narrator discovers "the portrait of a young girl just ripening into womanhood" (2:663), he responds impulsively, without deliberate thought. He is both attracted to the image of the woman in the painting and unaccountably frightened, and, unlike the artist whom Ehrenzweig describes, he struggles to regain rational control over his vision. He shuts his eyes in an "impulsive movement to gain time for thought—to make sure that my vision had not deceived me—to calm and subdue my fancy for a more sober and more certain gaze" (2:663). Poe's analysis of his narrator's mind in this scene suggests an opposition between reason and imagination, consciousness and the unconscious, and he explores how such an opposition impinges upon an image of woman, which becomes similarly divided. Shutting his eyes means breaking the link between mind and object—between the female image which provokes a deeply subjective response and the perceiving mind. It results in something of a short circuit, enabling the male character to regain control of the mind and mental process which have, in the presence of a woman, momentarily exceeded his control. It also makes the woman much more a product of the perceiving mind than a subject in her own right.

Anticipating the animated quality of the famous "chair-portrait" in *Pierre,* the portrait of the young woman is striking for its vitality and for its suggestion of a visual conflict between formlessness and form. Without sharp boundaries, the "arms, the bosom and even the ends of the radiant hair, melted imperceptibly into the vague yet deep shadow which formed the back ground of the whole" (2:664). That is, Poe offers the first of many examples of a woman's aesthetic image that dissolves the limits of artistic form; to be precise, the image of woman within the male mind refuses to conform to the objectifying "frame" of the male's thought. Instead of imprisoning and objectifying a woman, the painting seems to enhance her character, as if she refuses to be captured in two dimensions but inclines toward a condition of formlessness or fluidity and the suggestion of a reality beyond the reductive powers of art. In stark contrast to more typically diseased, dead, or imaginatively disembodied woman, this aesthetic image of a woman possesses a vitality which threatens to burst the circumscriptive bounds of aesthetic form.

In addition, the portrait enjoys a measure of autonomy; it insists, as it were, upon a viewing—like Ligeia or Madeline Usher forcing the male character to be a largely passive observer. With his gaze "riveted upon the portrait," the narrator admits, "I had found the spell of the picture in the absolute *life-likeliness* of expression, which, at first startling, finally confounded, subdued and appalled me" (2:664). Poe, of course, does not specify the portrait's "appalling" qualities, any more than he does those of Ligeia or Morella or Madeline Usher. As much as anything, it seems to me, it is the autonomy, the resistance of the portrait to objectification—its *"life-likeliness"*—that the narrator finds distressing. In this, the narrator resembles the narrator of "Ligeia," who had "no power" to describe the "vehemence" of Ligeia's "desire for life." To escape the frightening implications of the aestheticized female appallingly come to life, the narrator returns the candelabrum, the source of the light by which he has been viewing the painting, to its place beside his bed. That is, again he short-circuits the perceptual process in order to gain control of the imaginative process of response which is occurring in his mind. As he searches for some rationalization by which he can disregard the vitality of the woman's appearance, he feels certain that his imagination could not have caused the illusion. "Least of all," he says, "could it have been that my fancy, shaken from its half slumber, had mistaken the head for that of a living person. I saw at once that the peculiarities of the design, of the *vignetting,* and of the frame, must have instantly dispelled such idea—must have prevented even its momentary entertainment" (2:664). By appealing to the artificiality of art, by emphasizing the frame and the form, he is able to defend himself from its meaning. In this instance, aesthetic form is clearly used to circumscribe and devitalize content. Ironically, as viewer of the oval portrait, the narrator does to the woman in the painting precisely what, he comes to learn, her husband had done to the woman herself.

Reinforcing this opposition of woman and masculine art, the narrator seeks more objective information about the painting by consulting a book he notices beside the bed. He discovers in the history of the painter and his bride an archetypal version of the essential conflict in Poe's conception of art. As Patrick Quinn observes, "The theme of 'The Oval Portrait' is that both construction and destruction may inhere in the same process—even in the specifically creative process of art."[27] The woman is the epitome of female vitality, while her artist husband is committed to a creative process that robs her of all energy and life: "And evil was the hour when she saw, and loved, and wedded the painter. He, passionate, studious, austere, and having already a bride in his Art; she a maiden of rarest beauty, and not more lovely than full of glee: all light and smiles, and frolicksome as the young fawn: loving and cherishing all things: hating only the Art which was her rival: dreading only the pallet and brushes and other untoward instruments which deprived her of the countenance of her lover" (2:664–65). Blind to everything but his own method, Poe's artist anticipates the artist-scientists in Hawthorne's "The Birth-mark" and "Rappaccini's Daughter." Like them, he "became lost in reveries" and would not recognize that he "withered the health and the spirits of his bride, who pined visibly to all but him" (2:665). Furthermore, because he is so committed to creating a lifelike portrait, he literally (in the terms of the parable) transfers his wife's vital energy into her artistic image. Because he prefers an aesthetic version of woman, because he has a "bride in his Art," he "*would* not see that the tints which he spread upon the canvas were drawn from the cheeks of her who sat beside him" (2:665). Like Hawthorne's Owen Warland, Poe's artist loses himself in the creative process; like Owen, he is momentarily successful. He is able, "for one moment," to stand "entranced before the work which he had wrought" (2:665–66) before he recognizes that his "passion" for his aesthetic bride is ultimately inhuman. At the very moment he believes the artistic image of his wife is "*Life* itself," he also recognizes that "*She was dead!*" (2:666).

For this narrator and for others, the death of a beautiful woman is not only the most poetical theme for art, but also the means by which they can project an abstracted ideal of woman. Poe makes clear in "The Oval Portrait," as he does in "The Spectacles," that when they project such an ideal, male characters commit themselves to a creative process at once destructive and self-destructive, as the vital image of woman becomes imprisoned in the deadly forms of art.

Even though it is one of Poe's hoaxes, the story of a man who marries

his great-grandmother, "The Spectacles" also represents his last significant treatment of male relationships to women. In fact, Poe's choice of
genre enables him to remain more distanced than in any other tale from
his male protagonist, and thus to explore more objectively the perceptual and imaginative problems in male visions of women. Refusing to
wear spectacles to correct an admitted weakness of vision, Simpson, the
narrator, finds himself bewitched one evening at the theater by the
image of Eugénie Lalande, the "*beau ideal*" of his "wildest and most
enthusiastic visions" (3:889). Like most of Poe's female characters,
Madame Lalande is far less a real woman than she is an abstracted and
ideal figment of the narrator's desire. And like most of Poe's male characters, Simpson therefore falls in love not so much with the woman as
with an image of her he has created. "In the mad intensity of my devotion," he admits, "I forgot everything but the presence and the majestic
loveliness of the vision which confronted my gaze" (3:894). Although
the narrator's refusal to wear eyeglasses seems rather a mechanical device
for playing a joke on him, it does allow Poe to dramatize problems of
perception and to explore in very explicit terms the workings of the male
imagination, the ways men perceive and imagine women.

Especially fitting in this regard are the engagement presents that
Simpson and his fiancée exchange. Presenting Simpson with a miniature portrait of herself, she asks that, in return, he don a pair of spectacles on their wedding day. Contrived though they are, these two
offerings suggest the alternatives so many male characters face. Putting
on the glasses suggests a clarification of vision, a willingness to encounter a woman *as she is*. The miniature, by contrast, suggests circumscrip-
tion and idealization. Enclosed within an aesthetic frame—in this case
miniaturized and thus even more repressively contained—the woman's
image is thereby disjoined from her self and objectified for the wish-
fulfilling imagination of the male. The miniature perfectly reproduces
the vision which Simpson has of his beloved, depicting her, according
to the inscription on the back, in the beauty of her twenty-eighth year.
Such an image competes, in other words, with Madame Lalande's
effort to correct Simpson's defective vision, yet the latter remains the
chief motive behind the tale. "You shall conquer, for my sake," she
says, "this affectation which leads you, as you yourself acknowledge, to
the tacit or implied denial of your infirmity of vision" (3:907).

There are obvious sexual connotations to Madame Lalande's demand

and to the story as a whole, as there are in the numerous folktales with which the story can be compared. In "The Spectacles" these connotations are muted, but the coincidence of the wedding day and the donning of the spectacles, as well as the coy manner in which the narrator phrases his acceptance of the deal, encourage that interpretation. "I will place it upon my—upon my nose—and there wear it afterward" (3:908), the narrator vows, agreeing (although he does not know it at the time) to love an old woman, a mortal woman whose inevitable aging he would rather ignore. Not only does the tale play a joke on the self-deluded male, but it leads him to the brink of a kind of ultimate carnal knowledge: making love to an old woman. The spectacles, in short, do produce a radical clarification of vision. Rather than the object of his desire, however, Simpson encounters a toothless and "'villainous old hag'" (3:911) who is eighty-two years old—the language alone suggesting the spontaneous revulsion which the male imagination attaches to such a figure.

Simpson, of course, has been tricked—and tricked by a woman. Madame Lalande is in fact his great, great-grandmother, and she, along with his friend Talbot, has been in on the hoax from the beginning. Poe, however, has made his point, and the harmlessness of the joke (the marriage has been faked, and Simpson is finally rewarded with the hand of Madame Lalande's beautiful daughter Stephanie) in no way abrogates the narrator's self-deception. He has been tricked, in other words, by his own vanity and wish-fulfilling perception, his "infirmity" of vision. Refusing to acknowledge his infirmities—his failing eyesight—he projected an image of Madame Lalande that, narcissistically, complemented his ideal image of himself. But of course the narrator's "infirm" vision is not Poe's, even though his idealization of Madame Lalande links him with the narrators of tales such as "The Assignation," "Morella," and "Ligeia." That Poe has achieved such distance in "The Spectacles" from the attitudes he seemed to treat more seriously in earlier tales, however, suggests that he should not be so readily identified with those earlier narrators.

Indeed, it seems to me that Poe was consistent over the course of his career in illustrating and critiquing a male tendency to disembody women—the attempt to preserve, usually in the form of an art object or through some other act of imagination, an image of woman which denies her human complexity and represses those very aspects of human being which the male would rather not face in himself. Efforts to differentiate women into real and ideal "characters"—to separate women from their bodies—are unsuccessful precisely because they are deadly to men and women alike. In his best fiction—in "Ligeia" and "The Fall of the House of Usher"—Poe forces his male protagonists, against their will, to sit passively in the presence of powerful women who force themselves upon their imaginations. The result may be catastrophic—the breakdown of the narrators' minds and the subversion of their narratives—but the implication is clear. Rather than being mere ephemera, the creations of an idealizing male imagination, or beautiful aestheticized objects, Ligeia and Madeline Usher resist efforts to suppress, reform, or kill them. The death of a beautiful woman may have been the most poetical topic in the world for Poe, but his tales suggest an equal fascination with women who have life, if not lives, of their own.

CHAPTER THREE

Melville's Early Fiction

Creating the (Feminine) Creative

Melville's fiction calls to mind the all-male world of the sea; his most significant human relationships are male-to-male: Tommo and Toby, Redburn and Harry Bolton, White-Jacket and Jack Chase, and especially Ishmael and Queequeg. Gene Patterson-Black says that Melville "shows us a man seeking his satisfaction through other men," Charles Haberstroh adds that Melville invariably expressed "fear and distrust of females," while Joyce Warren simply dismisses Melville's female characters, citing his "failure to grant personhood to women." Melville's women, she says, "are either little more than animated memories—traditional images of femininity as conceived by men—or overpowering nightmare figures who threaten the autonomy of the male self." Indeed, Ann Douglas argues that Melville's fiction can be read as an effort to assert a "genuine masculinity" in the face of a culture that was growing increasingly "feminized." In her view, Melville savagely attacks gentility, sentimentality, and conventional morality—all identified with "femininity"—with a kind of "narcissistic rage."[1] All of these critics consider Melville fearful, distrustful, or openly hostile to women and all they represent.

While Melville's interest in masculine worlds is undeniable, he was also interested in the possibility of creative male-female relationships. Indeed, to turn a phrase, Melville had his "femininities."[2] He regularly blurred the gender boundaries of his male characters. Billy Budd, for example, possesses a "smooth face all but feminine in purity of natural complexion," and Melville even compares him to "the beautiful woman in one of Hawthorne's minor tales." In *Moby-Dick,* several male characters play female as well as male roles. Ishmael awakens in

Queequeg's "bridegroom clasp" in their room at the Spouter Inn; yet when Tashtego falls into the sperm whale's "Heidelberg Tun," Queequeg displays his skill in "midwifery" to rescue him.[3] Similarly, while Ishmael can identify with Ahab's masculine aggressiveness, he can also identify himself as Queequeg's "wife" (32). Even Ahab, who in many ways epitomizes the Jacksonian ideal of masculinity, can be a kind of mother to Pip, acknowledging the umbilical-like tie that binds them to each other: "Thou touchest my inmost centre, boy; thou are tied to me by cords woven of my heart-strings" (428).

Melville was perceptive enough to recognize that women, no less than men (for example, Bartleby, Babo, Billy Budd), were essentially unknowable, that women must necessarily be signs to male readers or interpreters. As the narrator of "The Encantadas" remarks about Hunilla, the Chola Widow, "She but showed us her soul's lid, and the strange ciphers thereon engraved; all within, with pride's timidity, was withheld."[4] Unknowability, for Melville, did not automatically translate into absence, however. If women presented only "strange ciphers" to men, they did not thereby lose all power to express and define themselves (or to withhold "all within"), nor did they surrender all power over men's imaginations and become mere projections or mirrors for men.

Melville's novels, in fact, evidence increasing complexity in his depiction of women, and several of them explore the possibility that a "genuine masculinity," as Douglas calls it, could depend upon an imaginatively open and sympathetic relationship to a woman. Those novels that include women—*Typee, Mardi,* and *Pierre* in particular—evidence his increasing sophistication in exploring male-female relationships, his discovery of a connection between relationships to women and creativity. The most important example, of course, is *Pierre*. The relationship between Pierre Glendinning and his half-sister Isabel is clearly the most important male-female relationship in Melville's fiction and offers one of the best examples we shall see of a male character's potentially creative relationship with a woman. But *Pierre* is not anomalous, for Melville paved the way for that novel's complexity in earlier works.

From the "mute enchantress" of an early fragment, through Fayaway, Yillah, and Hautia of his South Seas romances, to Isabel in *Pierre,* Melville's fiction shows a steady, if uneven, effort not only to achieve relationships with increasingly complex women, but also to understand the aesthetic implications of those relationships. Women are identified with the kind of art that Melville most wanted to create: spontaneous, fluid, self-creative and self-propelling, the product of deep "diving" and an imaginative openness to experience. Whereas the enchantress, Fayaway, and Yillah are associated with fantastical, freely associative powers of imagination, Hautia and Isabel are identified with a symbolic vision which transcends formal and linguistic limits. In two later stories ("The Piazza" and "The Tartarus of Maids"), the possibility of self-creative relationships to women diminishes; both protagonists feel estranged from women and from creative power. In every case, however, Melville uses female characters to test the elasticity—the "writerly" potential—of the male imagination, and, like Poe, he demonstrates that excessively structured works of art, like excessively structured relationships, can have disastrous effects on creativity.

Although Melville often addressed the issue pragmatically—as a conflict between what would and would not sell—he also distinguished theoretically between two kinds of art, two ways of thinking, and two modes of composition. Opposed to intentional, rationally ordered writing was a more passive state of mind in which the imagination operated as if with a will of its own. The result was an apparently formless, but actually organically formed, work of art.

The most explicit discussion of that writerly process is in *Mardi,* inarguably the pivotal work in Melville's career, the work in which he discovered his ability to "dive" as an imaginative writer. As Warner Berthoff argues, *Mardi* is "vibrant with Melville's awkwardly obtruding impulse to bear his witness and speak his truths. Stronger than any of its 'ideas' is the impression it delivers of the phenomenon of the formation of ideas in the human mind." According to Newton Arvin, Melville was able to "grope his way forward toward a new manner [of writing] by writing alternately in several manners, no one of them quite the right one." Above all, says Richard Brodhead, *Mardi* reflects Melville's discovery that writing could be a self-creative process: "his thought is in surging motion, always moving beyond its own attainments toward a further reach." And most important, Brodhead says, is Melville's "way of keeping his books open—open both to new information and to new ways of understanding information."5

Melville himself confirms these views. In a letter to Richard Bentley (5 June 1849) he indicated that he wrote *Mardi* under a kind of compulsion: "some of us scribblers, My Dear Sir, always have a certain something unmanageable in us, that bids us do this or that, and be done it must—hit or miss."⁶ Melville usually gave artistic license to that "something unmanageable" within himself, even when he knew that the results would be critically unpopular. As he added in a famous letter to Hawthorne (1 June 1851): "What I feel most moved to write, that is banned,—it will not pay. Yet, altogether, write the *other* way I cannot. So the product is a final hash, and all my books are botches" (*Letters*, 128). The price seemed worth paying because, torn though he was, Melville remained more interested in the process of writing than in the product. He believed, and devoted much space in his novels to showing, that a new self emerges through the artistic process, that a writer discovers himself in his words. Most important, he enjoyed the creative self that emerged during the writing process. He dated his life from his twenty-fifth year and told Hawthorne that he had "unfolded" within himself untold times since then (*Letters*, 130). He confessed to Evert Duyckinck (14 December 1849) that, despite *Mardi*'s unpopularity, if he had not written the book he would not be as "wise" (*Letters*, 96).

This is not to say, of course, that repeated self-evolution could not be frustrating, even horrifying.⁷ Three times in *Mardi* Melville described creativity as a dissociative state in which a second personality emerges to dictate or write the book. In a chapter simply entitled "Dreams," Taji characterizes writing as possession by a Dionysian tyrant: "My cheek blanches white while I write; I start at the scratch of my pen; my own mad brood of eagles devours me; fain would I unsay this audacity; but an iron-mailed hand clenches mine in a vice, and prints down every letter in my spite. Fain would I hurl off this Dionysius that rides me; my thoughts crush me down till I groan; in far fields I hear the song of the reaper, while I slave and faint in this cell. The fever runs through me like lava; my hot brain burns like a coal; and like many a monarch, I am less to be envied, than the veriest hind in the land" (3:368). Hardly a conventionally romantic account of Erato's descent, Taji's creative outburst is closer to Ahab's possession by a fiend, or to Pierre's compulsive, self-devouring writing in the later stages of that novel, or to the experience Roderick Usher describes when Monarch Thought is overridden in "The Haunted Palace." Melville emphasizes a feeling of entrapment and objectification—closure rather than a fluid or open form. More than anything else, the passage reveals fear of the radical transformation of the self that surrender to such volatile inner forces portends.

Because this account of the creative process is so ominous, Melville's second is notable for its comparative serenity. Responding to King

Media's query about man's moral sense, Babbalanja describes the feeling of not always being in control of his thoughts: "My most virtuous thoughts are not born of my musings, but spring up in me, like bright fancies to the poet; unsought, spontaneous" (3:456). Instead of suffering the violent conflict between Taji and his "iron-mailed" Dionysius, Babbalanja is apparently able to reconcile the two aspects of his own dissociated self—as if he were literally recognizing himself in an other. "I seem not so much to live of myself," he says, "as to be a mere apprehension of the unaccountable being that is in me. Yet all the time, this being is I, myself" (3:457).

Having posited extreme cases of essentially the same experience, Melville appears to reconcile the two in Babbalanja's account of the writer Lombardo, who labors tirelessly on his Koztanza, the magnum opus that bears obvious similarities to *Mardi* itself.[8] Surrendering to the "unaccountable being" that inhabits the self is an act of becoming in which the writer is a "mere amanuensis writing by dictation" (3:596). Ehrenzweig has noted the difficulty for most artists in tolerating the loss of ego control over the work of art, but such acceptance seems to account for Lombardo's success. He "did not build himself in with plans," Babbalanja says; "he wrote right on; and so doing, got deeper and deeper into himself; and like a resolute traveler, plunging through baffling woods, at last was rewarded for his toils" (3:595). The climax to the process, he announces, is, "I have created the creative" (3:595).

In all three passages, Melville defines creativity as an evolving and self-creative process; the writer remains passive while his thoughts assume form through a persona they bring into being. Joyce Warren has made a compelling case for Melville's radical egotism in relationships with others, comparing him with Thoreau in his desire for a friend "who would be a reflection of himself" and "damning" him for selfishness toward his wife and children. "For Melville," she says, "the claims of the other were always subordinate to the claims of the self" (*The American Narcissus*, 130, 131). It is especially interesting, therefore, that in the relation he maintained toward his writing Melville should have adopted such a selfless stance, that he should have viewed the texts he was in the process of creating as independent others that virtually created themselves. The key to creativity and to productive object-relations with the work of art, Melville suggests, is an imaginative openness that enables a creative self to emerge through the process of composition. The writer must tolerate the formlessness of the work—the tendency of the work (or relationship) to evolve by its own momentum. It is even more striking that Melville should identify this ideal creative state with women, that female others, Hautia and Isabel especially, should become the "unaccountable beings" with whom the male must try to achieve a productive relationship.

Although not associated with women, Melville's fascination with such aspects of the creative process is particularly evident in *Moby-Dick*. While the novel as a whole can be viewed as a long meditation on the "overwhelming idea of the great whale himself" (16), numerous scenes feature extended contemplations of objects that clarify the relationship of writer and reader to the literary text. In each case, Melville describes a passive condition in which the viewer surrenders his imagination to the object in his view. Staring down at the sea from the masthead, for example, Ishmael is "lulled into such an opium-like listlessness of vacant, unconscious reverie" that he is in danger of falling from his perch; he "loses his identity" and sees in the ocean "the embodiment of those elusive thoughts that only people the soul by continually flitting through it" (140). Staring into the fires beneath the great try-pots, he enters a similarly abstracted state: "The continual sight of the fiend shapes before me, capering half in smoke and half in fire, these at last begat kindred visions in my soul, so soon as I began to yield to that unaccountable drowsiness which ever would come over me at a midnight helm" (354). The novel offers many other examples: Ishmael's meditations on the "whiteness of the whale," the giant squid, and the "grand armada" of whale mothers and calves. In each case his passive attitude toward an object allows it to work upon his imagination. Resisting the temptation to impose meaning upon the object's surface, Ishmael achieves what Barthes calls a "writerly" relation to the "text."

Perhaps the best example in *Moby-Dick,* simply because it involves a bona fide art object, is the early scene in which Ishmael scrutinizes the painting in the entryway of the Spouter Inn. With its "unaccountable masses of shades and shadows," the painting resists comprehension. Only after "oft repeated ponderings" does Ishmael "arrive at an understanding of its purpose": "Ever and anon a bright, but, alas, deceptive idea would dart you through" (20). Ishmael's final interpretation anticipates the rest of the novel: he sees a whale "in the enormous act of impaling himself upon the three mastheads" of a ship in a storm (21). But equally important is his method of contemplation. The passage describing his prolonged viewing offers an object lesson in reading the novel or any other object, for here, too, meaning and form are fluid—product of an interaction or "conversation" between mind and object. Ishmael's interpretation may be subjective, a projection of what most concerns him, but it also evolves out of a sensitive and sympathetic experience of the painting itself.

Melville, of course, recognized the danger of formlessness in the world or in art; "The Mast-head" and "The Try-Works" chapters especially show Ishmael nearly losing his identity and moral compass as he surrenders to his vision. But he nevertheless returned again and again to such scenes of contemplation—to characters who assume an open imaginative stance toward works of art that, like the Spouter Inn painting, suggest "chaos bewitched" (20). A striking number of such scenes, furthermore, involve women. In his early "fragment from a writing desk" (1839), for example, Melville describes a writer's encounter with a mysterious woman of "transcendent charms" whom he identifies with imagination and inspiration (9:203). Reclining upon an ottoman in her country villa with a lute in one hand, the "queen" of Melville's tale is an obvious example of the woman-as-muse. Like one of Poe's arabesque chambers, however, the room in which the woman resides is designed to frustrate ordinary perception. Shape-shifting and fluid, it is furnished with mirrors, which "deceived the eye by their reflections" (9:202).

Like other male characters in such circumstances, Melville's narrator feels in danger of losing control of himself. "For a moment my brain spun round," he says, "and I had not at command a single one of my faculties." "A new dominion was creeping o'er my soul, and I fell, bound at the feet of my fair enchantress" (9:203). This moment of temporary imaginative surrender is short-lived and ultimately fruitless, however. The woman is "DUMB AND DEAF"; her lips move in apparent response to the narrator's "expression of a love, that rent [his] bosom like a whirlwind" (9:203), but they make no sound. While the reasons for this metamorphosis of muse to mute remain unclear in Melville's fragment, the phenomenon itself is familiar. Aesthetically considered, the protagonist does not achieve what Ehrenzweig calls a "conversation." He "listens" but does not hear. The fragment, of course, is a juvenile effort on Melville's part and also obviously derivative. Vaguely aware that such a female figure as the "enchantress" can symbolize artistic or creative power, he has clearly not fleshed out the idea. Yet it is interesting that, even at this point in his career, Melville associates inspiration with a woman—even if he cannot as yet imagine the woman speaking.[9]

He is only slightly more successful in *Typee* (1846). Despite its grounding in Melville's experiences of 1841–42, *Typee* also involves a journey to a kind of fairyland.[10] The Marquesas are an imaginary, fantastical world at least as much as an actual one, a world of noble savages, prelapsarian nakedness, and primitive religious ceremonies—in short, a "scene of enchantment" (1:5). Their chief attraction is their radical difference from ordinary experience, their resistance to missionary efforts of conversion and reform. They represent a non-Christian, non-Anglo Saxon, non-Western world view, and they offer the possibility of unconventional relationships between men and women.

Early in his narrative, for example, Tommo relates the story of a missionary who, "believing much in the efficacy of female influence, introduced among [the savages] his young and beautiful wife, the first white woman who had ever visited their shores" (1:6). Her spectacular appearance is like the descent of "some new divinity" (1:6), the epitome of social and formal grace. To the natives, however, the woman is an alien and artificial figure. Thus, "after a short time, becoming familiar with its charming aspect, and jealous of the folds which encircled its form, they sought to pierce the sacred veil of calico in which it was enshrined, and in the gratification of their curiosity so far overstepped the limits of good breeding, as deeply to offend the lady's sense of decorum" (1:6). Melville's diction—"form," "veil," "enshrined," "decorum"—and adoption of the natives' point of view offers an obvious example of objectification, of woman transformed into an icon or statue that incarnates cultural ideals. But in this guise the missionary's wife is clearly at odds with primitive values and with nature. The "efficacy of female influence" is counterfeit; the white woman, symbol of objectifying social forms and missionary reform, is a false "divinity." Contemptuously "stripped of her garments" (1:6–7) by the islanders, she is demystified as an idol and source of humanizing influence. Like other female characters we have seen, she represents an elaborately constructed form which is ultimately without energy—as vacuous, Melville implies, as Western religions which emphasize ritual over sacred meaning.

The tendency of Melville's fiction up through *Pierre,* however, is toward the liberation of a more complex woman. Native women in

Typee, for instance, suggest a natural order of experience largely impervious to the artifice of civilized manners and conventions. Immediately following his tale of the missionary's wife, Tommo recounts an experience two or three years later in which a group of American sailors meets a native king and queen. The Island Queen at first displays, much in the manner of the missionary's wife, the effects of French influence. Beneath her "gaudy tissue of scarlet cloth, trimmed with yellow silk" (1:8), however, she reveals two elaborately tattooed legs. Like the native girl Fayaway, the Queen exemplifies a life devoid of pretense and Western sexual taboos; in the elaborate decoration of her own body, she has made herself a living work of art. The abrupt revelation of those "hieroglyphics on her own sweet form" (1:8) sends a boatload of sailors into frenzied retreat. As she throws up the skirts of her mantle, in a gesture which suggests the association of art and female sexuality, the Queen "revealed a sight from which the aghast Frenchmen retreated precipitately, and tumbling into their boat, fled the scene of so shocking a catastrophe" (1:8).

In these two incidents Melville suggests a contrast between two kinds of art objects, both of them female. The missionary's wife, a Western cultural icon, is lifeless compared to the native queen. She is the product of externally imposed form and style, her veil of calico obscuring rather than expressing who she is. Conversely, the native queen casts off her fancy French clothing to reveal the work of art she has made of herself; she embodies an aesthetic, self-expressive reality which transcends conventional forms. And it is the latter female figure, identified with female sexuality and self-expression, which Melville consistently represents in his fiction.

Melville, in fact, repeatedly associates the Marquesan women with freedom of movement and expression and with freedom from externally imposed form—in other words, with the "open" aesthetic values he was beginning to value. Because of their almost constant swimming, the native girls always appear fluid in form and in motion. Describing the "whihenies" who swim out to greet the ship and clamber up the sides, Tommo notes, "they clung dripping with the brine and glowing from the bath, their jet-black tresses streaming over their shoulders, and half enveloping their otherwise naked forms" (1:14). The girls' virtue is their "artlessness," a natural, uninhibited self-expressiveness. "Their appearance perfectly amazed me," Tommo admits; "their extreme youth, the light clear brown of their complexions, their delicate features, and inexpressibly graceful figures, their softly moulded limbs, and free unstudied action, seemed as strange as beautiful" (1:15). In marked contrast to his description of the missionary's wife, Melville's language is as free as possible of objectifying terms; words such as "artless," "delicate," "inexpressibly graceful," and "unstudied," as well as Tommo's perplexity, suggest the girls' resistance to the codifying powers of language.

Although Tommo's first impression is entirely innocent, the girls' artlessness and seminudity do cause him some anxiety. Hautia and Isabel will offer sterner tests, but even this early in his career Melville clearly felt a link between women and a superior mode of artistic freedom and creativity. As the men good-humoredly yield themselves prisoners, as social proprieties give way to emotional license, Tommo reports that the native women are "passionately fond of dancing, and in the wild grace and spirit of their style excel everything that I have ever seen. The varied dances of the Marquesan girls are beautiful in the extreme, but there is an abandoned voluptuousness in their character which I dare not attempt to describe" (1:15). Like Melville's other male characters, Tommo resists the temptation to give his imagination free rein. Despite the obvious freedom he seeks in the Marquesas, there are clearly some things—the "abandoned voluptuousness" of women at the dance—which he is reluctant or unable to describe. Nevertheless, the meaning of the scene for Tommo and for Melville is clear: the dance is living art, uninhibited, sexually expressive, essentially formless or transcendent of conventional artistic form. "Not the feeblest barrier was interposed between the unholy passions of the crew and their unlimited gratification," Tommo continues. "The grossest licentiousness and the most shameful inebriety prevailed, with occasional and but short-lived interruptions, through the whole period of [the ship's] stay" (1:15). Tommo's obvious fascination as a spectator with his shipmates' "unholy passions," coupled with his desire to censure their "unlimited gratification," is important for understanding his subsequent relationship with Fayaway; for in contrast to the dancing girls, Fayaway appears to be an almost asexual ideal, an image of woman which has been purged of physical and sexual complexity.

A pure "child of nature" (1:86) who "clung to the primitive and summer garb of Eden" (1:87), Fayaway is clearly a projection of male fantasy (even if based in fact), who offers Tommo, in Ann Douglas's words, "exactly what the American Victorian lady would deny her male counterpart: unmoralized pleasure."[11] In the terms of Melville's contrast between the missionary's wife and the native Queen, Fayaway represents no opposition of appearance and reality. Her character has not been obscured by any artificial form, precisely because she is perceived through a pure medium of desire. "The face of this girl was a rounded oval," Tommo says, "and each feature as perfectly formed as the heart or imagination of man could desire" (1:85). Fayaway can remain such an ideal, of course, because Melville dissociates her from the sort of conflict he had dramatized in the other two women—and also from the latent eroticism of the dancing girls. Indeed, Fayaway's "free pliant figure" (1:85) suggests not the wild, Dionysian abandon of the dance (or of Melville's own most creative moments) but a tendency to conform to the uncomplicated needs of male fantasy.

One of Tommo's chief pleasures as a willing "captive in the valley" (1:119), is swimming with the native girls in a miniature, circular lake. Much like the men of the "captured" *Dolly,* though without the implicit threat, Tommo finds himself at the playful mercy of the "river-nymphs" who appear like so many supernatural creatures to his dazzled imagination. "The amphibious young creatures swarmed about me like a shoal of dolphins, and seizing hold of my devoted limbs, tumbled me about and ducked me under the surface, until from the strange noises which rang in my ears, and the supernatural visions dancing before my eyes, I thought I was in the land of spirits" (1:132). Here, too, Melville describes a scene which challenges the imagination and conventional categories. The women are hybrid creatures (amphibious) with the power to introduce Tommo to a kind of primitive, preliterate language, and extraordinary visions—a realm of experience which Poe's male characters also projected but less successfully realized in women. But it should be emphasized that this primitive language suggests regression, especially when contrasted to the powerful symbolic visions that later female characters evoke. The underwater sounds of the native girls can be compared to the prenatal sounds of the womb and, in contrast to the sounds produced by later characters (Isabel with her guitar, for example), encourage no creative response.

Tommo's sojourn in Happy Valley obviously suggests an inner journey to some deep part of the psyche, a realm of preconscious forms or archetypes that results in an at least temporary union of potential opposites. Melville offers a striking portrait of an ideal union of the sexes (and art) in the androgynous figure of Marnoo, a "Polynesian Apollo" who exhibits a "matchless symmetry" of form (1:135). With cheeks of a "feminine softness" he is "one of the most striking specimens of humanity" (1:135) Tommo has ever seen. In addition, in his elaborately tattooed body, Marnoo represents the epitome of that elusive union which Melville sought between social form and primitive energy. The "oval of his countenance and the regularity of every feature reminded me of an antique bust," Tommo says. "But the marble repose of art was supplied by a warmth and liveliness of expression only to be seen in the South Sea Islander under the most favorable developments of nature" (1:135). Instead of repressing or obscuring vitality, form serves the needs of self-expression; the "marble repose of art" does not deaden but enhances "warmth and liveliness of expression." In thus transforming himself into a living work of art, Marnoo becomes a native god. His person is "held as sacred" (1:140), and when he speaks, the "effect he produced upon his audience was electric," as if they were "listening to the inspired voice of a prophet" (1:138). Here, in short, is a kind of male ideal—a perfect marriage, so to speak, of man, woman, and art in which aesthetic form is divinely capable of expressing human nature. Here, too, is Melville's ideal artist, an idealized image of himself: inspired, electric, his powers of expression and prophecy deriving at some level from the inner union of masculinity and femininity in a self-expressive aesthetic form. In reserving that accomplishment for the South Sea Islander and then only under the "most favorable developments of nature," on the other hand, Melville suggests the difficulty of duplicating that "marriage" in civilized society.

Tommo's flight from Happy Valley stems from his fear of being irrevocably changed by a prolonged stay in the Marquesas, but more specifically, he flees with "terror and indignation" from the native tattoo artist, Karky, who, he fears, will transform his face into a savage's. He is convinced that he will be "disfigured in such a manner as never more to have the *face* to return to [his] countrymen, even should an opportunity offer" (1:219). In contrast to Marnoo, then, the "diabolical" Karky represents a frightening version of the artist. In later works (most notably in *Pierre*) Melville will represent this threat (and promise) of transformation in a female character, but in *Typee*, despite earlier associations of women and art, he is careful to dissociate the fantastical Fayaway from such dangerous aspects of art. It is interesting to note that Melville does not "tattoo" the native girls—except for the three dots that Fayaway and the others have on their lips and a small design on their shoulders.[12] He not only kept his primary male-female relationship free of sexuality, but he also seemed reluctant to explore the relationship between art and the self-transforming power of mature object-relations. "From the time of my casual encounter with Karky the artist, my life was one of absolute wretchedness," Tommo says (1:231), and to underscore that impression he discovers three shrunken heads, one of which is obviously a white man's, suspended from the ridge-pole of Marheyo's house. An almost Poe-esque example of that primal Western fear of the irrational—the diminishment or shrinking of the rational powers of a mind "gone native"—the shrunken heads illustrate the metamorphic powers of primitivistic art, a native sculpture that actually uses the human body as its material. "My imagination ran riot in . . . horrid speculations," Tommo exclaims, "and I felt certain that the worst possible evils would befal me" (1:233). Not surprisingly, soon after this nightmarish encounter Tommo makes his escape.

Tommo's flight from the Marquesas is only indirectly associated with anxiety about women—his seemingly idyllic relationship with Fayaway marred by a more general fear of savagism. Yet it is interesting that in the works by Melville examined thus far, the male character's journey to a place dominated by the presence of a woman ends with his rather abrupt departure. The reasons become clearer, however, as we approach *Mardi* and *Pierre,* both of which feature a more significant relationship between women and art.

Critics discussing the role of women in *Mardi* invariably cite the allegorical contrast between Yillah and Hautia, the conventional Fair Maiden and Dark Lady, and thus a thematic opposition between innocence and experience, purity and sexuality. Merrell Davis, for example, sees Melville's hero, Taji, as torn between the two women and all they represent; Hautia is a "phantom queen, a snake, a vipress, and a shining monster, who Lamia-like has lured the Narrator to her island bower to try his constancy to an ideal."[13] Several critics, moreover, connect Melville's light and dark women and his anxiety over his marriage to Elizabeth Shaw in August of 1847. Leon Howard has shown how Melville's composition of *Mardi* was influenced by that marriage and by his wife's pregnancy; their son Malcolm was born in

February of 1849, just two weeks after Melville had finished proofreading the manuscript. Melville, moreover, often read his day's work to his wife, while she helped copy the manuscript into its final form.[14] More pointedly, Newton Arvin has viewed Taji's relationship to Yillah as the "emotional history" of Melville's marriage. Yillah is an "embodiment of the pure, innocent, essentially sexless happiness which, given his relations with his mother, Melville longed to find in his relations with some other woman." Such happiness was soon destroyed, however, by Hautia, "by the intrusion of the sensual, the carnal, the engrossingly sexual" (*Herman Melville*, 95).

My purpose here is not to refute these ideas, but to show that they do not adequately describe the role of women in *Mardi*. The tendency of the narrative, it seems to me, is toward Taji's gradual recognition that Yillah and Hautia cannot be so neatly polarized. After Hautia disrupts his seemingly idyllic relationship with Yillah, Taji does spend the rest of the novel resisting her temptations and trying to find Yillah. But Melville makes it clear that this goal is ultimately untenable, and climactically Taji comes to realize that Yillah and Hautia are potentially one and the same—in other words, that his own imagination has kept them polarized: "in some mysterious way seemed Hautia and Yillah connected. But Yillah was all beauty, and innocence; my crown of felicity; my heaven below;—and Hautia, my whole heart abhorred. Yillah I sought; Hautia sought me. One, openly beckoned me here; the other dimly allured me there. Yet now was I wildly dreaming to find them together" (3:643).

Besides the story of Yillah and Hautia, Melville includes several vignettes of male-female relationships that show him exploring the effects of marriage. King Donjalolo, for example, has thirty wives, each named for a night of the moon, although his nightly labors have produced no children. In contrast, another king, Uhia, has given up women in favor of his life's work (which is moving the island of Ohonoo to the center of the lagoon). "They shall sap and mine me no more," he says, "my destiny commands me. I will don my manhood" (3:275). Although Uhia's life's work seems futile (and thus perhaps foreshadows Taji's quest for Yillah over an "endless sea"), the effect of celibacy on his person is startling and positive. "From that time forth," Taji is told, "young Uhia spread like the tufted top of the Palm; his thigh grew brawny as the limb of the Banian; his arm waxed strong as the back bone of the shark; yea, his voice grew sonorous as a conch" (3:275).

The most important marriage in the novel and certainly the most fearsome is that between Samoa and Annatoo. Annatoo is a tigress (3:90), a terrible and voracious woman who steals and hoards anything she can get her hands on. Samoa is a "hen-pecked husband" (3:97), whose wedding the narrator compares to suicide (3:69). He has lost an arm and is thus only a "large fragment of a man, not a man complete" (3:78). The fear of emasculation, emotional and sexual inadequacy, even the loss of identity, associated with marriage to a woman like Annatoo is obvious, and in this relationship Melville undoubtedly voiced some of his own fears. In Donjalolo's case he expresses a wish for sexual experience freed of the consequences of monogamous fidelity and family responsibilities. In Uhia's case he reveals a fear of physical and sexual emasculation and the suspicion that chastity and/or bachelorhood will enhance his physical and mental integrity. Marriage to a demanding woman can make a man feel incomplete, whereas refusing to "clasp a waist" (3:275) gives him "brawny" limbs and a "sonorous" voice.

According to my reading of *Mardi,* however, Melville only briefly indulged himself in these pessimistic views of women and marital relationships. In the story of Yillah and Hautia he attempted to work his way through such common fears to recognize the possibility of a more mature and self-enhancing relationship that would help his art, even though a thorough exploration of this possibility would have to wait until *Pierre.*

Taji's violent rescue of Yillah from the priest Aleema has been widely discussed in Oedipal terms, but equally important are the aesthetic implications of his relationship with Yillah.[15] Initially, Yillah is little more than an icon or art object. She is "like a saint from a shrine" with her hands "drooping"; she is passive, virtually without an imaginative life of her own—"snow-white" and enveloped in a "gauze-like robe" (3:136). Much like the later Isabel in *Pierre,* she has only the faintest ideas about her origin; her story—indeed, the self that her remembered story constitutes—has been written over by others like a palimpsest. She is undoubtedly of European origin, as Davis has argued (130), so her story of her olive skin being "washed white" (3:137) is a fabrication given her by the priests: "For ulterior purposes connected with their sacerdotal supremacy, the priests of these climes oftentimes secrete mere infants in their temples; and jealously secluding them from all intercourse with the world, craftily delude them, as they grow up, into the wildest conceits" (3:139). Melville deserves credit in his account of Yillah's childhood for exploring the way female psychology and identity are conditioned by environment and by male myths and ideals for women. Yillah exemplifies Judith Fetterley's complaint about women who are encouraged to "identify against themselves." Worshipped as if she were divine and prepared for sacrifice, she is encouraged by the priests to regard herself as an adorable object. Such "conceits of a state of being anterior to an earthly existence," Melville explains, "may have originated in one of those celestial visions seen transparently stealing over the face of a slumbering child. And craftily drawn forth and reechoed by another, and at times repeated over to her with many additions, these imaginings must at length have assumed in her mind a hue of reality, heightened into conviction by the dreamy seclusion of her life" (3:153).

In rescuing Yillah, Melville implies, Taji has given her the opportunity to discover herself—largely through the medium of language. Whereas Yillah first appears a kind of lifeless statue, as soon as Taji speaks to her in his "own tongue," she stirs and begins to tell her story. Evoking her buried memory of the native language she lost when captured by Aleema makes it possible to restore her own potential self; replacing one language with another is to substitute one story and self for another. Yillah is more than a passive Galatea to Taji's Pygmalion, however, because Melville also explores the reciprocal relationship between her power of language and Taji's. Like Poe's Ligeia (although with different physical characteristics), Yillah is not simply passive or ephemeral; she is invested with considerable power to penetrate beneath male consciousness and to provoke a visionary state of mind. Taji says that she "gazed so earnestly into my eyes, like some pure spirit looking far down into my soul, and seeing therein some upturned faces, I started in amaze, and asked what spell was on me, that thus she gazed" (3:152). Melville's imagery is interesting in this passage, because it anticipates the metaphor of the stranger within. Although Taji resists any knowledge of Yillah that sullies her purity, Melville implies that she as well as Hautia has the power to create the creative—if the male will only enter into a properly receptive relationship with her. Specifically, he identifies her with a self-creative power of language. "Often she entreated me to repeat over and over certain syllables of my language. These she would chant to herself, pausing now and then, as if striving to discover wherein lay their charm" (3:152). In keeping with her largely maternal role, Yillah is given the power to confer meaning upon the sounds that Taji makes, to transmute sound into language.

Yillah's identification with even this primitive power of language makes her more complex than most critics acknowledge and clearly links her with Hautia, not as part of a dichotomy, but as representative of an early stage of development. But despite Yillah's promise, Taji remains unreceptive. He is tempted to keep her in her "divine" and thus objectified state. When he transfers her to his own prow, he keeps her enclosed in her cocoon-like tent and invents a story of Aleema's being "dispatched on a long errand" to explain his actions (3:140). To keep her from being further alarmed at this abrupt change, he invents a story (not unlike Aleema's) of their common past: a fable of paradise in which the two of them, like Adam and Eve, romped in innocent bliss (3:142–43). From her point of view, then, Yillah has been rescued from one male myth only to be embedded in another, created by Taji's desire for an uncomplicated, exclusive relationship with a woman. Yillah will become the "earthly semblance," Taji says, "of that sweet vision, that haunted [his] earliest thoughts" (3:158). "Her dreams seemed mine," he continues. "We lived and we loved; life and love were united; in gladness glided our days" (3:159). In *Pierre* Melville parodies this sort of imaginatively incestuous relationship; Pierre must leave his mother and her Yillah-like choice for his wife.

But even in *Mardi* Melville does not allow this blissful relationship to last. The Oedipal desire sponsors what Melville later emphasizes is a "fictitious" and psychologically fraudulent relationship characterized by resistance to change or growth. That fiction objectifies male and female alike in a condition of perpetual innocence and ignorance; it is regressive because it features such complete identification with a projected image of woman instead of a mature object-relation. The two share their dreams, participating imaginatively in a mutual, self-enclosed fantasy, and even share a kind of private language. But Melville clearly recognized the puerility of his character's relationship with Yillah, for he abruptly disrupts it. He makes Taji discover more mature relationships—first with four male companions and finally with Hautia.

Alter egos who dominate the remainder of the narrative, Taji's four companions possess specialized knowledge and are thus associated with much more sophisticated powers of language. Mohi the historian is a "venerable teller of stories and legends," Babbalanja the philosopher is "learned in Mardian lore" and "much given to quotations from ancient and obsolete authorities," and Yoomy the poet is a singer of "amorous melodies, and rondos, and roundelays, very witching to hear" (3:197). Leon Howard has argued that including these characters in his narrative enabled Melville to incorporate his voluminous reading into his work: "With these as vehicles for the expression of his unassorted ideas, Melville let his hero lose most of his character as a sailor, take on the mythological name Taji, and fall as far into the background as the requirements of first person narration and a continued allegory would permit."16

Melville's abrupt shift in his novel makes sense in his exploration of Taji's developing powers of language. Relationship with Yillah encouraged an infantile, self-reflexive use of language—almost a prelanguage—to enclose the two of them in a fantasy world of Taji's own creation. In surrendering his narrator's voice to such knowledgeable spokesmen, on the other hand, Melville was able to incorporate a male authority into his narrative, to sublimate himself as a writer in the words of others. He was also able to move from the enclosed psychological world of Taji's fantasy to the world outside the self. But even though Taji's four alter egos dominate the narrative and effectively eclipse the search for Yillah by their informed exploration of the world, Melville at least implies in his use of Hautia that Taji must free himself from these authoritative voices as well. From his own point of view, excessive reliance on literary authorities obviously impedes discovery of an original voice and the sort of organic form that he sought. As Brodhead notes, "Melville clearly feels that to be properly judged *Mardi* needs to be taken on its own terms, seen as making its own formal model rather than imitating an already available one" ("*Mardi*: Creating the Creative," 32). That form and the voice required to create it, moreover, are associated with Hautia.

Melville, however, leaves Hautia rather vaguely defined. In fact, she hardly appears in the novel at all until the last few chapters, and those are so cryptic that it is difficult to define their significance. On the other hand, Melville does "haunt" the novel with her; she appears periodically to remind Taji of Yillah but also to represent an alternative to his juvenile infatuation. Structurally, she represents Taji's final encounter before he sets sail upon his "endless sea," and as such, it seems to me, she defines a stage in his development as narrator-artist. She is characterized in language linking her to the aesthetic values of spontaneity, depth, and fluidity with which Melville was coming to terms in the novel as a whole. Whereas Yillah is associated with juvenile fantasies of wish-fulfillment and a primitive power of language, Hautia represents a symbolic vision that challenges the denotative power of language. She is not merely Yillah's opposite but an aesthetic alternative both to Yillah and to Taji's four male companions. In moving Taji through relationships with Yillah, the four male guides, and finally Hautia, Melville was working his own way from self-enclosed and self-reflexive fantasy to the interpolated use of literary models and a male authority to the symbolic expression he would achieve in *Moby-Dick* and *Pierre*.

Beginning with chapter 189 Melville attempts to resolve the issues that Hautia's presence in the novel has raised. Even though he does not clarify the meanings of Yillah and Hautia, he does suggest their respective association with fixity and openness, concreteness and fluidity. For example, when Taji reports that he hears Yillah's voice calling him from the sea, he notes, "gazing whence that music seemed to come, I thought I saw the green corse drifting by: and striking 'gainst our prow, as if to hinder. Then, Then! my heart grew hard, like flint; and black, like night; and sounded hollow to the hand I clenched. Hyenas filled me with their laughs; death-damps chilled my brow; I prayed not, but blasphemed" (3:639). Yillah's image is still complicated by the "green corse" of the slain father-priest Aleema—a sign that Taji will be unsuccessful in rediscovering a relationship to a woman until he can overcome his regressive yearning for an uncomplicated union. Appropriately, Melville attributes to this complex image of Yillah a power to objectify Taji's imagination and emotions, suggesting that his longing for the self-enclosed relationship he enjoyed with Yillah is a psychological dead end that will turn his heart to "flint."

In the next short chapter ("They meet the Phantoms") Hautia's heralds reappear, bearing a "large and stately urn-like flower, white as alabaster, and glowing, as if lit up within. From its calyx, flame-like, trembled forked and crimson stamens, burning with intensest odors" (3:640). An ironic image of the idealized Yillah (here lit up from within by flames and passions), the flower also symbolizes Hautia. Melville links the two characters once again and suggests their dynamic quality. The remainder of the novel, in which Taji moves into closer contact with Hautia, is rife with similarly vibrant imagery. The herald's flower, which is "as an urn of burning niter," abruptly "changed, and glowed like Persian dawns; or passive, was shot over by palest lightnings;—so variable its tints" (3:640). Such protean images are among Melville's favorites, as we have seen, and from the painting at the Spouter Inn to the chair-portrait of Mr. Glendinning, he uses them to signify the sort of open-ended, open-minded art (ever "lit up within") he himself most respected and most wanted to create. But Taji's first instinct is to distance himself from everything that this "passion" flower portends. Rather than remaining open to what it suggests, he steels himself (in an act of radical self-objectification) against the threat he feels in Hautia. "Away!" he exclaims, "my eyes are frozen shut; I will not be tempted more" (3:640).

Yet Taji is still wracked by "conflicting emotions" that "tore up [his] soul in tornadoes" (3:643). In particular, he finds it increasingly difficult to maintain the distinction in his own mind between Yillah and Hautia. This indicates, it seems to me, that Melville wants his hero to discover his relationship to a more complex woman than Yillah had been at the beginning of the novel. Thus, even though Taji says that he still hates Hautia, he cannot escape the feeling that "in some mysterious way" the two women are "connected"; he cannot help "wildly dreaming to find them together" (3:643). Either Taji must forsake Yillah in favor of the more complex Hautia, or he must acknowledge and accept Yillah's potential to become like Hautia.[17] According to the aesthetic values Melville has defined, moveover, Hautia is close to an ideal. She is associated with emotional freedom, openness, vitality— with resistance to rigid formality. Not only is her eye "fathomless" (3:646), but she refuses to assume a single, comprehensible form in Taji's imagination. "I see ten million Hautias!" he exclaims, "all space reflects her, as a mirror" (3:647).

The climax of Taji's experience with Hautia occurs in the final two brief chapters, as Media, Mohi, and Yoomy leave him alone in Hautia's presence. Without their reasonable advice and cautions, Taji appears more open to the dynamic experience with which Hautia is associated. "As their last echoes died away down the valley," he notes, "Hautia glided near;—zone unbound, the amaryllis in her hand. Her bosom ebbed and flowed; the motes danced in the beams that darted from her eyes" (3:650). Hautia is consistently identified with depth, mystery, intensity of vision, and a metamorphic power. Whereas Yillah served as an echo chamber or sounding board, giving meaning to Taji's words, Hautia's linguistic power is more active and creative. She would bring a new Taji into being just by saying his name. " 'Taji! Taji!—as a berry,

that name is juicy in my mouth!—Taji, Taji!' and in choruses, she war-
bled forth the sound, till it seemed issuing from her syren eyes" (3:650).
Hautia is here associated with the "stranger" within the self that is
liberated during the creative process and with a specially self-creative
power of language. In keeping with that power to bring a new, creative
self into being, she asks Taji to "dive" with her in "deep waters"—an
activity to which Melville, of course, gives special privilege in his thinking and writing.18 In short, having brought a new, creative persona
into being, Hautia encourages that writerly self to explore new ideas
and experiences.

Although Taji does dive with Hautia, he emerges empty-handed,
hardening his imagination and emotions to protect himself from
change: "Down, down! down, down, in the clear, sparkling water, till
I seemed crystalized in the flashing heart of a diamond" (3:651).
Melville implies that his failure results from diving alone, for as Hautia
says, everything he seeks may be had "for the diving," but "through
[her] alone, may these be had" (3:651). Taji's self-reliance, coupled with
his quest for an idealized mate he can incorporate unresistingly into his
own fantasies, prevents his achievement of the kind of relationship
Melville emphasizes in *Pierre*. Twice, in fact, Hautia asks Taji to "join
hands" with her and dive. If he will only "join hands," she promises,
she will take him where he will "learn to love the living, not the dead"
(3:651). But Taji rejects her offer; he is "crystalized" in his purpose of
finding Yillah. "Better to me, oh Hautia!" he tells her, "all the bitter-
ness of my buried dead, than all the sweets of the life thou canst be-
stow; even, were it eternal" (3:651).

When he returns to Hautia's bower after his abortive dive, even
though he remains committed to Yillah, Taji feels drained of energy.
Instead of an inspiriting ideal, his image of Yillah has hardened him
into mere stubbornness. In contrast to Hautia, Yillah represents an
ideal that Taji has buried inside himself: "within my inmost vault, side
by side, the Past and Yillah lay:—two bodies tranced;—while like a
rounding sun, before me Hautia magnified magnificence; and through
her fixed eyes, slowly drank up my soul" (3:652). Hautia is more than
an "emasculating witch-woman who uses all of her powers to subju-
gate man to her will" (Warren, 117). Although Hautia's ocular vam-
pirism seems to link her with other evil temptresses, we must remember that the image is Taji's and the direct result of his fear of what
she offers. So powerful a figure does Hautia appear, in other words,

that Taji feels his own life, his own identity, to be in danger. Further-more, Melville seems to recognize Taji's imaginative limitations; he distances himself from his hero by continuing to associate Hautia with life and the future—and Yillah with death and the past. More impor-tant, he uses Hautia's voice to imply that Taji's stubborn devotion to Yillah is psychically suicidal. Pointing to another cavern in the hill, she tells him, "Go, go,—and slay thyself . . . go,—dead to dead" (3:653).

Taji's dive into this second lake is a desperate, nearly suicidal plunge. Hautia has given up on him, resigning in favor of the dead and ide-alized Yillah, whom Taji thinks he sees in the water. But in marked contrast to the fiery Hautia, Yillah is only a "revolving shade," a "gleaming form [that] slow circled in the deepest eddies:—white, and vaguely Yillah" (3:653). In a startling passage, Melville clearly suggests the futility of Taji's yearning, the complete objectification and enerva-tion of his imagined ideal. Pursuit of such an ideal, he implies, results in an arrested emotional condition and estrangement from all self-cre-ative forces: "As somnambulists fast-frozen in some horrid dream, ghost-like glide abroad, and fright the wakeful world; so that night, with death-glazed eyes, to and fro I flitted on the damp and weedy beach" (3:653).

According to my view, then, Taji's quest ends negatively because of his willful rejection of a potentially creative relationship with Hautia. Although Melville does not directly comment on the final episodes, as he does in *Moby-Dick* and *Pierre,* the evidence offered by the imagery he uses to describe Taji's experience and decision to leave leads to the conclusion that Taji has been unsuccessful in his quest. In other words, in his imagination Melville recognized that Taji's rejection of Hautia and endless pursuit of the vaguely ideal Yillah constituted a psychic and aesthetic dead end—that his flight at the end of the novel repre-sented only experience postponed. Indeed, in terms of its association with a woman, that experience would have to wait through three nov-els (*Redburn, White-Jacket,* and *Moby-Dick*) before receiving its climac-tic expression in *Pierre.*

CHAPTER FOUR

Pierre *and Melville's Later Fiction*

The Caster's Ladle and Female Form

When critics examine *Pierre* (1852) as a novel of male-female relationships, they commonly focus on the opposition of the Fair and Dark Ladies, Lucy and Isabel, and rarely do they consider gender as one of the novel's ambiguities. For Joel Porte, the novel expresses the illicit attractions of sexuality: Isabel "evokes the notion of wild sexual passion," while Lucy embodies "the reserve and chastity of the Anglo-Saxon fair maiden."[1] Judith Fryer considers Isabel "Eve the temptress"—"beautiful, witchlike in her magnetism, sexually alluring yet full of danger"—although she does credit Melville with making her more "complicated" than most Dark Ladies because he "incestuously unites in her the opposites of life and death, of heaven and hell."[2] For Michael Davitt Bell, on the other hand, Lucy and Isabel represent different varieties of Romantic art. In transferring his allegiance from Lucy to Isabel, Pierre is "moving from the calm, submissive romanticism of Wordsworth to the dark, defiant romanticism of Byron."[3]

From the beginning, Pierre's introduction to Isabel is clearly associated with his initiation into the mysteries of self and art. As Hershel Parker notes, the last half of *Pierre* was written amid dispiriting negotiations with the Harpers in January 1852, and certainly Melville's popular failure as a writer (as reflected in reviews of *Moby-Dick*) accounts for much of what happens to Pierre once he enters New York City.[4] At the same time, the shape-shifting quality of Isabel's appearance, Pierre's efforts to resolve her ambiguities, as well as to compose the work of art they inspire—all represent concerns Melville had had for some time. *Pierre,* in fact, offers one of the best examples we shall see of artistic creativity depending upon a relationship with a woman; Pierre's ability to manage such a relationship is intimately linked to his ability to succeed as an artist.[5]

Pierre's most important relationship at the beginning of the novel, however, is with his mother. Mary Glendinning plays sister and wife as well, and her relationship with her son recalls Yillah's with Taji in its innocent fantasy. As such, it represents something Melville had already questioned, if not repudiated. In addition to its incestuous quality, this mother-son relationship is artistically and psychologically unproductive, a creative dead end. As William Ellery Sedgwick argues, Mrs. Glendinning "would stunt [Pierre's] growth by possessing him entirely."[6] In contrast, despite the ambiguity of her true relation to Pierre, Isabel clearly encourages him to embark upon a psychological journey toward maturity and self-discovery characterized by the subversion of everything he has taken for granted. More profoundly than even Poe's narrators in "Ligeia" and "The Fall of the House of Usher," Pierre finds himself largely helpless before a dynamic image of woman that refuses to remain a projection of his rationalizing mind.[7] Coming to terms with Isabel, emotionally and aesthetically, means learning to cope with that "mysterious thing in the soul, which seems to acknowledge no human jurisdiction, but in spite of the individual's own innocent self, will still dream horrid dreams, and mutter unmentionable thoughts" (7:71). In Ehrenzweig's terms, Pierre must become able to tolerate the apparent disorder of the primary process; in Barthes', he must give the "texts" of woman and art alike a writerly reading.

When Isabel first appears to Pierre, she is only a strangely haunting "face," a form into which he can project everything that is different from Lucy. Whereas Lucy is Pierre's "heaven" (7:36), Isabel is frightening, dazzling, not because she incarnates forces of evil, but because of her ambiguity, her resistance to any such label. She is not Lucy's opposite so much as a composite figure whom Pierre himself comes to perceive as dangerous. Thus, whenever Pierre feels haunted by "the face," he feels beset by "invisible agencies" and "things [he has] no name for" (7:37)—things, that is, beyond his power of comprehension or the denotative power of his language.

Clinging to a Manichean vision of the world in which good and evil, heaven and hell, are separate and clearly recognizable opposites, Pierre has no desire to confront the idea of an undifferentiated universe—or the idea of an undifferentiated image of woman. Identifying with Lucy, he has no desire to imagine the self that a relationship with Isabel entails. Before Isabel actually appears, then, Melville has set the stage for a repetition of the phenomenon we observed in Poe's fiction. Attracted to the "heavenly" Lucy, Pierre becomes haunted by another image of woman. But whereas Poe normally ended his tales with the return of the repressed woman, Melville begins at that point and goes on to dramatize his hero's efforts to deal with such a complex image of woman in relation to his artistic development. More presciently than any of Poe's heroines, Isabel herself seems to realize that she must depend upon Pierre for her being and her form. "Thy hand is the caster's ladle" that "holds me entirely fluid," she tells him. "Into thy forms and slightest moods of thought, thou pourest me; and I there solidify to that form, and take it on, and thenceforth wear it, till once more thou moldest me anew" (7:324). Melville devotes almost clinical attention to the mental process by which Pierre molds Isabel, the tension between Isabel's "fluidity" and Pierre's tendency to "pour" her into increasingly objectifying forms. And in addition to illustrating her subversion of masculine forms, he makes Isabel an artist in her own right.

Challenging Pierre to the depths of his being, Isabel provokes a revolution in his mind and feelings in which both self and world become virtually unrecognizable. More than a passive reflector, Isabel models Pierre's newly emerging sense of self—his sexual maturity and developing creativity—in both cases, his desire to relate self to other. She encourages him to conceive of the self in a new way as a dynamic rather than static entity. Like the narrator of "Ligeia," whose attraction to Ligeia's eyes was to a depth of experience "more profound than the well of Democritus," Pierre sees Isabel as a space opening within himself. She suggests such an unknown or unacknowledged realm of experience that he "shrank abhorringly from the infernal catacombs of thought, down into which, this foetal fancy beckoned him" (7:51). As John T. Irwin says, "This sense of the self's inherent instability, of its ability to adopt any role or mask, to become anything, precisely because in itself it is nothing, comes more and more to dominate Melville's thought."[8]

Equally important is the revolution Isabel causes in Pierre's conception of himself as a writer. Her "face haunted him as some imploring, and beauteous, impassioned, ideal Madonna's haunts the morbidly longing and enthusiastic, but ever-baffled artist" (7:48), and throughout the novel Melville uses artistic metaphors—statuary, painting, reading and writing—to describe her effect on Pierre. Edgar A. Dryden points out that *Pierre* is "the story of a reader who attempts to become a writer. His growth is rendered in terms of the development of his interpretive faculties and his maturity is defined by his decision to 'give the world a book.'"9 Melville even represents Pierre's career as a fictional text and Isabel as a hidden meaning inscribed within it. Early in the novel he notes that "so perfect to Pierre had long seemed the illuminated scroll of his life thus far, that only one hiatus was discoverable by him in that sweetly-writ manuscript. A sister had been omitted from the text" (7:7). Appropriately, Isabel first announces herself to Pierre in a letter, a self-expressive text that he must read, and Melville emphasizes the power of Isabel's writing to re-create Pierre as a reader. Dryden calls the letter a "pre-text" that "renders intelligible textual details [from Pierre's experience] which to this point have been unreadable or misread" ("Entangled Text," 163, 164). But Pierre's first reaction is to resist the letter's meaning; he gives it a "readerly" reading, structuring the text self-protectively so that it will not disturb his unexamined image of himself. Simultaneously, the halting, fragmented quality of Pierre's response prefigures his failure to achieve a safe and self-satisfying reading. "'Myself am left, at least,' he slowly and half-chokingly murmured. 'With myself I front thee! Unhand me all fears, and unlock me all spells! Henceforth I will know nothing but Truth; glad Truth, or sad Truth; I will know what *is*, and do what my deepest angel dictates.—The letter!—Isabel,—sister,—brother,—me, *me*—my sacred father!—This is some accursed dream!—nay, but this paper thing is forged,—a base and malicious forgery, I swear'" (7:65).

Pierre's initial resistance to the letter's meaning is especially important to this study because of the specific demands that Isabel expresses in this written form. The letter, which a chemical reaction between tears and ink has made appear written in blood, "indeed seemed the fit scroll of a torn, as well as bleeding heart" (7:65). No temptress who speaks with a siren's voice, Isabel not only requires Pierre to become a sympathetic, or writerly, reader, but she writes honestly—from her "bleeding heart"—the kind of sincere text that will elude Pierre for the remainder of the novel. The demand she makes upon Pierre is precisely that which might enable him to realize himself as a man and as an artist. "I perish without thee;—pity, pity," she writes, "here I freeze in the wide, wide world; no father, no mother, no sister, no brother, no living thing in the fair form of humanity, that holds me dear" (7:64). In that heartfelt statement Melville clearly defines Isabel's role in Pierre's experience: to instruct her "brother" in the self-creative potential of a relationship with her.

Indeed, within the space of a single long paragraph, Pierre effectively rereads Isabel's letter; more precisely, he allows it to read itself into his mind, past the obscuring subtext of his first misreading, and he rationalizes his new reading by noting the letter's power to "move" him emotionally. "From all idols, I tear all veils," he vows, "henceforth I will see the hidden things; and live right out in my own hidden life!—Now I feel that nothing but Truth can move me so. This letter is not a forgery. Oh! Isabel, thou art my sister; and I will love thee, and protect thee, ay, and own thee through all" (7:66).

Melville explains Pierre's abrupt change of mind through artistic metaphor. For one thing, as Eric J. Sundquist notes, "the reading of Isabel's letter destroys the sacred text that appears as the memory of his father."[10] Previously, Pierre's father existed as an ideal, a "perfect marble form," "without blemish, unclouded, snow-white, and serene," the "fond personification of perfect human goodness and virtue" (7:68), but such selective remembrance is clearly objectifying and prevents the discovery of a more mature relationship to his father. "Thrown into that fountain, all sweet recollections become marbleized; so that things which in themselves were evanescent, thus become unchangeable and eternal" (7:68). Although Pierre witnessed his father's death and heard him unaccountably cry out for a daughter (7:70), the words were entirely without context. Only Isabel's letter, which put the "chemic key of the cipher into his hands," unlocks the meaning and enables Pierre to read "all the obscurest and most obliterate inscriptions he finds in his memory; yea, and rummages himself all over, for still hidden writings to read" (7:70). Isabel's letter, in other words, establishes the necessary context in which Mr. Glendinning's originally mysterious words ("My daughter") make sense; one text enables Pierre to read the other that he has preserved unread in memory.

Many of Melville's novels support the view that he preferred male-to-male relationships and found male-female relationships inhibiting. Ann Douglas considers *Pierre* the cynosure of such feelings: a "savage study of the conspiratorial interaction between genteel religion, feminine morality, and polite literature against the interests of genuine masculinity."[11] But it is important to recognize that Pierre must work out his relationship to a variety of women (and only indirectly to his deceased father), and while his mother and Lucy clearly represent genteel religion and feminine morality, Isabel does not. Isabel, in fact, actually displaces paternal authority; she takes his father's place in Pierre's imagination—her special female authority serving as a model for Pierre's own creative experience. Isabel hardly represents the sort of suffocating "feminine sensibility" that Mrs. Glendinning and Lucy certainly do, and following her artistic lead will not cause Pierre to write the sort of sentimental fiction that Melville was clearly attacking. She encourages precisely the sort of symbolic, open-ended, and self-creative book that Melville most wanted to write. When Isabel offers to go out and teach guitar and thus to sell her art, Pierre recognizes that her special talents are not commercially viable. In that recognition, Melville links Isabel's art not with the successes of Pierre's youth (encouraged by his mother) but with his own frustratingly unpopular writing. So it is not women per se whom Melville attacks in the novel. Indeed, the novel confirms his recognition that the achievement of "genuine masculinity" meant affirming a creative relationship to women.

Subjects (as well as objects) that exist outside the male self, women and art both possess meanings or intentions of their own which the male "reader" must try to understand. Almost all works of art in the novel are associated with Isabel, who, as an "other" herself, offers Pierre a text that he must read in order to discover himself. Melville further implies that the most satisfactory reading of any text is interactive, a writerly rereading of the "illuminated scroll" of the self stimulated by various art objects (letters, women, statues, or paintings). He develops this idea in the famous chair-portrait of Pierre's father, whose contemplation Isabel's appearance encourages, and in the contrast between Mr. Glendinning's public and private selves. While Pierre has identified his youthful self with the "marbleized" figure of virtue he has secreted in the "shrine" of his memory, the chair-portrait, like Isabel's letter, forces him to contemplate a very different picture, and clarifies, when juxtaposed with the public portrait Mary Glendinning displays in the great drawing-room, an opposition in Melville's own conception of art and "reading."

Whereas the drawing-room portrait displays the "truest, and finest, and noblest combined expression" (7:72) of Mr. Glendinning, the chair-portrait shows a "brisk, unentangled, young bachelor" (7:73), the secret lover of Isabel's French mother. Less subjectified an object than the painting in the Spouter Inn, the portrait nonetheless possesses a fluid life of its own and represents another of Melville's representations of an essentially open graphic form. Like Isabel, it seems to beckon Pierre's imagination into unknown depths, as if the artist had successfully pared away a patina of social manner—the "thousand proprieties and polished finenesses" which make us "abdicate ourselves, and take unto us another self" (7:83)—to reveal the core of human nature. In spite of all the mental blocks Pierre brings to the portrait, he cannot help himself from giving it a writerly viewing: "standing guard, as it were, before the mystical tent of the picture; and ever watching the strangely concealed lights of the meanings that so mysteriously moved to and fro within; thus sometimes stood Pierre before the portrait of his father, unconsciously throwing himself open to all those ineffable hints and ambiguities, and undefined half-suggestions, which now and then people the soul's atmosphere, as thickly as in a soft, steady snowstorm, the snow-flakes people the air" (7:84). Art does not objectify a particular meaning but forces a viewer—almost against his will—to confront that meaning within himself. As such, of course, it opposes in both form and content that rigid, "perfect marble form of his departed father," which Pierre has always cherished.

The portrait, moreover, acts both as objective correlative and omen, embodying Pierre's familial link to Isabel and that secret aspect of his father's nature (and of his own) from which he has hidden himself. Although this art object represents a man rather than a woman, Mr. Glendinning's startling appearance in the painting stems from his passionate relationship to a woman; as such, it represents the sexually and artistically mature self that Pierre himself can become. As Douglas points out, the "revelation of Mr. Glendinning's sexual trangressions provides Pierre, curiously enough, with his first real opportunity to replace his mother's idealized mannequin with a flesh-and-blood man. . . . Ironically, Mr. Glendinning becomes at this point just what Mrs. Glendinning claims he should be to his son: a model."[12] In the painting's "behavior" Melville brilliantly symbolizes the relationship among art, sexuality, and the achievement of mature selfhood, representing the self as an open or dynamic aesthetic construct rooted in a passionate relationship to a woman. As Pierre becomes the ideal viewer of the painting, he becomes the self that the painting represents. Gazing at it, he gradually recognizes, "by irresistible intuitions," that "all that had been inexplicably mysterious to him in the portrait, and all that had been inexplicably familiar in the face, most magically these now coincided" so that by "some ineffable correlativeness, they reciprocally identified each other, and, as it were, melted into each other, and thus interpenetratingly uniting, presented lineaments of an added supernaturalness" (7:85).

While the painting attracts his imagination, forcing him to recognize truths about himself, Pierre, like Taji, tries to avoid the experience. Feeling safer when he keeps his imagination under strict control, he "starts from these reveries and trances" in order to "regain the assured element of consciously bidden and self-propelled thought," and he promises himself "never again to fall into a midnight revery before the chair-portrait of his father" (7:84–85). Later, in fact, at the Black Swan Inn, when he rediscovers the painting in the blue chintz-covered chest, Pierre finds it "detestable" and "altogether loathsome" (7:196). Just as he had with the letter, he tries to dissociate his memory of his father (and the new self-image associated with him) from his father's painted self. To do that, he must split his father's image in two, objectifying in the work of art what he fears in order to control and ultimately to destroy it (when he burns the portrait upon his departure from the inn). In "his own memory of his father," Melville writes, "Pierre could not recall any distinct lineament transmitted to Isabel, but vaguely saw such in the portrait; therefore, not Pierre's parent, as any way rememberable by him, but the portrait's painted *self* seemed the real father of Isabel" (7:197).

In an important sense, of course, the painting *is* the father of Isabel; that is, Melville attributes to works of art a specially procreative and transforming power—if the viewer or reader remains sensitive to their meanings. Isabel encourages the sort of emotional and imaginative relation that produces this ideally receptive state. For the rest of the novel, especially when he attempts to write, Pierre experiences a conflict between an impulse to "throw himself open" to the ambiguities and "half-suggestions" which move beneath the surface of rational thought and a desire to "regain the assured element of consciously bidden and self-propelled thought"—and that conflict is most graphically represented in his progressive relationship with Isabel.

Isabel's musical, vaguely articulate voice could be thought to epitomize the exclusion of female intentionality from a male text; woman becomes an object for male contemplation without a subjectivity of her own.[13] But Melville clearly privileges Isabel's creative powers and criticizes Pierre's inability to "read" her correctly. While essentially nonverbal, Isabel's voice transcends the limitations of language and "speaks"

directly to the heart. At the same time, because Melville wishes to subjectify Pierre's experience as much as possible, he deliberately keeps Isabel's
background vague. She even describes her own developing sense of
identity in language that corresponds to Pierre's experience of his father's portrait. "I go groping again amid all sorts of shapes, which part
to me," she tells Pierre; "so that I seem to advance through the shapes;
and yet the shapes have eyes that look at me" (7:118). Not only as an
aesthetic object, but as a subject, Isabel experiences herself provision-
ally. She allows Melville to represent the essential indeterminacy, not
only of the world of objects, but of the self.

Most important, it seems to me, Isabel comes to symbolize a special
mode of artistic creativity, what Charles Feidelson calls the "full power
of symbolic vision."[14] Her guitar is a symbol-making instrument of
extraordinary power; like the chair-portrait, it possesses a life or mind
of its own. "The guitar was human," she tells Pierre; the guitar
"taught me the secret of the guitar; the guitar learned me to play on
the guitar" (7:125). In short, the guitar created its creator: "All the
wonders that are unimaginable and unspeakable; all these wonders are
translated in the mysterious melodiousness of the guitar. It knows all
my past history. Sometimes it plays to me the mystic visions of the
confused large house I never name. Sometimes it brings to me the
bird-twitterings in the air; and sometimes it strikes up in me rapturous
pulsations of legendary delights eternally unexperienced and unknown
to me" (7:125).

As Isabel plays, a largely passive Pierre witnesses a mergence of artist
and instrument in which the sounds of Isabel's voice become one with
the sounds of the guitar. Whereas in the chair-portrait Melville noted
the power of art to beguile a viewer, in Isabel's performance he portrays the creative potential of the self. Anticipating Ehrenzweig, he
describes a state of mind peculiar to the artist who is passionately en-
gaged with her composition—a kind of creative passion which is the
result of a surrender of "self-propelled thought" to deeper forces
within the imagination.

Although Melville clearly views the young Pierre and his juvenile
literary efforts ironically, Isabel's creative prowess offers a marked alternative to conventional nineteenth-century art. Pierre may have "conned
his novel lessons" and "read more novels than most persons of his years"
(7:141), but those lessons aid him little in coming to terms with Isabel—
emotionally or aesthetically. Safe and conventional, according to the

satirical chapter, "Young America in Literature" (7:245), these run-of-
the-mill novels represent "false, inverted attempts at systematizing
eternally unsystemizable elements" and an "audacious, intermeddling
impotency, in trying to unravel, and spread out, and classify, the more
thin than gossamer threads which make up the complex web of life"
(7:141). Such literature springs from the same needs suggested by
Pierre's previous efforts to maintain the illusion of an "undifferentiated" universe and, of course, is precisely the kind of novel Melville
could not let himself write even when he tried. Isabel, on the other
hand, comes to represent all that is "unsystemizable" in human experience, in human nature, and in art. As a dynamic art object in Pierre's
experience, Isabel embodies open form and a writerly "text"; as a subject, she inspires Pierre to attempt a similarly visionary creation. And
any efforts to systemize that aspect of her character, Melville makes
clear, will result in a decadent, ultimately self-destructive art.

An important part of Pierre's removal from Saddle Meadows and
his new life with Isabel in the city is the recognition that his youthful
literary efforts are "Trash! Dross! Dirt!" (7:272). Douglas argues, in
fact, that "in *Pierre,* Melville turned decisively and openly against the
middle-class sentimental-minded feminized reading public he had essentially tried to evade or educate in his previous work. It is as if their
interference with his creative effort has become so troubling that he
must deal with it, and he does so by making it, in curious ways, the
actual subject of his book."[15] Melville is clear and consistent, moreover, in defining the changes that must occur for Pierre to be
successful.

The first step is burning his Juvenilia, comparable in this novel with
Taji's loss of Yillah. (In both cases, the hero's juvenile language is
matched by his relationship with a female figure who provides a narcissistically self-indulgent relationship.) Just as the second stage for Taji
was represented by four male companions—and thus by an authoritative male language—the second stage of Pierre's literary development involves assimilation of his voluminous reading. In Book 21 of
the novel, Melville describes just such a stage of "transition" (7:283) in
his hero's career. But while Taji had spent most of his time in this stage,
Melville moves Pierre much more quickly through this anxiety of influence and toward the liberation of his own original thought. Pierre
"did not see,—or if he did, he could not yet name the true cause for
it,—that already, in the incipiency of his work, the heavy unmalleable

element of mere book-knowledge would not congenially weld with the wide fluidness and ethereal airiness of spontaneous creative thought" (7:283).

As Melville continues his prescription for artistic success, carried along by his own spontaneous thought, he grows increasingly pessimistic not so much about his hero as about the truth-telling power of art in general. Pierre "did not see, that even when [all existing great works are] thus combined, all was but one small mite, compared to the latent infiniteness and inexhaustibility in himself; that all the great books in the world are but the mutilated shadowings-forth of invisible and eternally unembodied images in the soul" (7:284). There is an obvious paradox in Melville's thought, as his own intellectual momentum reveals the "truth" that there is no single truth, but only "surface stratified on surface" and "nothing but superinduced superficies" (7:285). There is obvious irony as well, since he sets his hero on a writer's course, even as he complains of writing's inherent inability to express truth. But this transition stage is still important, because in Pierre's career, Melville explores the possibility that writing can do more than merely "shadow forth" the "unembodied images in the soul." Whether he is successful or not, he unmistakably identifies Isabel and her artistic mode with that effort—that is, with the third and final stage of Pierre's literary education. He had only vaguely outlined such a mode in the final pages of *Mardi*, when Taji entered Hautia's bower. In *Pierre*, he devotes the last half of the novel to his hero's efforts to write the book inspired by his relationship with Isabel.

Melville recognized that the artist cannot feed his "foetal fancy" solely from within. For "though the naked soul of man doth assuredly contain one latent element of intellectual productiveness; yet never was there a child born solely from one parent; the visible world of experience being that procreative thing which impregnates the muses; self-reciprocally efficient hermaphrodites being but a fable" (7:259). Melville's choice of words is striking. Not only does he affirm the artist's need for experience of the world, but he expresses that need in language which equates creativity with female sexual identity and relationship. The artist's encounter with the "visible world of experience," however shape-shifting, results in newly creative, "procreative," power. If the work of art is the artist's "child," it cannot be the product of his self-sufficient imagination or "foetal fancy"; it must be the progeny of a mature relationship with another. In Pierre's case, that means discovering and accepting his relationship to Isabel, his father, and their common past.

It is this sort of new knowledge that Pierre vows to incorporate into his writing—"I will write it!" (7:273)—even though he conceives of "deeper truths" as leading to a kind of moral chaos in which Virtue and Vice are but "two shadows cast from one nothing" (7:274). But this is precisely Melville's goal: the ability to accept ambiguities and to avoid structuring the texture or text of experience excessively. And in expressing such an "open" view of life, Pierre earns Isabel's praise. She has held such a view for some time, and her role in this part of the novel is almost parental. More than merely Pierre's inspiration, she serves as a guide to a condition of social alienation but private, male-female relationship. "When thou just hovered on the verge," she tells him, "thou wert a riddle to me; but now, that thou art deep down in the gulf of the soul,—now, when thou wouldst be lunatic to wise men, perhaps—now doth poor ignorant Isabel begin to comprehend thee" (7:274).

At the same time, for all the good she does in leading Pierre away from the youthful platitudes of Saddle Meadows, Isabel, much like the later Bartleby, speaks in a tone of fundamental cynicism that can be deadly to art. Despite her sense of human sin and alienation, Isabel cannot transcend her condition or actually teach Pierre to translate his new experience into literary art. Her image is essentially passive (as she herself noted), so it is up to Pierre, if he can, to integrate her meaning into his art and thus give it a coherent form. Even though she plays her "mystic guitar" until Pierre feels "chapter after chapter born of its wonderful suggestiveness," the music is "eternally incapable of being translated into words; for where the deepest words end, there music begins with its supersensuous and all-confounding intimations" (7:282). As he does elsewhere in *Pierre,* Melville here obviously gives voice to his own frustration in trying to give verbal form to his "vision." Poe had characterized Ligeia's voice and the mystery behind her eyes in much the same manner, and here, too, the infinitely suggestive voice or expression of a woman does not quite assume a comprehensible form in male consciousness. The male listens but he does not quite hear.

In fact, instead of maintaining imaginative contact with Isabel, Pierre withdraws from her, writing, for example, behind the closed door of his frigid room. Emphasizing her potentially salutary influence, Isabel wants him to keep "her connecting door open," so that "the heat of her room might bodily go into his" (7:297). The symbolism is obvious. Isabel's "heat" is imaginative as well as sexual and encourages the sort of communicative circuit, or conversation, that in

Melville's view formed the pretext for creativity. By contrast, Pierre's cold room, in which he sits virtually immobile, slowly freezes his physical, emotional, and imaginative vitality. By the end of the novel, in fact, he reduces himself to a helpless, childlike condition; just to begin writing each day, he requires elaborate preparations by Isabel and Delly Ulver: a cloak filled with hot bricks, a bedstead moved within arm's reach, a crook-ended stick to reach anything his two nursemaids have forgotten. Melville himself was used to such attentions from Elizabeth, who "kept his inkwell filled and his paper in order," but Pierre is far more dependent.[16] Sitting for eight and a half hours each day, he has "no power over his condition" (7:303). In repudiating his ties to the past, rationalizing his relationship to Isabel, and "renouncing all his foregone self," he cuts his imagination off from those "procreative" forces which can be discovered through relationships. For her part, Isabel conforms herself, her own self-image, to Pierre's new attitude towards her; as she had promised, she "solidifies" into the "forms and slightest moods of thought" into which Pierre pours her (7:324). Indeed, when Pierre attempts to affirm the bond he feels to her, Isabel recognizes that his words lack sincerity. "Pierre," she says, "once such syllables from thee, were all refreshing, and bedewing to me; now, though they drop as warmly and as fluidly from thee, yet falling through another and an intercepting zone, they freeze on the way, and clatter on my heart like hail" (7:334).

Because Pierre's relationship to Isabel mirrors his relationship to his writing (and to the most creative part of the self), alienating himself from Isabel means alienating himself from his art. In effect, Melville observes, he is writing two books, "of which the world shall only see one, and that the bungled one. The larger book, and the infinitely better, is for Pierre's own private shelf. That it is, whose unfathomable cravings drink his blood; the other only demands his ink" (7:304). Part of the reason for the splitting of texts is Pierre's (and Melville's) contempt for his audience and for the pressure of forcing himself to write what would sell.[17] It is important, however, to distinguish Melville from Pierre. Despite obvious identification with his hero's heroic failure, he remains able to analyze his protagonist and, by implication, himself.[18] Most important, he gains remarkable insight into the emotional and psychological relationship between the writer and his writing, anticipating Ehrenzweig's concept of a creative "conversation" between the artist and the work of art. In effect, Pierre's failure to cope emotionally (and verbally) with his relationship to Isabel prevents his developing an honest relationship to his writing. As Melville observes, "the one [book] can not be composed on the paper, but only as the other is writ down in his soul" (7:304). Pierre's inability to define (and "publish") his relationship to Isabel is linked to his failure to publish his work-in-progress, the "child" of his artistic labor. The book involves that relationship, but in composing it Pierre seeks less to reconcile his conflicting feelings than to repress or obscure them. The book gradually "born" of his creative effort actually prevents the other book, the "infinitely better" book, from being written. Both woman and book remain ambiguous and concealed.

Melville, in fact, repeatedly characterizes Pierre's relationships to women as fictitious, the products of language. Pierre and his mother were "wont to call each other brother and sister" (7:5), he notes, and he terms Pierre's marriage to Isabel a "nominal conversion of a sister into a wife" (7:177). Dangerously, Pierre attempts to live up to his fictions and at the same time to use fiction to obscure the truth; "the same powerful motive which induced the thought of forming such an alliance, would always thereafter forbid that tacit exposure of its fictitiousness" (7:175). Although obviously the manifestation of an otherwise unacknowledged desire, this particular fiction becomes an interpolated secret text that gradually supplants the text of the brother-sister relationship. In fact, both of Pierre's acknowledged relationships to Isabel are fictitious. Essentially, his acceptance of Isabel as his sister derives from an inference that makes sense in the story Pierre has suddenly revised about his father. Of course, that story, as well as Isabel's character in it as his sister, is also designed to sublimate Pierre's erotic attraction to her. But calling her his wife in New York is no less fictitious; rather than getting closer to the truth, it makes a fiction out of a fiction.

In describing the chair-portrait and Isabel's music, Melville suggests the instructive power of art. Pierre's double fabrication of his relationship with Isabel, which is evasive rather than instructive, thus bodes ill for the integrity of his work in progress. Fiction does not encourage him to discover his right relation to Isabel; it obscures that relation. Because "man's moral texture is very porous, and things assumed upon the surface, at last strike in," Melville explains, "hence, this outward habituation to the above-named fictitiousness had insensibly disposed his mind to it as it were; but only innocently and pleasantly as yet" (7:177). One fiction or text gives way to another; Isabel's fictional character as wife becomes her real character, and the problem for Pierre is how to act the part of husband that he himself has created. In burning the contents of his trunk at the Black Swan Inn, including the chair-portrait and packages of family letters, he had reasoned that he now had "no paternity, and no past," and that he now stood "untrammeledly his ever-present self!—free to do his own self-will and present fancy to whatever end!" (7:199). Isabel's presence obviously complicates his freedom to indulge his "present fancy," and Melville makes clear that he fools himself in thinking that he can "self-will" any relationship and any book.

Cutting himself off from all outside relations, Pierre becomes a writing automaton, an amanuensis for a "stranger" that inhabits him. Unlike Taji or Lombardo, however, he does not thereby create a truly creative self. Instead, he increasingly experiences himself as double—as both writer and reader of the text he writes. Unfortunately, those two roles are now incompatible. Like Melville himself, Pierre suffers from a peculiar eye ailment that renders him nearly blind, so he is unable to read what he has written. His newly created writerly self, in other words, is now alienated from the self that reads, just as he has become increasingly alienated from Isabel and from what he writes. His eyes become so bad, Melville says, in a strikingly appropriate metaphor for the excessively structured text, that "some days he wrote with the lids nearly closed, fearful of opening them wide to the light. Through the lashes he peered upon the paper, which so seemed fretted with wires. Sometimes he blindly wrote with his eyes turned away from the paper;—thus unconsciously symbolizing the hostile necessity and distaste, the former whereof made of him this most unwilling states-prisoner of letters" (7:340). After Pierre's night of wandering the city, in fact, his eyes "absolutely refused to look at paper." He can only sit at his writing desk—"suspended, motionless, blank" (7:341). Yet it is of course during this "suspension" of conscious awareness and insight that Pierre dreams the story of Enceladus, which Joel Porte has called the "romance that eludes his waking skill" (183).

In addition to the sexual symbolism of the giant "fast frozen into the earth at the junction of the neck" (7:345), the rock is a giant art object, perhaps "some stern thing of antediluvian art" (7:345). Indeed, the entire landscape which Pierre recalls in his "state of semi-consciousness" (7:342) exemplifies the kind of symbolic art to which Isabel introduced him. Here, however, the symbolizing process is reflexive and ironic, expressing the death of the imagination rather than its dynamic powers—a case of the artist representing his inability to write.

Enceladus, on which Pierre's "own duplicate face and features magnifiedly gleamed upon him with prophetic discomfiture and woe" (7:346), suggests the petrification of creative impulse, the fate of the artist who has "fast frozen" those forces which promised to generate artistic vision. If Pierre had earlier wanted to "behead himself" in order to ease the pain in his "aching head" (7:305), in his dream he projects himself as dead from the neck down, reduced to a perpetually "aching head." Operating reflexively, Pierre's writing, estranged as it is from creative relationship, creates an uncreative self.

Leaving his closet immediately after the dream ends, Pierre cannot bear to look at himself in the mirror: "dreading some insupportably dark revealments in his glass, he had of late wholly abstained from appealing to it" (7:347). In this reference to the mirror, Melville encourages us to recall Pierre's actions just before he read Isabel's letter, the incident that set him upon his writerly course. Then, too, he had been frightened by his mirrored image; here, so far has he alienated himself from others, he is virtually without a mirrored self. In sacrificing relation, Pierre mistakenly believes that he can "feel himself in himself, and not by reflection in others" (7:261); by his own logic, he also believes that he can write his book from his own "foetal fancy," as a "child born solely from one parent." But Melville had clearly repudiated that notion in the very act of mentioning it, so Pierre's radical self-reliance and self-enclosure illustrate his downward drift toward failure in the terms Melville has set forth.

Melville has thus made the novel come full circle. Whereas Isabel had introduced Pierre to a dynamic art and the possibilities of open form, Pierre's effort to control his experience encloses him—his own self-image—within an excessively structured mental form. Whether or not his story also reflects Melville's commentary on his own creative efforts is another matter. Arvin has argued that "there is something in the violence, the overheatedness, the hysterical forcing of now one note, now another, in the novel, that inescapably suggests a doubleness in the mind of the man who wrote it, a bitter distaste of and disbelief in his own book in the very process of writing it, and a half-confessed intention to invoke ridicule and even contempt on the literary act itself."[19] But it seems to me that Melville's account of Pierre's novelistic career is consistent from beginning to end and that, whatever its wildness, the novel shows him struggling to achieve the same kind of open form, the same writerly relation to his material, to which he introduces his hero. This is not to say that he simply treats Pierre ironically, for there can be little question that he identifies with his character. But he is still able to view that character and his own literary efforts from a critical perspective.

Even more than the myth of Enceladus, which culminates his career as a writer, Pierre's visit to the picture gallery with Lucy and Isabel climaxes his experience as a "reader" of women and art. In Painting No. 99, a "Stranger's Head, by the Unknown Hand," he comes face to face with another chair-portrait, the "resurrection of the [painting of his father] he had burnt at the inn" (7:351). Unable to escape his father's secret self, unable to escape that part of himself which he finds projected in the portrait, Pierre also discovers that the painting square-ly faces one of the most problematical women for the male imagina-tion—Beatrice Cenci. The portrait, in short, forces Pierre to face his attitudes toward women. Lucy first discovers the painting of the Cenci, and although the portrait recalls the painted image of Pierre's father and thus of Isabel, it also bears a remarkable resemblance to her. In both cases, Melville forces his characters to find themselves in art, and the Cenci in particular provides a kind of archetypal aesthetic image of woman, whose complexities and apparent contradictions perfectly ex-press the conflicts in the male imagination. With "blue eyes and fair complexion, the Cenci's hair is golden—physically, therefore, all is in strict, natural keeping; which, nevertheless, still the more intensifies the suggested fanciful anomaly of so sweetly and seraphically *blonde* a being, being double-hooded, as it were, by the black crape of the two most horrible crimes . . . possible to civilized humanity—incest and parricide" (7:351). In *Mardi* Melville had hinted that the "maidens of Hautia are all Yillahs held captive, unknown to themselves"; here he implies that even the angelical Lucy might rival the legendary Cenci in complexity. More importantly, the Cenci's combination of Lucy's fair complexion and Isabel's history suggests the futility of any superficial polarization of women into dark and light, good and evil. No matter what woman he imagines or seeks, the portrait seems to say, Pierre will end up contemplating the same problematical experience. The conflicts that he projects onto women, after all, are subjective; resolution of those conflicts, like the resolution of differentiated aspects of woman into a single image, depends far less on any change in woman's nature than on the male coming to terms with himself.

That, indeed, seems to be the conclusion toward which Pierre him-self moves at the end of the novel. If the portrait of a "complete stranger" (7:353) can inspire the same thoughts as the chair-portrait and the same associations with Isabel, then perhaps something in Pierre's own nature sponsors the correspondence. The "original of this second portrait was as much the father of Isabel as the original of the chair-portrait," Pierre thinks. "But perhaps there was no original at all to this second portrait; it might have been a pure fancy piece" (7:353).

After he has shot Glen Stanly and been imprisoned, Pierre seems to achieve a certain peace with himself. Whereas he once felt compelled to choose between Lucy and Isabel, now he feels estranged from both. He is "neuter now" (7:360). Both women, moreover, reflect Pierre's deadened state of mind. When he leaves on his suicidal quest for Stanly, he leaves Isabel, "without the power to stir toward him," sitting "petrified in her chair, as one embalmed and glazed with icy varnish," while Lucy appears as a "marble girl" (7:357). Unreconciled, these differentiated images of woman have become petrified, "solidified" into "forms of thought"—the most common way, as we have seen, for a male author to represent the objectification of women by the male imagination. With a logic as unswerving as Poe's in "The Fall of the House of Usher," however, Melville clearly suggests that this process is self-destructive, that the male artist who alienates himself from a woman by projecting her into a devitalizing aesthetic form will find that image returning vengefully upon him. When she visits him with Lucy in his cell, instead of bringing the inspiration she has promised for much of the novel, Isabel bears in her bosom a vial of poison by which both of them will die. Having created the creative, Isabel finally molds herself to the form that the "caster's ladle" of Pierre's imagination establishes for her.

The short fiction that Melville wrote between 1853 and 1856 is marked by obvious cynicism toward human relationships and the possibilities of communication. From the cranky marriage in "I and My Chimney" to the abandonment of Jimmy Rose, the solipsism of Bartleby, and the desperation of Benito Cereno, Melville portrays isolated individuals and failures of communication. As Berthoff says of this later fiction, "We are never again to get from his writing that impression of expansiveness and superfluent energy which all his earlier books deliver. The letters surviving from the summer and fall of 1852 show a tiredness and even apathy, at the least a reserve, which are suddenly prophetic of the remaining forty years of his life."[20] For our purposes the two most important stories from this period are "The Paradise of Bachelors and the Tartarus of Maids" (1855) and "The Piazza" (1856). Both follow logically from *Pierre,* for they reveal obvious pessimism about the possibility of mutually creative male-female relationships. Both depict men estranged from women and from the sort of creative mood that women can evoke. Both show Melville having a final word, so to speak, upon the issues he had treated in his earlier work.

Although "The Paradise of Bachelors and the Tartarus of Maids" contains no fully drawn female characters (only anonymous working girls), the diptych does deal directly with the issue of women and creativity. William Bysshe Stein cites the bachelors' "estrangement from any form of creative *eros,*" while W. R. Thompson argues that the bachelors of the tale's first half are so "devitalized" that their "libidinal instincts have become enervated; their physical life they sublimate by living vicariously in the pages of literature."[21] "The Tartarus of Maids" is an obvious sexual allegory, set in a nightmarish landscape conceived as a gigantic female anatomy. But the story is more than a "grotesque mockery of the birth and sexual processes" and more than a nearly pathological account of fears of female genitalia and the violent facts of sex and birth.[22] Most important for our purposes is Melville's continued exploration of a relation between women and art.

Despite the sportiveness of the writing, the obvious desire to fool editors and readers cool at best to his latest literary efforts, the journey to Tartarus is remarkably similar to the other journeys we have observed in Melville's fiction. Many of Melville's works can be viewed as attempts to *con-fuse* art and sexuality: to explore the artist's sexual experience—no matter how indirectly imaged—as a source and subject of art. And except for the much longer *Pierre,* that theme is most graphically explored in "The Tartarus of Maids"; symbolically, the narrator's penetration of this anatomized landscape means seeking a kind of literary womb, a large whitewashed building where paper is manufactured.

In portraying the narrator as a "seedsman" who comes to the paper mill to purchase seed envelopes manufactured by women, Richard Chase observes, Melville makes a "conscious connection between sex and literary activity."[23] During this period of his career, Melville experienced acute frustration as a writer; after the failure of *Pierre* (itself an account of failed writing), writing became an evil business as much as a creative act. It is commonly acknowledged that such stories as "Bartleby, the Scrivener," "Jimmy Rose," and "The Fiddler" reflect such frustrations, and it is not surprising that through the narrator of "The Tartarus of Maids" Melville should comment ironically upon the business that writing and publishing had, unfortunately, become for him. When filled, the narrator comments, the seed envelopes are "all but flat, and being stamped, and superscribed with the nature of the seeds contained, assume not a little the appearance of business-letters ready for the mail" (9:324–25). The paper mill, according to this view, transforms the essentially creative act (the seeds) of the writer-seedsman into a business venture. The seeds of creativity are flattened and devitalized until the creative impulse becomes objectified and packaged for sale.

"The Tartarus of Maids," however, is more than some aesthetic version of a *vagina dentata* legend, for besides depicting a threat to masculinity, the story also shows the diminishment of the women themselves. The maids are victimized by a technology which is conceived, at least in part, as male.[24] Melville demonstrates the interdependence of men and women, the destructiveness and self-destructiveness of those processes by which women are rendered less threatening to men. The dehumanization of women, he implies, has similar consequences for the creative process.

Midway through his tour of the factory, for example, the narrator comes upon a gigantic machine whose function is simply to stamp the "impress of a wreath of roses" on pieces of "rose-hued note-paper." With its "vertical thing like a piston periodically rising and falling" (9:328) upon sheets of paper, this "iron animal" equates male sexuality and creativity, as the driving thrusts of the phallic "pen" imprint the paper. The machine is being fed by women, and the paper, with its rosy hue, suggests some vital feminine object. Yet, as he looks from the paper to the girls, thus confirming the identification, the narrator notices that the women appear "blank-looking" (9:328)—in fact, "sheet-white" (9:330)—and the brow of one girl even appears "ruled and wrinkled" (9:328). Feeding the iron animal, in other words, results in the gradual devitalization of the women. As in Poe's "The Oval Portrait," the women's vitality is being transferred into art objects which remain under male control. Specifically, it is the women's expression which is silenced by the iron machinery. "Not a syllable was breathed," the narrator notices. "Nothing was heard but the low, steady, overruling hum of the iron animals. The human voice was banished from the spot" (9:328). Besides the obvious social criticism of women's lot in American factories, it is tempting from a feminist perspective to see another example of woman's self-expression being excluded from a male text. We must keep in mind, however, Melville's identification of male creativity with female creativity, so that this oppression of women in the factory redounds directly to the narrator. Stifling women's creativity, Melville demonstrates, means stifling men's.

The tour of the paper mill culminates in the narrator's introduction to the "great machine" that actually makes the paper. Unlike the stamping machine, this one appears female—an ultimate source of female creativity. Located in a room "stifling with a strange, blood-like, abdominal heat," the machine is actually fed its supply of pulp by two huge vats—two gigantic ovaries "full of a white, wet, woolly-looking stuff, not unlike the albuminous part of an egg, soft-boiled" (9:331). Despite the gestational imagery, however, the great machine's operation does not exemplify vast creative power, but "unvarying punctuality and precision," and it produces only "foolscap," because that, according to the guide, is in "chief demand" (9:333). Melville thus comments pointedly on the publishing industry and its readers, scoring their demands for derivative, mass-produced literature.

The narrator's experience with the machine reaches its climax when he tests its precision by dropping a slip of paper, upon which he has written his guide's name, Cupid, into the pulp. This effort to write—to inscribe himself on paper in an act of love *and* creativity—requires a commitment of masculinity to femininity and thus suggests a special sort of creative surrender. Yet, as the machine gives birth to the narrator's creation—announced by a "scissory sound," as "of some cord being snapped"—it produces only an "unfolded sheet of perfect foolscap, with [his] 'Cupid' half faded out of it, and still moist and warm" (9:332). The female machinery of creation, it seems, profanes the narrator's creative efforts, confirming the threat he had perceived in the nightmarish landscape.

Throughout his tour, in fact, the narrator has felt the enervating influence of the paper mill. His cheeks have been frozen the whole time, and he is sure that only by leaving this Devil's Dungeon will he be able to "feel them mending" (9:335). In the end, then, Melville offers two distinct images of women in the story: the pale and sickly maidens whose lives are drained by the machines, and also the great machine itself, the conceiving woman, effectively corrupted by industrial impersonality, who produces foolscap and enslaves men and women alike. Thus, in the wild "disorder of a dream," Melville seems to have captured as forcefully as Poe a central truth about the male experience of woman: that in the devitalization of women (whether by the male imagination or by the "iron animal" of male technology) the male's own vitality and creativity become frozen and diminished. The problem that Melville finally dramatizes in "The Tartarus of Maids" is not the feminization of American culture, but the alienation of men and women from each other and from their sexuality. The tale anatomizes the poetics of gender, demonstrating in its special allegorical terms the impact of culturally engendered differences on the creative process. In the gigantic male *and* female machinery of the paper mill, he suggests that sexual energy—potentially the source of creative and procreative effort—has become mechanical and produces foolscap. Melville has come a long way from the sense of promise he depicted in the male-female relationships in *Mardi* and *Pierre,* which were at least potential sources of language, creativity, and symbolic expression.

Although not as graphic, "The Piazza" is no less pessimistic. As in the early fragment, the narrator's removal to the country brings him (like Melville in the Berkshires) to a world of art, a "paradise of painters" (9:1).[25] The surrounding limestone hills are "galleries hung, month after month anew, with pictures ever fading into pictures ever fresh" (9:2). Indeed, as he contemplates the mountains from his piazza, he is most impressed by their kaleidoscopic quality. The mountains, he says, "play at hide-and-seek, and all before one's eyes" (9:4). More than merely an exotic background, Melville's "fairyland," like one of Poe's arabesque chambers or Hawthorne's "neutral territory," represents an intermediate world of the imagination, a visionary realm with a "mind" of its own before which the viewer is largely passive. Marianna, the woman who lives in the mountain fairyland, becomes the product, as well as the prisoner, of this world, but Melville's emphasis is on the alienation—a mutual alienation—of the male imagination from this aesthetically dynamic realm associated with a woman.

Unlike the mute enchantress of the fragment, Marianna is not deaf and dumb. Indeed, reversing the relationship in his early fragment along gender lines, Melville here describes his male narrator as "mute" while Marianna speaks (9:9). Although she has "strange fancies" (9:10) as she sews by her window, she is isolated from the narrator's world, maintaining the same enchanted illusion about his house down the mountain that he does about hers. A mirror *of* rather than *for* the narrator, Marianna is another of Melville's portraits of the lonely artist, cut off from the outside world and at the mercy of a shadowy world within. "Have you, then, so long sat at this mountain-window, where but clouds and vapors pass," the narrator asks, "that, to you, shadows are as things, though you speak of them as phantoms; . . . that, to you, these lifeless shadows are as living friends, who, though out of sight, are not out of mind, even in their faces—is it so?" (9:11). A world of shadows and haunting faces—the world shared by Ishmael as he peers into the depths of self and sea after his "ungraspable phantom of life" and certainly by Pierre when he first beholds Isabel.

Like Isabel, Marianna is an ominous figure, a female double who places the stability of the male self in jeopardy. Although the narrator wishes that, for Marianna's sake, he could be "that happy one of the happy house" she dreams that she sees, he abruptly breaks off his visit and any possible relationship with her, vowing to launch his "yawl no more for fairy-land" and to "stick to the piazza" (9:12). Emphasizing the unbridgeable gap between the two characters and their worlds, Marianna points out a "small garden, where, side by side, some feet apart, nipped and puny, two hop-vines climbed two poles, and, gaining their tip-ends, would have then joined over in an upward clasp, but the baffled shoots, groping awhile in empty air, trailed back whence they sprung" (9:12). Faintly recalling the divided graves of Hester Prynne and Arthur Dimmesdale, Melville makes clear that there will be no union of male and female, no imaginative synthesis of the mundane world of the piazza and the shadowy realm of fancy and fairyland. Like the "baffled" vine, the narrator is content to return to his house below.26 His piazza becomes his "box-royal." He will observe Marianna's world from a distance, because from there the "illusion" is "so complete" (9:12). Although he notes that, "every night, when the curtain falls, truth comes in with darkness," although he admits being "haunted by Marianna's face, and many as real a story" (9:12), "The Piazza" ends in estrangement. As clearly as in "The Tartarus of Maids" or the final pages of *Pierre,* furthermore, that estrangement is gender-inflected—a mutual alienation of men and women from the creative possibilities of relationship.

Melville, it seems to me, deserves more credit than he has received for his efforts to bring his male characters into creative relationships with women who clearly do not conform easily to type. As I have attempted to show, up through *Pierre,* Melville seemed to be coming closer and closer to that goal. The "mute enchantress" of his early fragment gives way to the child-like Fayaway and the other "whihenies" of *Typee,* who in turn give way to Yillah and the much more provocative Hautia in *Mardi.* Pierre's relationship with Isabel obviously climaxes this "movement" in Melville's fiction; indeed, *Pierre* remains something of a tour de force of male efforts to explore the connection between male-female relationships and the complex relation between the male writer and his work. For reasons located as much in his frustration as a publishing author as in his psychology, Melville could not finally achieve the creative relationship between Isabel and Pierre that he set up as an ideal. His subsequent fiction reflects a loss of faith both in relationships and in the very possibility of communication. Nevertheless, Melville came much closer than most writers—closer certainly than Poe—to realizing that through relationships with women, male authors could create the creative.

CHAPTER FIVE

Hawthorne's Letters and Tales

Writing and Relationship

*I*n a letter to Sophia Peabody about a month before her marriage to Hawthorne, Margaret Fuller praised her friend's fiancé. "If ever I saw a man who combined delicate tenderness to understand the heart of a woman, with quiet depth and manliness enough to satisfy her, it is Mr. Hawthorne." Eight years earlier, Fuller had written enthusiastically about Hawthorne's anonymously published "The Gentle Boy": "it is marked by so much grace and delicacy of feeling, that I am very desirous to know the author, whom I take to be a woman."[1] Fuller was not alone, moreover, in perceiving a feminine quality in Hawthorne and in "The Gentle Boy." In a review of *Twice-Told Tales* (*North American Review*, April, 1842), Henry Wadsworth Longfellow noted the "strength and beauty of a mother's love" that Hawthorne "poured over" that story, as well as the "minute delicacy of touch, and womanly knowledge of a child's mind and character" evident in "Little Annie's Ramble." Hawthorne's "genius," he concluded, was "characterized by a large proportion of feminine elements, depth and tenderness of feeling, exceeding purity of mind, and a certain airy grace and arch vivacity."[2] Although we might wonder how the writer who would complain about a "d——d mob of scribbling women" would have reacted to such compliments about his "feminine" qualities, it is difficult to think of another American writer as concerned as Hawthorne with coming to terms with women in his fiction, or of one who so often associated women with specially creative powers.[3] And the fact that writers such as Longfellow and Fuller noted a mixture of gender characteristics in Hawthorne's personality and prose encourages a reexamination of his masculine poetics.

Like Melville, in fact, Hawthorne often blurred conventional gender boundaries in his characters, creating "masculine" women (Ann Hutchinson, Hester Prynne, Zenobia) and "feminine" men (Arthur Dimmesdale, Clifford Pyncheon, Miles Coverdale). Despite his fragility, it would be going too far to say that Dimmesdale plays a kind of pale maiden to Hester's dark lady, but *The Scarlet Letter* does feature some measure of gender reversal—especially obvious in Dimmesdale's plea to Hester in the forest: "Think for me Hester! Thou art strong. Resolve for me!" (1:196)[4] Dimmesdale's dependency, moreover, anticipates that of one of Hawthorne's seemingly much stronger male characters: Hollingsworth, as he appears leaning on Priscilla's arm in the final scene of *The Blithedale Romance*. But, well before that scene of pathos, Hawthorne had revealed that even the hypermasculine Hollingsworth had his feminine side. When Miles Coverdale takes to bed with a fever shortly after his arrival at Blithedale, Hollingsworth's "more than brotherly attendance" gives him "inexpressible comfort" (3:41). There was "something of the woman moulded into the great, stalwart frame of Hollingsworth," Coverdale observes; "nor was he ashamed of it, as men often are of what is best in them" (3:42).

With his "full, tender lips and beautiful eyes" that "indicate not so much capacity of thought, as gentle and voluptuous emotion" (2:32), Clifford Pyncheon is surely Hawthorne's most feminine male character, just as *The House of the Seven Gables* represents the novel in which he most thoroughly researched alternative gender identities and roles. At one extreme among the male characters is the effeminate Clifford, whose maleness is so dispassionate that he is incapable of forming any productive ties with a woman. Clifford's "images of women," Hawthorne notes, "had more and more lost their warmth and substance, and been frozen, like the pictures of secluded artists, into the chillest ideality" (2:140). At the other extreme is Jaffrey Pyncheon, whose "sex, somehow or other, was entirely too prominent" (2:118), who has worn out a wife in three or four years after giving her a "death-blow" on their honeymoon and compelling her to "serve him with coffee, every morning, at his bedside, in token of fealty to her liege-lord and master" (2:123). Hawthorne casts Holgrave squarely between these radically opposed, but equally unsatisfactory, models of masculinity—in a position to synthesize both extremes within his own personality into a masculinity that incorporates the feminine. Holgrave proves himself, as we shall see, by refusing to pursue the seductive advantage that his art (his story of Alice Pyncheon) gives him over Phoebe.

Over the past two decades Nina Baym has led the way among Hawthorne's critics in examining the role of women in his fiction. In a series of articles later incorporated in *The Shape of Hawthorne's Career,* she established a central conflict in Hawthorne's work between female passion and male authority, and she has argued in a more recent essay that "the question of women is *the* determining motive in Hawthorne's fiction."[5] Less interested than previous critics in allegorical contrasts, she argues that " 'woman' stands for a set of qualities which the male denies within himself and rejects in others. She represents warmth, imagination, intuition, and love; identified with nature and the heart, she also implies the nonrational complexities of the self."[6] Baym emphasizes male characters' resistance to relationships with such women and what she regards as Hawthorne's judgment of their failures. Women, she says, "represent desirable and valuable qualities lacking in the male protagonist. They offer him the opportunity to attain these qualities through erotic alliance or marriage. The man's invariable failure to take the opportunity is harshly judged by the narrator in fiction after fiction" ("Thwarted Nature," 60).

I would like to extend Baym's insights into the potential complementarity of Hawthorne's male and female characters by exploring a connection in his writing between male responses to women and the achievement of selfhood and creative power—the way relationships with women can bring a creative male self into being. More specifically, it seems to me that Hawthorne's fiction can be read as a progressive effort to liberate a powerful female figure, clearly identified with his own creative power. That effort begins in the love letters he wrote to Sophia Peabody in the three and a half years before their marriage in 1842.

The 109 letters that remain from the courtship and engagement period show Hawthorne attempting to address many of the same problems he addressed in his fiction. As a first-person narrator who adopts various personae, he finds himself confronted by a woman (Sophia) who alternates between opposed "characters" ("the Dove" and "naughty Sophie") while he struggles with the feelings she evokes. In the process of writing this epistolary narrative, moreover, Hawthorne tested the limits of conventional discourse: the power of words to express what was obviously an emotional and sexual awakening; the power of literary "characters" to express the complexity of a woman's being and to represent his ambiguous feelings for her. Through that experimental process, moreover, Hawthorne explored the connection he felt between his relationship to Sophia and his power as an artist. In being irreducible to a single word or image, Sophia encouraged him to research the very basis of creativity—the intimate connection between writing and relationship.

Although allowances should be made for a lover's enthusiasm, the letters testify to Sophia's remarkable power to make him know himself—to make him "be." In an oft-quoted letter from 4 October 1840, for example, he admits, "I used to think that I could imagine all passions, all feelings, all states of the heart and mind; but how little did I know what it is to be mingled with another's being!" He tells Sophia that she has "taught me that I have a heart," and "thrown a light deep downward, and upward, into my soul" (15:495). Describing an androgynous ideal of reunion, he credits her with restoring him to himself and anticipates the language he would use at the beginning of his introduction to *The Scarlet Letter*. There, as he reflected upon his relationship to the novel he had written, he conceived of it as a type of love letter, an agent or even substitute for his male ego that, in his place, would court that "one heart and mind of perfect sympathy" from which he felt himself divided. The "printed book," he could imagine, might "find out the divided segment of the writer's own nature, and complete his circle of existence by bringing him into communion with it" (1:3–4). Writing and relationship—both were specially creative. As he told Sophia in the same letter of 4 October: "Thou only hast revealed me to myself; for without thy aid, my best knowledge of myself would have been merely to know my own shadow—to watch it flickering on the wall, and mistake its fantasies for my own real actions. Indeed, we are but shadows—we are not endowed with real life, and all that seems most real about us is but the thinnest substance of a dream—till the heart is touched. That touch creates us—then we begin to be—thereby we are beings of reality, and inheritors of eternity" (15:495).

Hawthorne was thirty-six when he wrote this letter; his zeal suggests a longstanding ideal belatedly realized, a change within himself that must have seemed like a rebirth. Indeed, self-creative relationship requires Hawthorne's self-surrender; he becomes a form that Sophia will fill and then quicken into life—a male Galatea to her Pygmalion.

In fact, Hawthorne found himself with little imaginative power to comprehend or control this new relationship. Although Baym considers the letters "elaborately artificial" because Hawthorne is simply "playing at being a lover" and "playing at being in love," the letters show him recognizing the inadequacy of conventional figures and conventional language, struggling for words to express his feelings (*Shape*, 86). Such a complaint is itself conventional, but it also suggests frustration with the language he had inherited and his desire to discover an alternative. Indeed, it can be argued that he uses the derivative, sentimental language of love, characterized by abstraction, idealization, and euphemism, in order to test and even to subvert its limitations. By repeatedly lamenting the impotence of words available to him, Hawthorne invites Sophia to look behind those words. Similarly, he uses euphemism self-consciously to signal feelings and experiences— shared emotions and fantasies—which his words cannot denote. In the process of subverting the very discourse he employs, moreover, Hawthorne suggests the possibility of a superior language that incorporates emotion, a language composed of "heartfelt words," created by "dipping our pens as deep as may be into our hearts" (15:295), words that do not simply express but actually embody their author. Fretting over his distance from Sophia, Hawthorne imagined his words bringing them literally *and physically* together. On one occasion he kisses the words he wrote to her ("mine own Dove") and invites her to "kiss them too" (15:327).

But such "heartfelt" writing was clearly difficult. The "soul" of his thought, he complains, will not readily assume the "earthly garments of language" (15:306). His feelings will not, "of their own accord, assume words—at least, not a continued flow of words" (15:316). "I would fain sit still," he tells Sophia on 15 April 1840, "and let thoughts, feelings, and images of thee, pass before me and through me, without my putting them into words, or taking any other trouble about the matter" (15:440). He goes on at such length to explore his notion of extra-verbal communication that the rest of the letter represents an extended effort to use language against itself by circling an emotional and sexual reality that it cannot denote:

> In truth, I never use words, either with the tongue or pen, when I can possibly express myself in any other way;—and how much, dearest, may be expressed without the utterance of a word! Is

there not a volume in many of our glances?—even in a pressure of the hand? And when I write to thee, I do but painfully endeavor to shadow into words what has already been expressed in those realities. In heaven, I am very sure, there will be no occasion for words;—our minds will enter into each other, and silently possess themselves of their mutual riches. Even in this world, I think, such a process is not altogether impossible—we ourselves have experienced it—but words come like an earthy wall betwixt us. Then our minds are compelled to stand apart, and make signals of our meaning, instead of rushing into one another, and holding converse in an infinite and eternal language. Oh, dearest, have not the moments of our oneness been those in which we were most silent? (15:440)

Hawthorne's reluctance to put his obviously passionate feelings for Sophia into words suggests a certain prudery; yet he clearly despairs of the distance he feels between them—a distance created by words—at the same time that his language closes that distance in a deliberately physical way. His view of a kind of semiotic heaven in which "our minds will enter into each other, and silently possess themselves of their mutual riches," his belief that their minds are capable of "rushing into one another, and holding converse in an infinite and eternal language," ascribes a reciprocally erotic power to language that helps us to understand his fascination in his fiction with mutually creative relationships between men and women: Hester's ecstatic effect on Dimmesdale in the forest, Zenobia's power over Coverdale's imagination, Miriam's inspiration of creative passion in Kenyon. In contrast to those occasions in male-authored literature when women are silenced in order to be reduced to signs and mirrors for men, Hawthorne seeks moments of "oneness" and perfect, nonverbal communication—not because he has possessed Sophia's mind, but because he shares it.

Such self-expression and communication did not occur without anxiety, of course. Hawthorne was frustrated, as well as fascinated, by the gap between what he felt and what he felt he could write. In affirming the limitations of language to express his increasingly erotic feelings, he was also inviting Sophia to share the feelings he could not put into words. By 20 January 1842, six months before their wedding, Hawthorne's feelings have clearly exceeded his ability or willingness to put them into words. In a fascinating way, however, Hawthorne's very wordlessness thereby becomes a secret language. Sophia, in effect, must read between the lines, understanding her fiancé's silences by reading or projecting what she feels in her own heart. Repression becomes expression, as "writing grows more and more an inadequate and unsatisfactory mode of revealing myself to thee. I no longer think of saying anything deep, because I feel that the deepest and truest must remain unsaid" (15:606). Again and again Hawthorne laments the limitations of the language at his disposal, its powerlessness to express the facts and feelings of relationship. Yet he goes on to make the very process of recognizing his linguistic impotence a virtue, circumscribing his meaning in the very act of inscribing its absence. For of course if writing is more and more inadequate, saying so implies a better, more adequate mode. If the "deepest and truest" must remain "unsaid," the statement itself—the unsaying—implies what it cannot name. "Looks—pressures of the lips and hands, and the touch of bosom to bosom—these are a better language," he goes on; "but, bye-and-bye, our spirits will demand some more adequate expression even than these." On one level, of course, he refers to a spiritual communication in some Platonic realm where nothing has embodied life; on another, his intentions are more earthly. He means the opposite of what he says because, as he himself had admitted, words are "more and more an inadequate and unsatisfactory mode of revealing" himself. "And thus it will go on," he concludes, in obviously suggestive language, "until we shall be divested of these earthly forms, which are at once our medium of expression, and the impediments to full communion. Then we shall melt into another, and all be expressed, once and continually, without a word—without an effort" (15:606).

In addition to struggling to find an adequate language for his passionate feelings, Hawthorne also had difficulty finding language to describe Sophia. Her image in the love letters is more dynamic than static, the result of obvious inner conflict. His best-known formula for understanding Sophia's character is his repeated distinction between "naughty Sophie" and "the Dove." Although he referred to Sophia as his Dove from the very beginning, it was several months (21 August 1839) before she became his "naughty wife" (15:337) and a month after that when he first discovered the implications of the two "characters."

Hawthorne's letter of 23 September 1839, coming nearly a year after he had first met Sophia, clearly marks a turning point in his feelings, his first unabashed acknowledgement of erotic attraction. The letter, which began with a lengthy review of their "blessed relationship," was interrupted by supper-time, and when he returned to his writing Hawthorne clearly felt the pangs of a different appetite. He has read her recent letter over again, he says, and "meeting with Sophie Hawthorne twice [that is, with the words 'Sophie Hawthorne'], I took the liberty to kiss her very fervently." Very "strong," he admits, "is the consciousness that I am truly your husband! Dove, come to my bosom—it yearns for you as it never did before. I shall fold my arms together, after I am in bed, and try to imagine that you are close to my heart. Naughty wife, what right have you to be anywhere else? How many sweet words I should breathe into your ear, in the quiet night—how many holy kisses would I press upon your lips" (15:348). Words and kisses in apposition—Hawthorne was close to putting his feelings into words, close enough that the rest of the sentence and most of the next were excised by Sophia. But the eruption of such feelings also clearly put a strain on Hawthorne's own language, for he concluded the letter two days later with his first overt differentiation of Sophia into two characters. "Dove," he says, "I have but a single moment to embrace you. Tell Sophie Hawthorne I love her" (15:349).

More interesting than this conventional opposition, however, is the difficulty Hawthorne had in maintaining the distinction between his own Dark Lady and Fair Maiden. Fascinated by Sophia's resistance to type, he relishes her vitality as an image in his mind. Try though he might to comprehend her, he repeatedly finds himself in the presence of a woman, in Roland Barthes' term, who "dazzles" his lover's discourse.[7] As he admits, "It seems as if Sophie Hawthorne fled away into infinite space, the moment I strive to fix her image before me in order to inspire my pen;—whereas, no sooner do I give myself up to reverie, than here she is again, smiling lightsomely by my side" (15:384). Whether or not Hawthorne really possessed a "delicate tenderness to understand the heart of a woman," as Margaret Fuller told Sophia he did, he clearly found it difficult to reify Sophia into opposed characters.

Hawthorne revealed this difficulty most intriguingly in his letter of 23 October 1839. Although he addresses his "Dear little Dove" and wishes she was present, he is not sure about the "character" in which she should appear. "And now if my Dove were here," he exclaims, "she and that naughty Sophie Hawthorne, how happy we all three—two—one—(how many are there of us?)—how happy might we be!" (15:357). He goes on, in fact, in the most explicit terms to be found in the love letters, not only to express his feelings about the characters he has conceived for Sophia, but to analyze the reasons he finds both characters necessary to their relationship. Imagining Sophia asleep, he imagines himself entering "beneath the dusky veil of sleep and find[ing] himself in the midst of her enchantments." Yet he wonders if "Sophie Hawthorne" will "be there too." "Shall she share our nuptial couch?" The answer, he explains, is an emphatic "Yes." Whether his "own Dove" likes it "or no, that naughty little person must share our pillow," because she has "contrived" to make herself "absolutely necessary" to him (15:357). "His heart," he says, "stirs at her very name—even at the thought of her unspoken name" (15:357–58). Obviously, as Hawthorne's feelings for Sophia became increasingly erotic, he worried that those feelings, which he identified with "naughty Sophie" but preferred to leave "unspoken," would jeopardize the Dove's character.

Moreover, try as he might to keep that "little Dove" before his mind's eye, he found his thoughts turning more and more to "naughty Sophie." "Sometimes, while your husband conceives himself to be holding his Dove in his arms," he admits, "lo and behold! there is the arch face of Sophie Hawthorne peeping up at him. And again, in the very midst of Sophie Hawthorne's airs, while he is meditating what sort of chastisement would suit her misdemeanors, all of a sudden he becomes conscious of his Dove, with her wings folded upon his heart to keep it warm" (15:358). The important point is that, while Hawthorne does see double, something in his imagination resists the two images remaining mutually exclusive. For he concludes by explaining that he considers a "true woman holier than an angel": a woman "who should combine the characteristics of Sophie Hawthorne and my Dove would be the very perfection of her race. The heart would find all it yearns for, in such a woman, and so would the mind and the fancy" (15:358). Most important, Hawthorne seemed to recognize that his own well-being was best served by focusing his vision of Sophia. Although he admits that he has "reason to apprehend more trouble with Sophie Hawthorne than with [his] Dove" (15:359), he says that he loves her the more because she is both. "Which do I love the best, I wonder—my Dove, or my little Wild-Flower?" he asks. "I love each best, and both equally; and my heart would inevitably wither, and dry up, and perish utterly, if either of them were torn away from it" (15:359).

Finding his command of language inadequate to express the feelings Sophia evoked and conventional figures of speech inadequate before her dynamic character, Hawthorne gave up the effort to comprehend the relationship in conventional terms. He opened his imagination to her influence and even looked to her for words. He went so far in his letter of 20 December 1839, in fact, as to suggest a desire to surrender his writing to her entirely. Because his deep feelings for her will not form themselves into words, he says, he wants her to enter his imagination, or "heart," in order to "read" his feelings directly:

> Blessedest wife—has not Sophie Hawthorne been very impatient for this letter, one half of which yet remains undeveloped in my brain and heart? Would that she could enter those inward regions, and read the letter there—together with so much that never can be expressed in written or spoken words. And can she not do this? The Dove can do it, even if Sophie Hawthorne fail. Dearest, would it be unreasonable for me to ask you to manage my share of the correspondence, as well as your own?—to throw yourself into my heart, and make it gush out with more warmth and freedom than my own pen can avail to do? (15:388)

Not only did Hawthorne admit Sophia's power to make him "be," in other words, but in this passage he granted her an ability to make him write. Opening his heart to her would make his brain and heart "gush out" with more "warmth and freedom." That is, in identifying himself with her, he might be able to bring a newly creative self into being and so achieve a new verbal power.

In inviting Sophia to "manage" both shares of their correspondence from a privileged position in his "inmost regions," Hawthorne does more than simply invoke a conventional muse. He was exploring the possibility of identifying his own creative power with a woman—not with a feminized, narcissistic self-image, but with an autonomous female other. Sophia would not inspire creativity but be creative, inscribing herself, so to speak, in and through his imagination or "heart." Nancy K. Miller refers to a "pseudo-feminocentrism," or "female drag," to characterize male writers who impersonate women by adopting female personae—for Miller simply another way to deny women the pen and appropriate their discourse.[8] But compared to the writers Miller discusses (e.g., John Cleland in *The Memoirs of Fanny*

Hill), who use the "amorous discourse of the Other" narcissistically to ensure their own "irresistibility" as lovers (51), Hawthorne seems without such ulterior motives. Indeed, it might be more accurate to invert Miller's terms in Hawthorne's case, as he seems to offer Sophia a kind of "male drag." He resigns control over his own interior space and invites her to take his place, speaking and writing in her own voice— but through him. The imagery he employs, furthermore, is striking for its suggestion of gender reversal. Instead of penetrating Sophia, Hawthorne himself is penetrated and virtually—verbally—impregnated. With Sophia empowered in his "inmost regions," he will in effect give birth to a new, more self-expressive kind of writing—a writing in the feminine—gushing out in "warmth and freedom" as he has not been able to do before.⁹

Hawthorne goes a long way in his love letters, then, toward identifying creativity with an ability to share power with a woman or even to surrender power to her. And it seems to me that he attempts to fulfill something of his wish in his fiction—particularly in several tales he wrote at the Old Manse during the first years of his marriage—by including female characters who not only embody the deepest truths of his heart, but also possess creative power to which he can surrender the narrative. In spite of obvious anxiety, a temptation for "heavenly language," Hawthorne seemed to recognize the importance of allowing his deepest thoughts and feelings about women—however "naughty"—to emerge into his writing. Even though, exactly a month before his wedding, he closed a letter to Sophia with the observation, "I have no more words, but a heart full of love" (15:629), over the next two decades his creative output would testify to his discovery that writing could begin, not end, with relationship—that a "heart full of love" could express itself in words. It is no accident that his most fascinating female characters (Beatrice, Hester, Zenobia, and Miriam) clearly possess the power to evoke "heartfelt words," to make the "inward regions" of his male characters "gush out" in "warmth and freedom."

This is not to say, of course, that Hawthorne's male characters are uniformly successful in achieving the sort of creative and self-creative relationships with women that Hawthorne evidently found in his marriage to Sophia. In fact, Hawthorne's fiction includes many failed relationships, and his writing evidences wild extremes in male attitudes toward women, including the male tendency to objectify women in order to protect the fragile self from penetration and change. Scientific experimenters such as Aylmer and Rappaccini are the prototypes, but the *English Notebooks* contain an extraordinary passage in which Hawthorne himself advocates a kind of sculptural murder of women who do not represent a preconceived ideal. An English woman of forty or fifty, he observes, is the "most hideous animal that ever pretended to human shape." Characterized by "horrible ugliness" and "all manner of fleshly abomination," these "grim, red-faced monsters" illustrate the "penalty of a life of gross feeding." "Surely," he reasons, "a man would be justified in murdering them—in taking a sharp knife and cutting away their mountainous flesh, until he had brought them into reasonable shape, as a sculptor seeks for the beautiful form of woman in a shapeless block of marble. The husband must feel that something alien has grown over and incrusted the slender creature whom he married, and that he is horribly wronged by having all this flabby flesh imposed upon him as his wife."10 Even allowing for the obvious hyperbole, this is strong stuff indeed—a radical example of male fears of women's bodies and of what Simone de Beauvoir calls "woman's first lie."11 And Hawthorne's "final solution" to this problem of the flesh is nothing short of murder—an aesthetic murder that makes Aylmer's surgery upon his wife's birthmark seem tame by comparison. It would be wrong, of course, to make too much of this isolated passage, and thankfully Hawthorne's writing offers many other descriptions of women to counteract it. The bulk of Hawthorne's fiction, in fact, seems to me to belie the violently objectifying wishes of the notebook passage. Even Hawthorne's fictional sculptors (Drowne and Kenyon) are more effective in creating statues of women when they surrender conscious control over their medium and allow the woman's creative power to shape her own image in their minds and in their art.

Although Rita Gollin argues that the ideal creative state for Hawthorne was the daydream, because "the imagination can operate freely; but since the will retains control, unpleasant thoughts cannot gain dominion,"12 it seems to me that the most dazzling works of art in the fiction are those created when the artist is in least control of the creative process. As much as Melville and Poe, in other words, Hawthorne experimented with the imaginative possibilities of creative surrender, describing states of mind within his characters that anticipate what Ehrenzweig calls "passive watchfulness." He broaches the idea in the love letters, as Sophia becomes an other within the self who takes responsibility for writing, and his fiction includes numerous characters, usually women, with similarly creative powers. At the same time, of course, Hawthorne did feel some anxiety about what he called the "passive sensibility." He recognized the potential of creative surrender—becoming the writer as dreamer—at the same time that he experienced such a state as a severe test of will. His "passive sensibility" was always in danger of becoming the "haunted mind": "In the depths of every heart, there is a tomb and a dungeon, though the lights, the music, and revelry above may cause us to forget their existence, and the buried ones, or prisoners whom they hide. But sometimes, and oftenest at midnight, those dark receptacles are flung wide open. In an hour like this, when the mind has a passive sensibility, but no active strength; when the imagination is a mirror, imparting vividness to all ideas, without the power of selecting or controlling them; then pray that your griefs may slumber, and the brotherhood of remorse not break their chain" (9:306).

Hawthorne's sentences swing back and forth between phrases of delight and phrases of anxiety. The openness of his mind's "receptacles" is modified by the word "dark," the "passive sensibility" is qualified by its lack of "active strength," and the vitality or "vividness" of his imaginative power is qualified by its inability to select or control. Indeed, he concludes almost abjectly that one can only "pray" that this passive state will not offer an excuse for "grief" and "remorse" to take over his mind. This tension between imaginative openness and fear of victimization by the mind's own "dark" imaginings can be seen whenever Hawthorne writes about creativity. As we have seen in his letters to Sophia, he could identify creativity with relationships to others—particularly a creative female other who entered his "inward regions," causing the receptacles of his mind to open and "gush out" with "warmth" and "freedom."

Consistently, that is, he invested his heroine with the sort of creative power he had projected in Sophia, while his hero assumed his own largely passive stance as sympathetic spectator of the heroine's creative efforts. Hawthorne's fiction, moreover, grew increasingly open to his heroine's creative power; her character came to have more influence—a greater voice—in the text and in the hero's imagination. More and more forcefully Hawthorne's heroine demands the right to express and define herself; she thereby challenges his hero to become an ideal reader, "the one heart and mind of perfect sympathy."

It is worth examining the passage in "The Custom-House" in which the latter phrase appears; for even though it does not explicitly refer to women, it does define an ideally sympathetic audience for the artist's creative effort. Hawthorne begins by recalling the "autobiographical impulse" which for the second time in his life has "taken possession" of him (1:3). He goes on in very subtle terms to discuss the relationship that exists between the self-revealing author and the "few who will understand him." He distances himself somewhat from his discussion by referring to "some authors" who "indulge in such confidential depths of revelation as could fittingly be addressed, only and exclusively, to the one heart and mind of perfect sympathy" (1:3). He himself apparently is not such an author—he wants more than one reader for his book—but his fiction does include numerous characters who seek such an exclusive audience. The result, as Hawthorne goes on to suggest, is that their words "find out the divided segment of the writer's own nature, and complete his circle of existence by bringing him into communion with it" (1:3–4). For his part, Hawthorne finds it "scarcely decorous" to "speak all," but in recognizing that "thoughts are frozen and utterance benumbed, unless the speaker stand in some true relation with his audience," he proceeds to imagine a friend, "though not the closest friend," as his ideal reader. It is worth noting Hawthorne's characterization of the cost of a false relation with his audience, for, as we shall see, his heroines are regularly "frozen" and "benumbed" when they fail to achieve a "true relation" with his heroes. To pursue the metaphor a bit playfully, Hawthorne of course is skating on some thin ice in this passage. His "true relation" by his own definition is to be a false relation; even though he expects his friendly auditor to "thaw" his "native reserve," he looks forward to keeping "the inmost Me behind its veil. To this extent and within these limits," he concludes, an author "may be autobiographical, without violating either the reader's rights or his own" (1:4).

Hawthorne does not identify the creative impulse he describes in "The Custom-House" as feminine, although he did clearly recognize that his chosen profession deviated from a certain masculine standard. In acknowledging that his two earliest Salem ancestors, those "stern and black-browed Puritans," would think little of an "idler" like himself (1:10), he implicitly identifies with other victims of their scorn and punishment—which means, of course, with women such as Ann Coleman, the Quaker woman whom William Hathorne sentenced to a whipping, or the witches whom John Hathorne sentenced (many of whom were women). Similarly, his remark in the sketch of "Mrs. Hutchinson" (1830) that "delicacy" perceives "a sort of impropriety in the display of woman's naked mind to the gaze of the world, with indications by which its inmost secrets may be searched out," obviously anticipates the reluctance he expresses in "The Custom-House" to reveal his own naked mind or "inmost Me." However mixed his feelings, moreover, Hawthorne was clearly fascinated by women capable of dazzling a male audience with their discourse. Like Hester at the Governor's mansion or Zenobia at Eliot's Pulpit, Ann Hutchinson stands "loftily" before her male judges, whom "her doctrines have put in fear." The "deepest controversialists of that day," Hawthorne notes, "find here a woman, whom all their trained and sharpened intellects are inadequate to foil."[13] Raining down accusations upon their heads, Hutchinson anticipates the Quaker woman who usurps male prerogatives and the pulpit in "The Gentle Boy" (1832) in order to harangue the congregation. In several details Catharine's ursurpation of the male pulpit anticipates Ligeia's rejuvenation in Poe's tale. As she takes off her cloak and hood, for example, "her raven hair fell down upon her shoulders" (9:81), while the minister, like Poe's narrator, sits in "speechless and almost terrified astonishment" (9:80).

Although he questions her motives, Hawthorne clearly admires her power, unmistakably identifying it with the "heart-felt" and essentially extra-verbal prose he idealized in his love letters: "it was a vague and incomprehensible rhapsody, which, however, seemed to spread its own atmosphere round the hearer's soul, and to move his feelings by some influence unconnected with the words. As she proceeded, beautiful but shadowy images would sometimes be seen, like bright things moving in a turbid river; or a strong and singularly shaped idea leapt forth, and seized at once on the understanding or the heart" (9:81). Consistently identifying gushes of heartfelt language with women, Hawthorne tried over the course of his fiction to accommodate that "feminine" element in his own imagination by surrendering his narratives to powerfully creative female characters within them.

It is certainly no accident that those tales in which Hawthorne most directly engages the connection between male-female relationships and the achievement of creative power—"The Birth-mark" (1843), "The Artist of the Beautiful" (1844), "Drowne's Wooden Image" (1844), and "Rappaccini's Daughter" (1844)—should have been written at the

Old Manse during the early years of his marriage.[14] Indeed, while Hawthorne composed very little during his courtship of Sophia (he was working hard to make marriage economically feasible), the Old Manse period shows a veritable "gushing out" of creative effort: the publication of twenty-one new tales and sketches.[15] Marriage, of course, gave him an economic motive to publish, and a settled domestic life gave him the opportunity, but most important, his relationship with Sophia inspired him to center his attention, more than he ever had before, on the creative possibilities and the problems of relationship. While "The Birth-mark" and "The Artist of the Beautiful" depict the dangerous effects of male power, "Drowne's Wooden Image" and "Rappaccini's Daughter" illustrate the potential of creative surrender to women.

Aylmer, the scientist in "The Birth-mark," performs the sort of surgery on his wife Georgiana that Hawthorne advocated in his *English Notebooks* entry, killing her in the act of reforming her according to a preconceived ideal. Judith Fetterley argues, in fact, that the story is a "brilliant analysis of the sexual politics of idealization." Georgiana epitomizes "woman as beautiful object, reduced to and defined by her body," and the story demonstrates that "the idealization of women has its source in a profound hostility toward women."[16] Fetterley is right, but she stops short of crediting Hawthorne with the same insight or with more than an "implicit feminism" (31). In my view, Hawthorne explicitly criticizes his protagonist and indicts his sadistic treatment of his wife.

A type of Pygmalion (10:41), Aylmer views the "hideous" hand on Georgiana's cheek as "one of those small blue stains, which sometimes occur in the purest statuary marble" (10:38), and he gives his wife such a deadly look that he changes the "roses of her cheek into a deathlike paleness, amid which the Crimson Hand was brought strongly out, like a bas-relief of ruby on the whitest marble" (10:39).[17] Hawthorne's interest is in the operation of the male imagination on an aestheticized woman, and he makes it clear that Aylmer deforms the relationship. Selecting the birthmark "as the symbol of his wife's liability to sin, sorrow, decay, and death, Aylmer's sombre imagination was not long in rendering the birth-mark a frightful object, causing him more trouble and horror than ever Georgiana's beauty, whether of soul or sense, had given him delight" (10:39). Although Hawthorne treats the idea with more sophistication in *The Scarlet Letter,* here too he illustrates the failure, in effect, of a male reader. Much like the townspeople of Boston, Aylmer is guilty of letting a sign express a woman's whole being. He mistakes projection for interpretation.

In bringing Georgiana to the isolated laboratory in which he works, Aylmer lures her to an artist's chamber of illusion and horror not unlike one of Poe's. In order to "release her mind from the burthen of actual things," for example, he creates a kaleidoscope of "airy figures, absolutely bodiless ideas, and forms of unsubstantial beauty" (10:44), archetypes of his disembodied ideal of womanhood which rival Roderick Usher's "pure abstractions." To climax this art show and prefigure the consequences of his final operation on the birthmark, Aylmer tries to take Georgiana's picture, to capture her being in two dimensions. Yet as he tries to transfer her image to a "polished plate of metal," he is "affrighted to find the features of the portrait blurred and indefinable; while the minute figure of a hand appeared where the cheek should have been" (10:45). That is, this aesthetic image of woman, which nearly always in Hawthorne's fiction reveals the "secret soul," here reflects a radical division in the artist's mind. Within the picture, the woman's being has seemingly decomposed, while the scientist succeeds, beyond his intention, in copying only a magnified impression of the birthmark he most fears. In making the hand and all it represents the center of his attention, he discovers that his wife has been eclipsed by the emblem which has displaced her in his mind.

Although Fetterley is right that "Georgiana is co-opted into a view of herself as flawed and comes to hate herself as an impediment to Aylmer's aspiration" (*The Resisting Reader*, 32), "The Birth-mark" is not an exclusively androcentric tale. In effect, Hawthorne has anticipated Fetterley's reading of the story and actually built that reading into his narrative. In recounting Aylmer's experiment, he subtly shifts his focus from the scientist to Georgiana, showing her response to her fate and, from her point of view, qualifying our attitude toward Aylmer. While Aylmer prepares for his experiment, Georgiana reads his journal, "the history and emblem of his ardent, ambitious, imaginative, yet practical and laborious, life." But Georgiana's response to her husband's writing is not entirely naïve. Even though, "as she read, [she] reverenced Aylmer, and loved him more profoundly than ever," she does maintain some aesthetic distance, admiring her husband, Hawthorne notes, "with a less entire dependence on his judgment than heretofore." In effect, she becomes a resisting reader, interpreting this male-authored text as "the sad confession, and continual ex-emplification, of the short-comings of the composite man" (10:49). Not simply a story about the "sickness of men" (Fetterley, 27), "The Birth-mark" reveals the difficulty, from a woman's point of view, of being a resisting reader. Georgiana, for example, is intensely moved by this honest record of her husband's failure, so much so that she "laid her face upon the open volume, and burst into tears." Despite her recognition of Aylmer's limitations, she does not lose her faith in his male authority. Even when he confesses that "there are pages in that volume" that he himself cannot read without risk, even when he warns her to "take heed lest it prove as detrimental to [her]," she admits that it has made her "worship" him more than ever (10:49).

When Georgiana "joyfully" stakes all upon Aylmer's "word" and drinks the potion that will kill her (10:53), she commits herself not only to a male scientist but to a male writer. The drink has the effect of silencing her, as she speaks her "last words" before falling asleep "with a gentle reluctance, as if it required almost more energy than she could command to pronounce the faint and lingering syllables" (10:54). Silent and unconscious, she ceases to exist except as the site of Aylmer's experiment. As inexorably as the great machine in Melville's "The Tartarus of Maids," which causes the word "Cupid" to fade out of the paper it produces, Georgiana's birthmark fades into Aylmer's written account of her dying. Her sexuality becomes textuality. As a character inscribed in her husband's text—a text whose pages she, like Isabel in *Pierre,* has stained with her tears—she becomes her physical symptoms, regardless of whether the experiment should prove a success or a failure. "A heightened flush of the cheek—a slight irregularity of breath—a quiver of the eyelid—a hardly perceptible tremor through the frame—such were the details which . . . he wrote down in his folio volume" (10:54). In this respect, Aylmer's experiment reverses the process that the narrator of "Ligeia" describes; instead of bringing a woman to life part by part, he records her death.

Because Aylmer resists the idea of a woman who unites an "angelic spirit" and a "mortal frame" (10:55), he fails to achieve what Hawthorne pointedly terms a "profounder wisdom" (10:56). Hawthorne expresses that wisdom, furthermore, through Georgiana, who recovers her voice long enough to utter some final words. Her closing statement reflects her allegiance, her loyalty and her skepticism, her ability to identify with and participate in Aylmer's experiment and the recognition that she is its victim. "Do not repent," she says, "that, with so high and pure a feeling, you have rejected the best that earth could offer" (10:55). She may acquiesce in the operation that kills her, but her words subtly condemn her husband and exalt herself.

In the final paragraph, moreover, Hawthorne himself partially echoes her words—partially, because he does not excuse Aylmer. In place of Georgiana's "Do not repent," he substitutes an unequivocal condemnation of Aylmer's failure to "find the perfect Future in the present" (10:56). Distancing himself from both Aylmer and Georgiana—victimizer and victim—he aims a warning at all men, including himself, about the destructive and self-destructive effects of idealizing women. As he had observed earlier, "Perhaps every man of genius, in whatever sphere, might recognize the image of his own experience in Aylmer's journal" (10:49).

Although Owen Warland exercises none of Aylmer's sadistic power— he deforms himself more than he harms Annie Hovenden— "The Artist of the Beautiful" also illustrates a man's aesthetic detachment from a woman and failure to achieve a creative relationship. Instead of operating directly on a woman's body to make it perfect, Owen sublimates his love for Annie in an aesthetic quest for ideal beauty.[18] Successful in his quest, as every reader knows, he is a failure in love; the child of Annie's marriage to the blacksmith Robert Danforth—the creation of a "true relation"—destroys Owen's mechanical butterfly. Well before this incident, however, Hawthorne discourses at some length about the relationship between Annie and Owen's art. The passage clearly anticipates the opening to "The Custom-House," for Owen apparently discovers "the one heart and mind of perfect sympathy" that will make all of his artistic efforts worthwhile. Looking at Annie, "the thought stole into his mind, that this young girl possessed the gift to comprehend him, better than all the world beside. And what a help and strength would it be to him, in his lonely toil, if he could gain the sympathy of the only being whom he loved." Indeed, Hawthorne uses much the same language as in the "Custom-House" preface to describe the cost of Owen's failure to cultivate this sympathetic relationship, as he experiences "a sensation of moral cold, that makes the spirit shiver, as if it had reached the frozen solitudes around the pole" (10:459). But when Annie inadvertently ruins the miniature object that Owen has devised, he abruptly concludes that she lacks the "talisman" that would admit her into his "secrets" (10:460), and that forever closes off the possibility of their relationship.

The story, of course, is not as simple as that. Owen, after all, finally succeeds as an artist without any help from Annie, and even the destruction of his beautiful butterfly does not discourage him. For her part, Annie seems more suited to be a blacksmith's wife than an artist's; she possesses none of the power of Hawthorne's most creative heroines. Subtly, however, Hawthorne suggests that Owen himself is to blame for her failure of sympathy. When Owen dismisses her, Hawthorne comments that he "erred, yet pardonably; for if any human spirit could have sufficiently reverenced the processes so sacred in his eyes, it must have been a woman's. Even Annie Hovenden, possibly, might not have disappointed him, had she been enlightened by the deep intelligence of love" (10:460). Owen fails to love and to communicate his feeling in such a way that it evokes a sympathetic response, and so fails to create the "reader" he needs for his art. The "career of his passion," Hawthorne observes, "had confined its tumults and vicissitudes so entirely within the artist's imagination, that Annie herself had scarcely more than a woman's intuitive perception of it" (10:464).

Owen, however, does not thereby sacrifice all relations. He not only discovers a Bride in his art; he also discovers one in his imagination. Dismissing the "real" Annie, he conjures up a fantastical replica as a kind of secret muse. "Forgetful of the time when she had shown herself incapable of any deep response, he had persisted in connecting all his dreams of artistical success with Annie's image" (10:464). But in so doing, Hawthorne makes clear, he has deceived himself. Whereas Aylmer substituted the birthmark for Georgiana, Owen eclipses Annie with a fantasy of his own creation—and then effectively brings that fantasized image to life in the figure of his mechanical toy. "She, in the aspect which she wore to his inward vision," Hawthorne notes, making precisely this connection, "was as much a creation of his own, as the mysterious piece of mechanism would be were it ever realized" (10:464). Instead of achieving a relationship with a creative other who can make his mind "gush out" with "warmth and freedom," Owen has substituted a relationship with a mechanical contrivance of his own invention, an image of woman that is essentially a "plaything" and a "gem of art" (10:473).

In "Drowne's Wooden Image" and "Rappaccini's Daughter," by contrast, women exercise more active power. The woman who animates Drowne's wooden carving provokes the kind of creative outburst that Hawthorne associated with Sophia, while, with a voice of her own, Beatrice anticipates the heroines of the novels in challenging Giovanni's imagination to respond openly and sympathetically to her words.

Despite its startling verisimilitude, Drowne's carving lacks a "deep quality, be it of soul or intellect, which bestows life upon the lifeless, and warmth upon the cold, and which, had it been present, would have made Drowne's wooden image instinct with spirit" (10:309). As he falls under the spell of a mysterious Portuguese woman, however, Drowne becomes an "inspired artist" (10:311). His art is "transformed," as Nina Baym comments. "Wood becomes an expressive form, fluid to his emotions as it never was to his tools" (*Shape,* 111). While this striking female figure anticipates Hester, Zenobia, and Miriam, the method of her creation is most important. Instead of merely imposing an idea on a block of wood, Drowne has surrendered his conscious designs to his medium. He experiences just the sort of creative surrender—a "gush" of "warmth and freedom"—that Hawthorne anticipated if Sophia were to enter his "inward regions." "A well-spring of inward wisdom gushed within me," he confesses, "as I wrought upon the oak with my whole strength, and soul, and faith!" (10:313). Indeed, no less an artist than Copley, the most famous painter of his day, perfectly glosses the process which produced the wooden image: so powerful was the image of the woman, he suggests, that it "first created the artist who afterwards created her image" (10:319). Hawthorne makes clear, moreover, that feelings of love sponsor this creative outburst, that "expression of human love" is the "secret of the life that had been breathed into this block of wood" (10:314). As Drowne himself says, "this work of my hands" is also the "creature of my heart" (10:313). Drowne thus realizes Hawthorne's ideal: a reciprocal relationship between the male artist and his female subject in which a woman's self-image brings a creative self into being to form the work of art that embodies her. Drowne may be Pygmalion, but he does not seek creative and possessive power over a woman through his art. Rather, by surrendering control over the creative process, he becomes the agent or medium of a woman's self-creation. She creates herself through him.

Like most of Hawthorne's stories about art, however, "Drowne's Wooden Image" apparently ends unhappily; the "brief season of excitement, kindled by love" (10:320), does not last. The woman herself appears and, passing through Drowne's workshop, absorbs the life from his statue and leaves Drowne the "mechanical carver that he had been known to be all his lifetime" (10:319). Here, then, Hawthorne suggests the opposition we have observed before between a "real" woman and her aesthetic image; as in the case of Poe's oval portrait, there is only enough life for one or the other. But unlike Poe's artist, Drowne does not discover a "Bride in his art" at the expense of his wife's life. Instead of being "killed into art," her identity eclipsed by an art object the male artist substitutes for her, the Portuguese woman retains her integrity. Its vitality absorbed by the real woman, the statue "dies" instead, so from the woman's point of view, if not from Drowne's, the effect is a happy one. Indeed, the story can be read as a remarkably positive example of a woman's ability to commit herself, as it were, to the confines of masculine art without sacrificing her power to recover and be herself.

Drowne is one in a long line of Hawthorne's male artists whose loss of a woman's inspiration has disastrous effects on his art. The story explicitly identifies the importance of women to art and implies that the artist who fails to nurture that inspiration will become a mere mechanic. If he only surrenders himself to the creative impulse that the woman inspires, the artist can become a genius whose work seems imbued with divine fire. Such potential is readily apparent in such artist-heroes as Miles Coverdale and Kenyon and, in a different sense, Arthur Dimmesdale. At least briefly, they, too, enjoy creative relationships with women before repressing the self-creative impulse within themselves which the woman evokes. "Yet who can doubt," concludes Hawthorne, thereby establishing the elusive ideal his own fiction would attempt to fulfill, "that the very highest state to which a human spirit can attain, in its loftiest aspirations, is its truest and most natural state, and that Drowne was more consistent with himself when he wrought the admirable figure of the mysterious lady, than when he perpetrated a whole progeny of blockheads?" (10:320).

Although he is ultimately no more successful in cultivating the creative relationship he has opened with Beatrice, Giovanni Guasconti in "Rappaccini's Daughter" responds more sympathetically to a woman than any other male character in Hawthorne's short fiction. Although he is "one of Hawthorne's 'empiricists,'" according to Hyatt Waggoner, Giovanni is destined for an experience in which reason and imagination, consciousness and the unconscious, become confused.[19] On the one hand he wants to bring Beatrice "rigidly and systematically within the limits of ordinary experience"; on the other he is fascinated by the "wild vagaries which his imagination ran riot continually in producing" (10:105).

Hawthorne's most creative heroine before those in the novels, Beatrice epitomizes female vitality and self-expression. "She looked redundant with life, health, and energy," he says; "all of which were bound down and compressed, as it were, and girdled tensely, in their luxuriance, by her virgin zone" (10:97). Her portrait offers an example of form barely able to contain the energy of her being, and this image of female vitality and sexuality troubles Giovanni. He wonders if his senses have been deceived, and, like Hawthorne with Sophia's letters, he has the impression that Beatrice is to be "touched only with a glove, nor to be approached without a mask" (10:97). Almost in spite of himself, however, he comes to view the girl as in some way essential to his own being. "The instant that he was aware of the possibility of approaching Beatrice, it seemed an absolute neccessity of his existence to do so. It mattered not whether she were angel or demon; he was irrevocably within her sphere, and must obey the law that whirled him onward, in ever lessening circles, towards a result which he did not attempt to foreshadow" (10:109). According to Roy Male, Hawthorne "knew that in order to find a home and a hope of heaven—in order, that is, to develop his full human potential—man must accept either the woman or the dual promise she represents: tragic involvement with sin but also the consequent possibility of redemption."[20] But Hawthorne goes further than this, setting the stage for his hero's transcendence of positive and negative female stereotypes and his achievement of a relationship with Beatrice herself. With remarkable precision, however, he goes on to trace the imaginative process within his hero that makes such an achievement so difficult.

Even though Beatrice warns Giovanni to believe nothing "save what [he can] see with [his] own eyes" (10:111), that is precisely the problem Hawthorne dramatizes: the clouding of human vision by projection. Richard Brenzo argues that Giovanni is never entirely successful in liberating Beatrice from sexual stereotypes: "Swinging between the two classic extremes of viewing woman as demon or as saint, he never finds a basis in reality for his feelings about Beatrice."21 Nonetheless, at selected moments Giovanni comes much closer than his predecessors in Hawthorne's fiction to achieving an honest vision of a woman. He seems ready to act on Beatrice's own advice to forget "whatever you may have fancied in regard to me. If true to the outward senses, still it may be false in its essence. But the words of Beatrice Rappaccini's lips are true from the depths of the heart outward. Those you may believe" (10:112).

Whereas Georgiana "learned to shudder" at Aylmer's "gaze" (10:39) and gradually came to hate her birthmark (and herself) as much as he (10:48), Beatrice more successfully maintains her integrity and even responds to Giovanni's "gaze of uneasy suspicion with a queen-like haughtiness" (10:112). Whereas Georgiana accepted her appearance for Aylmer as her own reality, Beatrice asks Giovanni to ignore appearances and his own misapprehensions. More demonstrably than Isabel in *Pierre,* she asks for the right to define herself in her own words. At least briefly, Hawthorne has turned over the narrative to a woman, giving her the power to lead his hero toward a new awareness and a new relationship with her—the power, too, to define the imaginative prerequisites for that relationship: an open, sympathetic attitude, a surrender of preconceived categories and stereotypes. And momentarily Giovanni appears sensitive to such an outpouring from the heart. As a "fervor glowed in her whole aspect, and beamed upon Giovanni's consciousness like the light of truth itself . . . [he] seemed to gaze through the beautiful girl's eyes into her transparent soul, and felt no more doubt or fear" (10:112). Temporarily, Giovanni dissociates his image of Beatrice from the fear that it had provoked. "Whatever had looked ugly, was now beautiful; or, if incapable of such a change, it stole away and hid itself among those shapeless half-ideas, which throng the dim region beyond the daylight of our perfect consciousness" (10:114).

Because Giovanni is finally unable to overcome his fears, he reneges on the relationship he has initiated. In failing to subordinate his anxiety to the "light of truth" with which Beatrice tries to define herself, he effectively consigns her to the poisonous influence of her father. Though he still considers their meetings the "whole space in which he might be said to live" (10:115), he will not touch what he views as poisonous. "At such times, he was startled at the horrible suspicions that rose, monster-like, out of the caverns of his heart, and stared him in the face; his love grew thin and faint as the morning-mist; his doubts alone had substance" (10:116). Although Beatrice has revealed "something truer and more real, than what we can see with the eyes, and touch with the finger," Giovanni's imagination is "incapable of sustaining itself at the height to which the early enthusiasm of passion had exalted it; he fell down, grovelling among earthly doubts, and defiled therewith the pure whiteness of Beatrice's image" (10:120).

Hawthorne could not be clearer in suggesting that Beatrice is victimized by a male imagination that cannot overcome its own fears of woman. Although he uses the term "whiteness" to characterize Beatrice's image, we cannot interpret that to mean something like angelic or otherworldly purity. Hawthorne is not reverting to the terms of a binary opposition—woman as angel or demon. Not only has he clearly shown by Beatrice's assertion that such an opposition is irrelevant to her character, but he also gives her a sexual identity incompatible with conventional or stereotypical standards of female purity. Indeed, his description of the attraction between Giovanni and Beatrice represents one of his most forthright accounts of sexual passion—aroused but not consummated.22

Most importantly, Hawthorne's language clearly links eroticism and the sort of artistically creative surrender we have seen before. Experiencing sexual passion, he implies, causes a verbal, as well as emotional, outpouring from the heart and mind. The two characters, he says, had "spoken love, in those gushes of passion when their spirits darted forth in articulated breath, like tongues of long-hidden flame; and yet there had been no seal of lips, no clasp of hands, nor any slightest caress, such as love claims and hallows" (10:116). At this point in the story, Hawthorne describes an ideal, the complete sublimation of passion in expression, the achievement of a perfect circuit of communication.

But Giovanni cannot finally consummate the relationship, because, Hawthorne stresses, of the "horrible suspicions that rose, monster-like, out of the caverns of his heart," that make his love grow "thin and faint as the morning-mist" (10:116). Above all, he fears the change in himself that an intimate relationship with a woman entails. As he ponders a recent meeting with Beatrice, he contemplates the new self that his relationship with her has brought into being: he "grew white as marble, and stood motionless before the mirror, staring at his own reflection there, as at the likeness of something frightful" (10:121). In the same sort of reversal Poe depicted at the end of "Ligeia" and "The Fall

of the House of Usher," Hawthorne's male character is here objectified—turned to marble—by his thoughts of a woman.

It is not surprising then that Giovanni should defend himself from
such a transformation by working the same effect on Beatrice. As
Laing has said, "the man who is frightened of his own subjectivity
being swamped, impinged upon, or congealed by the other is frequently to be found attempting to swamp, to impinge upon, or to kill
the other person's subjectivity."[23] Giovanni becomes convinced that he
has been infected by Beatrice's poison and feels himself transformed
into a kind of statue by the frightening implications of what his image
of Beatrice reveals about himself. Hawthorne's use of the mirror in this
scene suggests another of those doublings back upon the self of the
"horrible suspicions" which have risen out of the "caverns of the
heart"—a perception of the self as other in which the thoughts previously projected upon Beatrice are now projected upon the self's own
mirror-image. As Giovanni breathes upon a spider, which he finds suspended from the ceiling of his apartment, he seems to be exhaling his
own evil thoughts about the girl. His breath is "imbued with a venomous feeling out of his heart" (10:122). To demonstrate Giovanni's
subjectivity, Hawthorne implies that Beatrice herself remains un-
changed. He gives his hero "recollections which, had Giovanni known
how to estimate them, would have assured him that all this ugly mystery was but an earthly illusion, and that, whatever mist of evil might
seem to have gathered over her, the real Beatrice was a heavenly angel"
(10:122). Those recollections, which grow increasingly faint, involve
just those sacred qualities that Hawthorne identifies with the most creative and self-creative state of mind: "recollections of the delicate and
benign power of her feminine nature" and "recollections of many a
holy and passionate outgush of her heart" (10:122). But his hero, he
observes, is incapable of the "high faith" that would allow him to
bring to the surface and then act upon such "recollections." The result
is irreparable damage to Beatrice.

Soon after the incident with the spider, the venom from Giovanni's
heart finds its way to his tongue; he speaks with "venomous scorn and
anger" (10:124). In an obvious example of projection, he accuses Beatrice of being the frightful object he fears himself to be. "Thou hast
made me as hateful, as ugly, as loathsome and deadly a creature as
thyself," he rages, "a world's wonder of hideous monstrosity!"
(10:124). Giovanni's accusation bespeaks his own fear of experience

more than Beatrice's poisoned nature. For Hawthorne clearly suggests that Giovanni has the potential, even the responsibility, to redeem her from the curse under which she suffers. She sees her own body as "nourished with poison," but her spirit, she says, "is God's creature, and craves love as its daily food" (10:125). It is precisely that love, however, that Giovanni is incapable of giving.

The final pages of the story, in fact, link Giovanni with Rappaccini and Baglioni in a conspiracy against Beatrice. All three characters, according to Brenzo, "'project' upon Beatrice impulses they are unwilling to acknowledge as their own" (153). As Giovanni flirts with the idea that there might "still be a hope of his returning within the limits of ordinary nature, and leading Beatrice—the redeemed Beatrice—by the hand" (10:125–26), Hawthorne observes his failure to recognize that, having "bitterly wronged" Beatrice's love, no hope of "earthly union and earthly happiness" remains (10:126). Denied in her fully embodied being, Beatrice must "pass heavily, with that broken heart, across the borders of Time—she must bathe her hurts in some fount of Paradise, and forget her grief in the light of immortality—and *there* be well" (10:126). Hawthorne suggests, in brief, that Giovanni's failure stems directly from his desire to "redeem" Beatrice and separate her from the physical experience which he perceives as poisonous. In offering her Baglioni's antidote, which he suggests they "quaff together," Giovanni insists that they will be "purified from evil" (10:126). The result, of course, is that Beatrice becomes so purified—her "earthly part" so "wrought upon by Rappaccini's skill" (10:127)—that she dies. Though he is less brutal than Aylmer, his antidote for what he perceives as woman's imperfect nature is no less deadly.

"Rappaccini's Daughter" reveals the consequences for a woman of a man's failure to accept her as she is. Though the competitive scientists are more directly to blame for Beatrice's fate, Giovanni is the object of her final words. If her father initially poisoned her nature, if Baglioni provided the "purifier" that actually killed her, Giovanni fails to transcend his divided vision of self and experience and to accept Beatrice in the terms in which she would define herself. Like Aylmer or the painter in "The Oval Portrait," Giovanni destroys Beatrice in the act of trying to save her—or at least a purified and objectified image of her. Hawthorne, of course, is typically ambiguous about whether Giovanni has actually been poisoned or has only introjected his fear of Beatrice and of relationship with her. In either case, Hawthorne has played a perverse joke on his protagonist and served him an irremediable dose of his own medicine. By rejecting Beatrice and then, in effect, being rejected by her, Giovanni is condemned to take her place. In saving his life by drinking the deadly antidote first, Beatrice condemns him to live out his life, not exactly as a woman, but as her male double—*le beau empoisonneur.* Whether or not he remains in the garden, he must remain alone for fear of infecting another with the poison he cannot be sure he has absorbed.

In switching his male victimizer and female victim, Hawthorne anticipates the more subtle shifts along gender lines he will make in his four completed novels: Dimmesdale's climactic substitution of himself for Hester, Holgrave's complex identification with Phoebe, Coverdale's incorporation of Zenobia's feminist discourse, Kenyon's inspiration by Miriam. The novels, moreover, make more explicit the aesthetic implications engendered in the tales. Beatrice's potential to define herself is realized much more fully (though in different degrees) by the heroines of the novels, who are more successful, not merely in expressing themselves but also in compelling a sympathetic hearing from their male auditors. Whereas the tales emphasize a male character's often sadistic control of a woman's character, figures identified with such power (Chillingworth, Matthew Maule, Westervelt, Miriam's model) appear only in the background of the novels. Hawthorne places in the foreground a sympathetic, if timid, male character, who, like Giovanni Guasconti, has the potential for achieving a truly creative relationship with the heroine. The problems of sympathetic response or "reading" dramatized by the young Giovanni, however, are no less present in the older heroes of the novels.

CHAPTER SIX

The Scarlet Letter *and* The House of the Seven Gables

Resisting the Seductive Power of Art

As early in his career as "Alice Doane's Appeal" (1835), Hawthorne examined the potentially seductive power of art—the power of words spoken by a male narrator to mesmerize a female listener or listeners. As he nears the climax of his story of Leonard and Alice Doane, the narrator glances at his two lady companions to gauge what he hopes is the mounting effect of his tale.[1] "Their bright eyes were fixed on me," he notes, "their lips apart" (11:275). And at the end of the story, after he has had to resort to a much more transparent narrative in order to convince his listeners of the presence of the past, he must actually break off his narrative when his companions seize his arms. Their "trembling" nerves make clear what he pointedly calls a "sweeter victory." "I had reached the seldom trodden places of their hearts, and found the wellspring of their tears" (11:280).[2]

The power of male art to reach the heart or "wellspring" of a female audience looms large in both *The Scarlet Letter* and *The House of the Seven Gables*. Indeed, as we know, *The Scarlet Letter* had such an effect on Sophia that it "broke her heart and sent her to bed with a grievous headache"—a reader response that Hawthorne considered a "triumphant success," a "ten-strike" (16:311). Within that novel, Arthur Dimmesdale wields similar power. After his forest walk with Hester, in a stunning example of the seminal power of language, he is tempted to "drop" into the "tender bosom" of the "youngest sister" of his congregation a "germ of evil that would be sure to blossom darkly soon, and bear black fruit betimes" (1:219–20). So "potent" does Dimmesdale feel that he is sure "one wicked look" and a single word will be enough to "blight" the girl's innocence (1:220). Similarly, in *The House of the Seven Gables,* as Holgrave tells Alice Pyncheon's story to Phoebe, he is conscious of his "power" over his listener and recognizes that "one wave of his hand" will be enough to "complete his mastery over Phoebe's yet free and virgin spirit" (2:211–12). In each case, male discourse possesses an essentially phallic power to penetrate and "master" the mind of a female listener; both cases invert the ideal Hawthorne had suggested in his love letter: Sophia's penetration of *his* "inward regions" to make *his* heart and mind "gush out" in "warmth and freedom." Even though Dimmesdale's perverse impulse is directly inspired by his "walk" with Hester, even though Holgrave's recognition of power depends upon Phoebe's behavior, neither character truly surrenders his imagination to a woman's influence. Neither, certainly, empowers a woman to speak for him or to take over a share of his discourse. At the same time, neither pursues his seductive advantage. Dimmesdale masks himself from his parishioner and rushes on with no sign of recognition; Holgrave has too much "reverence" for Phoebe's "individuality" (2:212) to use her the way Matthew Maule used Alice. Though hardly feminist, this reluctance to prosecute the seductive power of language represents an important step in Hawthorne's effort to explore the reciprocal connection between writing and relationship.

Most critics consider Hester Prynne Hawthorne's most complete and convincing female character. Compared to Hester, so opinion goes, the heroines of subsequent novels seem partial characters—either light or dark—and thus less powerful. "Because Hester is not split into schizophrenic segments," argues Judith Fryer, "she comes across as a whole person, one who elicits the reader's sympathy and admiration." Joyce Warren considers Hester "a woman of strength, intelligence, and resourcefulness, whose very existence gives the lie to those who would argue the natural inferiority of women." And Carolyn Heilbrun terms her the greatest "central female character" in American fiction because she most nearly fulfills an androgynous ideal. In that respect, she says, *The Scarlet Letter* is "unique in its author's career."3

Nina Baym, too, considers *The Scarlet Letter* the high point of Hawthorne's career, largely because Hester is his strongest heroine: "'Hester' gave Hawthorne the fullest command of his artistic powers that he had yet known. And, as events proved, the fullest command he was ever to know." The reason is that the "narrator allies himself with her and, despite occasional adverse judgments, devotes himself to her cause," forcing the reader "to accept Hester's reading of her letter as a badge of honor instead of a mark of negation" ("Thwarted Nature," 73). In Baym's view, in other words, Hester not only defines a self and a role exempt from the letter's implicit restrictions, but she forces the Puritan community (and the reader) to acknowledge the authority of her self-definition. "By making the letter beautiful, Hester is denying its literal meaning and thereby subverting the intention of the magistrates who condemn her to wear it." Rather than being objectified by aesthetic form, she is able to "play with that form in order to loosen it, expand it, undercut it, and thereby make it capable of a sort of many-layered communication" (*Shape,* 132, 133). In effect, Baym argues that Hawthorne's identification with Hester and with her subversion of authority augmented his own artistic power. Surrendering control of the letter (and the narrative named by the letter) to Hester means identifying his creative self with his heroine. Baym's view of Hester's creative role in *The Scarlet Letter* would seem to support my claims about Hawthorne's masculine poetics. In allowing Hester to "play with" the letter, Hawthorne seems to invite her, as he had Sophia, to "manage" his "share" of it, as if in this case, too, he felt confident that, while the "deep meaning" of the scarlet letter might have evaded the "analysis" of *his* mind, a woman could better express truths that his "heart would recognize as existing within its depths, yet which can never be clothed in words of [his] own" (15:388).

Hawthorne's relationship to Hester, to the scarlet letter and *The Scarlet Letter,* is more complicated than this, because the aesthetic issues he raises in the novel are more complicated. For example, while he certainly portrays Hester as an artist, he also uses her as a kind of art object—the creation not only of the Puritan community (through the medium and signifying power of the letter), but of Arthur Dimmesdale (through his commitment and withdrawal of emotional commitment to her). From my point of view, Hawthorne carefully measures his "artistic powers" between Hester and Dimmesdale, and thus between a strong femininity and a weak masculinity. Additionally, he uses his two main characters to explore the relationship he himself felt between the artist and his or her audience, the tension between the "inmost Me" and the "veil" or signs that express it. In each case, moreover, he marks the relationship with gender. Hester, for example, is both a sign and a generator of signs. As an artist, she tests the Puritan community's "reading" or interpretive powers and thus the self-expressive power of symbolic discourse (through the letter A, Pearl's attire, her own acts and works). As an art object, she measures the sincerity of Dimmesdale's discourse by registering its emotional subtext. Clearly, the townspeople are poor readers of the signs they encounter, and Hawthorne criticizes them again and again; but it is also true that Dimmesdale exploits their blindness.[4] He veils his "inmost Me" and his masculinity by establishing a false "relation" both to his audience and to the other (Hester) on whom that "inmost Me" depends. He clearly cannot speak from that relationship—only in opposition to it. Avoiding Hester, he sublimates creative energy in his profession and, indirectly, in the condemnation of his relationship to her. Dimmesdale's public discourse seems selfless and self-censuring, but he must know that his listeners will translate self-abasement into self-aggrandizement. Condemning himself means enhancing his public image.

According to Hawthorne's comments in "The Custom-House," *The Scarlet Letter* originated as a meditation on a symbolic object, a "certain affair of fine red cloth" (1:31), the scarlet and gold letter A. The longer he looks at the letter, the more it changes: from an object that is "little other than a rag" to a "mystic symbol" from which "some deep meaning . . . streamed forth" (1:31). Simply in looking at the letter, he has achieved a state of "passive sensibility" or creative surrender. He even uses a passive construction to describe his fixation: "My eyes fastened themselves upon the old scarlet letter, and would not be turned aside." The letter's deep meaning, he says, was "subtly communicating itself to my sensibilities, but evading the analysis of my mind" (1:31). The world that Hawthorne creates, says Charles Feidelson, is "generated by contemplation of the symbol, not by the yoking-together [as in allegory] of two realms which by definition are different in kind." "Every character," he concludes, "re-enacts the 'Custom House' scene in which Hawthorne himself contemplated the letter, so that the entire 'romance' becomes a kind of exposition of the nature of symbolic perception."5 When Hawthorne places the letter on his own breast, he assumes the burden of its meaning and identifies himself with Hester, as well as with Pearl and Dimmesdale. Burning like a "red-hot iron" (1:32), and identified with male and female, the symbol creates the book—and the book's creator. To paraphrase Copley's remark about woodcarver Drowne, the letter first creates the artist who afterwards creates its story. The challenge for Hawthorne is to keep his symbolic letter burning, to remain open to the meanings that "stream forth" from the "mystic symbol, . . . evading the analysis of [his] mind" (1:31)—and that, as we shall see, means achieving a creative "relationship" with the woman and man identified with the letter.

Hawthorne, of course, found more than the letter in the Custom House; he found a narrative—Hester's story—wrapped around it. Thus, the effort to understand the "deep meaning" streaming forth from the "mystic symbol" entails an effort to understand Hester. The novel as a whole can be viewed in terms of the tension between Hester's story and the letter—between "woman" and artistic form. Hawthorne shows himself aware of that tension throughout the novel in the attention he pays to Hester's "objective" status. Despite her independence and her relative success in "writing" her own character, she suffers progressive devitalization over the course of the novel—a surrender of energy to an objectifying aesthetic form. The letter with which she is identified undergoes a similar process, from the burst of energy and potential associated with its discovery, through the epiphany of its embroidery and the multiplication of its often opposed meanings, to the negation implied by its final office as a marker or signifier—on a "simple slab of slate" (1:264)—for the grave that Hester shares with Dimmesdale.

The letter, upon which all eyes are "concentred" (1:57) at the beginning of the novel, is at first an allegorical emblem confidently imposed by the Puritan community. Attending church, Hester often finds herself "the text of the discourse" (1:85); she wears and becomes the community's "birth-mark," a sign of its liability to sin. From the beginning the community attempts to contain Hester's meaning by "inclosing her in a sphere by herself" (1:54) and by "concentrating" her identity in an art object that eclipses her efforts to define herself. As Baym has

so convincingly shown, of course, Hester never entirely conforms herself to the prescribed meaning of the scarlet letter; she embroiders the
A even before she first emerges from the prison until it blazons forth
manifold symbolic meanings and implicates the whole community, despite the allegorical distance its members would maintain. Her whole
attire, Hawthorne notes, is "modelled much after her own fancy" and
"seemed to express the attitude of her spirit, the desperate recklessness
of her mood, by its wild and picturesque peculiarity." Attempting to
make a "halo of the misfortune," she is thus partially successful in
transfiguring herself through the "fantastically embroidered" letter
(1:53).

Eric Sundquist has argued, in fact, that the scarlet letter finally becomes an indeterminate symbol. It "refuses to assume the function of
the thing it symbolizes, that is, so refuses to stand reliably for any one
thing and thus draws all significance into itself that all referents disappear into the function of symbolizing."[6] If that is true, then Hester
would succeed in subverting the community's effort to denote her
character and make her simply a sign of sin. She would so fragment
the power of signification that it would disappear; all signs would be
called into question. But in fact, even though the scarlet letter accommodates additional meanings (or readings), it never loses its original
meaning entirely—not even for Hester. As she tells Chillingworth,
"Were I worthy to be quit of it, it would fall away of its own nature, or
be transformed into something that should speak a different purport"
(1:169). Such a conditional statement does look forward to a time
when the letter will cease to mark her or at least will change meaning.
But Hester despairs of living to see that time, and missing from her
expression is any faith that she can actively alter her essential relationship to the letter.

Not satisfied to embody creative energy in a single female character,
Hawthorne doubles his heroine; while Hester wears the scarlet letter,
Pearl *is* the letter, the "scarlet letter endowed with life" (1:102), a living
art object that embodies her mother's creative power and represents an
alternative, potential version of her. That is, Hester reserves the right
and power to express herself through Pearl. Symbolically, Hawthorne
thus intensifies the female creative power incorporated in the novel,
attempting to ensure that it will last beyond a single generation. In the
process, however, he also explores the pressures that work against that

happening. In the sentence immediately following his description of Pearl as the scarlet letter "endowed with life," for example, he comments upon Hester's reasons for modeling her daughter after the letter: it is "as if the red ignominy were so deeply scorched into her brain, that all her conceptions assumed its form" (1:102). Instead of emphasizing Hester's rebelliousness, in other words, Hawthorne emphasizes her surrender of originality, illustrating the insidious effect of received or inherited forms, their power to determine the character of thought. Thus, even though Pearl provides a medium, an alternative scarlet letter, through which Hester can express herself, Hester cannot prevent her thoughts, even her subversive ones, from assuming a form provided by the community.

As an artist in her own right, Pearl possesses a power similar to her mother's. "The spell of life went forth from her ever creative spirit," Hawthorne writes, "and communicated itself to a thousand objects, as a torch kindles a flame wherever it may be applied. The unlikeliest materials, a stick, a bunch of rags, a flower, were the puppets of Pearl's witchcraft, and, without undergoing any outward change, became spiritually adapted to whatever drama occupied the stage of her inner world" (1:95). Unmistakably, Hawthorne identifies his own imaginative method as a romancer with Pearl; the "bunch of rags" and "flower" in particular hint at the scarlet letter and the roses that appear often in the text.[7] Enfigured throughout the novel by flame imagery, Pearl is also associated with precisely those creative forces Hawthorne had portrayed in the tales as the products of the "passive sensibility" and the "haunted mind." At once a divine child and a "devil in manuscript," Pearl is "offered to the world," Hawthorne says, as a "living hieroglyphic, in which was revealed the secret [Hester and Dimmesdale] so darkly sought to hide—all written in this symbol, all plainly manifest,—had there been a prophet or magician skilled to read the character of flame!" (1:207).

From her own point of view, however, even though she lacks "reference" to the world in which she has been born (1:91), even Pearl cannot entirely escape the shadow of the letter. Despite her independence, the letter remains a sign which confers a sense of self. At one point, for example, she fashions her own letter out of seaweed, a material more appropriate to her "natural" character, but the form she gives that letter—the letter A—is that prescribed by the community. Up until the end of the novel and her removal to England, Pearl as hieroglyphic must be interpreted and must interpret herself in the context of Puritan Boston.

It is no accident that Hester's most powerful speech occurs at the Governor's mansion, when she prevents the Puritan magistrates from taking Pearl away from her. To do that, of course, she must convince Dimmesdale to help her, to speak for her, and she does that by virtually threatening to expose him. In effect, she forces him to act as Pearl's father by tacitly agreeing to let him remain—officially—not Pearl's father. Hester's speech, moreover, offers a brilliant example of the way Hawthorne manipulates point of view in the novel. Since readers will readily recognize the hidden subtext of Hester's speech (her threat to expose Dimmesdale), Hawthorne invites us to identify with her and with Dimmesdale in opposition to the other Puritans who obviously do not understand. When she commands him to speak for her because he was her pastor and had "charge" of her soul, because he knows her better than the other men—indeed, because he knows what is in her heart—Dimmesdale is quick indeed to come to her aid (1:113). Of course, under the circumstances, he speaks as much for himself as he does for Hester or for Pearl, but this forced cooperation with Hester—lending her his more authoritative voice—does offer an interesting example of creative surrender. Most important, perhaps, by preventing Pearl's re-education by Puritan society, this parental cooperation makes possible her escape from that society and discovery of an alternative life in England. Hawthorne, then, has made a start, in this novel of male-female estrangement, in the direction of male-female cooperation. The harmony of voice is ironical, to be sure, since Dimmesdale's speech derives its energy from his desperate effort to leave his relationship to Hester and Pearl unspoken.

Whereas Pearl's condition improves over the course of the novel (enabling her to escape Boston by the end), Hester's vitality withers under the ignominy of the letter. She suffers a "sad transformation" (1:163) under social pressure; temporarily, she accepts the role and identity that the community has assigned her and conforms herself to the parameters of the art object by which she is "inclosed." Even though the letter comes to stand for "Able" (1:161), Hester encourages that redefinition largely by conforming to community expectations. As Hawthorne comments, the townspeople's new "regard" for her arises from the fact that "She never battled with the public, but submitted uncomplainingly to its worst usage" (1:160). In private, of course,

Hester does engage in a certain "freedom of speculation," but she is content with radical thoughts. She has no need for "the flesh and blood of action." She is one of those people "who speculate the most boldly [but] often conform with the most perfect quietude to the external regulations of society" (1:164).

The personal cost of her new status is the repression of her sexuality and the suppression of the kind of verbal passion she had expressed at the Governor's mansion. Some "attribute had departed from her, the permanence of which had been essential to keep her a woman" (1:163). Despite her efforts to embroider the scarlet letter, to "loosen" that imprisoning form, she seems to harden gradually into the kind of objectified marble form we have seen in previous works. "Statue-like" in appearance (1:163), she becomes a devitalized art object whose "marble coldness," Hawthorne says, requires some "magic touch" to effect her "transfiguration" into vital womanhood (1:164). Hawthorne thereby suggests, of course, that relationship is essential to selfhood, though as we shall see his point is not that only women are so dependent; Dimmesdale, too, loses certain attributes that are essential to keep him a man.

In spite of her imaginative and intellectual self-reliance, Hester needs and wants Dimmesdale to provide a "magic touch" that will restore her womanhood—just as the minister requires a similar gesture from her. Based on their experience in the forest later in the novel, we must assume that both enjoyed a "transfiguration" before the novel began. Hawthorne makes it clear that no such emotional ecstasy attended Hester's marriage to Chillingworth and sees in that lack of passion a general rule for male-female relationships. "Let men tremble to win the hand of woman," he warns, "unless they win along with it the utmost passion of her heart! Else it may be their miserable fortune, as it was Roger Chillingworth's, when some mightier touch than their own may have awakened all her sensibilities, to be reproached even for the calm content, the marble image of happiness, which they will have imposed upon her as the warm reality" (1:176–77). But if Dimmesdale once offered a "magic touch" and a "warm reality," in place of the "marble image of happiness" that Chillingworth "imposed" upon Hester, he clearly has withdrawn such magic from her during the present time of the novel. Indeed, the frequent comparison of Hester to cold marble is often associated with Dimmesdale's refusal to touch or come near her at all.

In this respect Dimmesdale clearly anticipates Clifford Pyncheon. Though not as effeminate as Clifford, the minister has a similarly chilling effect on "images of women"—as Hester's behavior registers. The scene in the forest reveals the full potential of Hester's humanity and the sacred nature of her relationship with Dimmesdale, but it only intensifies the inner conflicts that the clergyman feels. In denying both Hester and Pearl, Dimmesdale has denied part of himself and so lives a sterile life of inner torment and guilt marked by Chillingworth's persecution. Unlike Hester, who, in embroidering the letter, partially transcends the identity she has been granted, Dimmesdale can neither say nor feel that what they did "had a consecration of its own" (1:195). According to Hester, they once "said so to each other" and "felt it so," but now she alone has the power to express those feelings. Hawthorne emphasizes Dimmesdale's loss of the power of emotionally informed speech at the same time that he gives Hester increasing responsibility for expressing the "deep meaning" of the novel. Dimmesdale "gazed into Hester's face with a look in which hope and joy shone out, indeed, but with fear betwixt them," he observes, "and a kind of horror at her boldness, who had spoken what he vaguely hinted at, but dared not speak" (1:199). Only briefly, by apparently reenacting his original "sin" with Hester, can Dimmesdale feel released from public and private censure. He feels "risen up all made anew" (1:202); he experiences the "exhilarating effect—upon a prisoner just escaped from the dungeon of his own heart—of breathing the wild, free atmosphere of an unredeemed, unchristianized, lawless region" (1:201). In telling Hester to "speak" for him, Dimmesdale reverses their roles at the Governor's house when he spoke for her. In effect, he asks her to re-create him through the power of her speech, and she obliges by imagining his assumption of a new name (1:198). Becoming a kind of mirror for woman, Dimmesdale's agreement to Hester's proposal enables her to remove the scarlet letter and, as she lets down her hair, to reclaim her full sexual nature, her identity as a woman. In contrast to her former "marble coldness," she reanimates her person with a sacred flame, a measure of the self-creative power Hawthorne attributed to male-female relationships. With her "bold" speech, she has created the male "artist" who then creates her. "Her sex, her youth, and the whole richness of her beauty, came back from what men call the irrevocable past, and clustered themselves, with her maiden hope, and a happiness before unknown, within the magic circle of this hour" (1:202). Most important, a scene that began with Dimmesdale deferring to Hester's power of speech ends in an apparent mutuality of voice: "Then, all was spoken" (1:198).

Hawthorne not only allows the two characters a sense of liberation but also comes close to moving his novel into a new path. In freeing Hester from the various forms that confine her character, he is also on the verge of opening up the narrative to the values with which she is identified: in particular, a sexually freer, but still "consecrated" relationship between a man and a woman. In Hester's suggestion that they escape either to the wilderness or to Europe, of course, he is also on the verge of allowing his heroine to shape the plot, breaking it free from the paradigm of sin-guilt-penitence that governs it. As Terence Martin has pointed out, however, in agreeing to accompany Hester to Europe, Dimmesdale plays the hypocrite, subverting her plot even as he apparently acquiesces in it. In making sure that they will not disembark until after he can preach the Election Sermon that will climax his public career, Dimmesdale tries to "have it both ways, to leave, but to leave with his duty well performed—which is to say, with the congregation marveling at their saintly, inspired minister."[8]

Hawthorne does not, therefore, give Hester absolute power to shape the story. Besides his subtle account of Dimmesdale's duplicity, he has Chillingworth book passage on the ship as well, ensuring that all the principle characters and the problems their conjunction embodies will be exported. There can be no escape. Dimmesdale's problem is internal, and only by reconciling his public role and his private self can he experience the exhilaration of full selfhood. And Hester, as Pearl reminds her, can only discover her full humanity by replacing the scarlet letter on her breast, by asserting her character within a social context. A major part of Pearl's function is encouraging her parents to a public acknowledgment of their relationship and thereby of her identity as their daughter. Hence, she will not recognize their reunion in the midnight privacy of the scaffold, nor will she accept their escapist indulgence in the freedom of the forest. When Dimmesdale allows himself the "mockery of penitence" (1:148) on the scaffold, Pearl insists that he embrace her and her mother in the same place during the day. Here in the forest, as her parents remove to their "magic circle," she stands estranged from them across the brook, on the other side of the "boundary between two worlds" (1:208). In thus straddling this symbolic stream of consciousness, the child and the letter with which she is identified—the sign and its meaning—remain abridged and uninte-grated. As the embodiment of all that the scarlet letter means, Pearl demands a full public confession and the assimilation of the letter's meaning into the imaginative life of the future. Not by escaping the implications of the letter, but by researching its meaning, Pearl seems to say, can any of them realize their human potential.

If this is the ideal toward which Hawthorne pushes the novel, he falls just short of its realization. Despite the epiphany of recovered energy and speech in the forest (or perhaps because of it), the balance of power between Hester and Dimmesdale shifts markedly in the last part of the novel. Dimmesdale is finally overwhelmed by his experience in the forest and by the image of himself that it reveals. He "seemed to stand apart, and eye this former self with scornful, pitying, but half-envious curiosity. That self was gone! Another man had returned out of the forest; a wiser one; with a knowledge of hidden mysteries" (1:223). Yet Dimmesdale is unable to reconcile his relationship with Hester and his role as keeper of the public morality. Returning to town, he feels bewildered and "in a maze." Unable to discover a viable outlet for his "knowledge of hidden mysteries," in his imagination he scandalizes his parishioners with illicit whisperings from his own haunted mind. As Michel Small has pointed out, "Dimmesdale's use of language, which elsewhere serves his spiritual ideal, has in these blasphemies come to express his aggression against that ideal." He has discovered the power to imagine, if not actually express, feelings that he has been repressing for years. "The power of obscene words to call up concrete sexual content," Small concludes, "allows him to sub-stitute them for forbidden sexual impulses." Dimmesdale, of course, does not act out his fantasies; the words he imagines do not actually pass his lips. He does not, for example, actually "drop" a "germ of evil" into the "tender bosom" of the young girl he encounters (1:219–20); he only imagines doing so. As Small says, "Sensing that language is temporarily enslaved to desire, he simply mumbles or says nothing until he can fully re-impose control."[9] As much as anything else, Dimmesdale is terrified by the image of himself that his own language reveals; the devil in the "manuscript" of his imagination, he recog-nizes, is himself. The self-image he prefers is the one "enshrined within the stainless sanctity of [the maiden's] heart" (1:219), and rather than jeopardize that objectified figure, he will suppress the linguistic power that creates another self. In repressing the seductive power of language and the masculine self empowered by that language, Dimmesdale moves toward a more feminine discourse, signalled by the almost vampirish transfer of energy from Hester to himself—and to his "art."

Dimmesdale's experience in the forest does finally assume a verbal form. Temporarily abandoning his mind to impulses he perceives as evil, he writes his final Election Sermon as a compulsive effort both to express and to exorcise the "fiend" which possesses his "foul imagination" (1:220, 221). Dimmesdale's response to his forest walk, in fact, could be considered the archetype within Hawthorne's fiction of the deep ambivalence we observed in several of the tales. Like the sinful thoughts that haunt Mr. Smith in "Fancy's Show Box," or the demonic "characters of fire" that "gush" out onto Oberon's writing paper in "The Devil in Manuscript" (10:174,175), Dimmesdale's sermon comes to him largely unbidden, the product of forces within himself released by his temporary reconciliation with Hester. Like Oberon or Mr. Smith, moreover, Dimmesdale gives in momentarily to an "impulsive flow of thought and emotion" (1:225) and becomes an inspired, visionary artist. That is, the conflict between those previously buried feelings and the pressure of his professional office generates so much internal energy that he is finally able to write in "words of flame" (1:248). Yet so alien are the impulses which converge upon his soul that he can only view himself through his society's eyes as a madman, and he "only wondered that Heaven should see fit to transmit the grand and solemn music of its oracles through so foul an organ-pipe as he" (1:225). In eschewing the seductive power of language on his walk through the "maze," however, Dimmesdale does not become more open to the creative potential of relationship. The "impulsive flow of thought and emotion" that generates his revised sermon is no gushing out of "warmth and freedom." Hawthorne does not share the text of that sermon with the reader, but the language he uses to describe its composition certainly implies that, rather than celebrating his "consecrated" union with Hester, Dimmesdale condemns it. If he resists the temptation to seduce the "youngest sister" of his congregation with his "potent" art, in other words, it is largely because he seeks a larger audience. He will seduce the congregation as a whole. Repressing the impulse to scandalize his parishioners one at a time, he sublimates that impulse in a sermon that condemns himself, but in precisely the form that will elevate him to the highest public stature he has yet enjoyed. In the process, of course, he effectively kills himself—ironically, ensuring that he will live on in the community's collective imagination in the form his words have established.

Although he cannot live through the experience, Dimmesdale seems to discover the courage to confess his relationship to Hester and Pearl, to make restitution to the female characters who have been victims in some sense of his timid imagination. Just as Hawthorne had placed the scarlet letter upon his breast and felt its searing heat, Dimmesdale assumes the burden of the letter's meaning in the final scaffold scene. He admits his own experience of the truth which the letter symbolizes; he tells the townspeople that "it is but the shadow of what he bears on his own breast, and that even this, his own red stigma, is no more than the type of what has seared his inmost heart!" (1:255). In so doing, he apparently offers his audience a lesson in interpretation, asking them to review the scarlet letter with minds open to its many meanings.[10] Yet as Hawthorne observes, the townspeople resist Dimmesdale's message. They misread the letter on his breast, just as they have misread the one on Hester's. Some suggest that Dimmesdale has selflessly assumed responsibility for Hester's sin, some that Chillingworth has caused the mark to appear, and that the "ever active tooth of remorse" has gnawed its way "from the inmost heart outwardly" to exemplify a heavenly judgment (1:258). Some spectators even deny "that there was any mark whatever on his breast, more than on a new-born infant's. Neither, by their report, had his dying words acknowledged, nor even remotely implied, any, the slightest connection, on his part, with the guilt for which Hester Prynne had so long worn the scarlet letter" (1:259). More than mere coyness on Hawthorne's part, this failure of interpretation is central to the novel's meaning. It suggests a pessimism similar to Melville's in *Pierre* about the power of language to express "deep meaning" and to discover a sympathetic audience, that "one heart and mind of perfect sympathy."[11]

Dimmesdale's confession also bears directly on Hester's status in the novel, suggesting, it seems to me, her failure to "subvert" the meaning of the scarlet letter and use it to express herself. In this scene, Dimmesdale, in effect, has expropriated the letter for his own purposes. Hester may, in some sense, inscribe her letter and the story it represents on her lover's bosom, but the speech he makes before revealing the letter belies its meaning. At best, Dimmesdale's speech and revelation are ambiguous, encouraging a diffusion of understanding; at worst, they are deliberately duplicitous, designed to confirm his canonization in his listeners' hearts. Dimmesdale, in short, writes his own story on the letter over Hester's. He has still not found the words to reiterate what he felt and evidently said in the novel's prehistory: "What we did had a consecration of its own" (1:195). Just as he had turned the reunion in the forest to his own uses, here he uses the letter itself to express something other than the "consecration" of their relationship. In failing to discover an unambiguous language by which Hester and their relationship can speak through him, he subverts Hester's intentions, in effect, if not in design. Indeed, rather than unambiguously uniting himself with Hester (and with Pearl), he substitutes himself for Hester, feminizing his discourse and himself in order to unite himself—alone—with God.

Hawthorne, moreover, makes very clear Hester's loss of vitality and self-expressive energy. Having undergone a "sad transformation," she seemed to regain her identity as a woman in the forest through Dimmesdale's "magic touch." In the final scene, too, her stature seems to depend on Dimmesdale's behavior, his willingness to free her from the "circle" of her self-enclosed and alienated life and to bring her within the "sphere" of the Puritan community. Yet Hawthorne's description of Hester throughout the scene of this "New England Holiday" suggests her loss of energy. As she enters the market-place, she has resumed her character as pariah. Her face shows a "marble quietude" and is like a mask, "or rather, like the frozen calmness of a dead woman's features" (1:226). Dimmesdale, on the other hand, appears to have gained the vitality that Hester has lost. Never, Hawthorne notes, "had he exhibited such energy as was seen in the gait and air with which he kept his pace in the procession" (1:238). The euphoria of their forest walk rapidly dissipates as Hester recognizes that, in so energetically fulfilling his public role, Dimmesdale is estranging himself from her. As she watches him from afar, she feels a "dreary influence come over her, but wherefore or whence she knew not; unless that he seemed so remote from her own sphere, and utterly beyond her reach" (1:239).

As we have seen before, the result of such male distancing from a woman is the woman's increasing objectification. And so it is with Hester. She can scarcely forgive Dimmesdale, Hawthorne says, "for being able so completely to withdraw himself from their mutual world; while she groped darkly, and stretched forth her cold hands, and found him not" (1:240). While Dimmesdale is inside the church preaching his sermon, Hester is relegated to a position outside at the foot of the scaffold—ironically, the very spot where she was first punished. Although she cannot hear Dimmesdale's words, she registers his sermon's underlying meaning "in the shape of an indistinct, but varied, murmur and flow of the minister's very peculiar voice" (1:242–43). As Hawthorne notes, "the sermon had throughout a meaning for her, entirely apart from its indistinguishable words" (1:243). That meaning inheres in the "plaintiveness," the "expression of anguish," the "deep strain of pathos," and the "cry of pain" with which Dimmesdale seeks forgiveness for his sins (1:243). In an ironic version of the "silent" communication he sought with Sophia, Hawthorne keeps the text of Dimmesdale's sermon a secret from the reader and from Hester, allowing his heroine to "read" an emotional subtext beneath Dimmesdale's words that confirms her sense of his estrangement from her. If Dimmesdale's energetic pace in the procession were enough to turn Hester's hands cold, the "statue-like" appearance she assumes as she listens to his sermon (1:244) is a sure indication that, whatever its power, it does not celebrate its speaker's passionate relationship with her. Hester may have contributed the energy for Dimmesdale's sermon, in other words, but she obviously has not contributed the text.

After the sermon, moreover, Hester is as alienated from the community as she has ever been. Outward from the "magic circle of ignominy" (1:246) in which she stands there radiates a simultaneously attractive and repulsive power. It is both ironic and prophetic that the same people who listen to Dimmesdale's "words of flame" still resist any implication in Hester's "sphere by herself." As they throng around her, they are "fixed" at a distance by the "centrifugal force of the repugnance which the mystic symbol inspired" (1:246). Hawthorne's diction is especially important here, for he had used the term "mystic symbol" to express his own sense of awe (in the Custom House) at what the scarlet letter inspired. Here, that sense of openness to various meanings "streaming" forth from the symbol has devolved into closed-minded "repugnance." Most important, that revulsion has been inspired at least in part by Dimmesdale's sermon. There could not be a greater or more tragic irony for Hester, since the energy that "wrote" the sermon was inspired by her forest walk with the author.[12] Thus, whatever her temporary success in expanding or even subverting the given meaning of the letter, Hester appears in this final scene as the letter's victim. It defines her more effectively than ever before. "At the final hour, when she was so soon to fling aside the burning letter, it had strangely become the centre of more remark and excitement, and was thus made to sear her breast more painfully, than at any time since the first day she put it on" (1:246).

Even in death, Hester discovers an ambiguous relationship to the letter. She shares a plot with Dimmesdale marked by a single tombstone on which the scarlet letter is "one ever-glowing point of light gloomier than the shadow." But even though the letter is her literary legacy, she has not been successful in writing her own personal meaning into it. The letter may glow on the "simple slab of slate" that serves as a tombstone, but the "curious investigator" of its meaning can only "perplex himself with the purport" (1:264). Just as it has been throughout the novel, the scarlet letter is still without a truly sympathetic reader, that "one heart and mind of perfect sympathy." As I noted earlier, in this final image *The Scarlet Letter* comes full circle, returning, as it must, to the beginning.[13] The "deep meaning" that "streamed forth" from the "mystic symbol" in the Custom House was rigidly contained within the letter-as-emblem which the Puritans imposed upon Hester. Although Hester was able to embroider the letter and wear it in such a way that it defied a single interpretation, she was never able to transcend it. Indeed, the letter's appearance on her tombstone had been anticipated by none other than Chillingworth as early as the second scene of the novel. Regarding the letter as a "living sermon against sin," he also looked forward to the day that "the ignominious letter [would] be engraved upon her tombstone" (1:63). In thus fulfilling a prophecy made early in the novel, the letter on Hester's grave has been denied some of its power to suggest indeterminate meanings. Despite being "ever-glowing," its final office is to mark the location of her dead body.

The House of the Seven Gables seems to pose a problem for this study, largely because the heroine, Phoebe Pyncheon, is so unlike Hawthorne's other major female characters. Hawthorne was determined to write a novel different from *The Scarlet Letter,* a work that he could consider a "more natural and healthy product" of his mind.[14] To do that, it seems clear, he had to create a heroine different from Hester Prynne. While she is not as pure or as purifying as Hilda in *The Marble Faun,* Phoebe obviously shares few characteristics with

Hawthorne's strong, dark women. Spirited and active, she is dynamic within her chosen domestic circle, but Hawthorne seems deliberately to narrow her sphere of influence. Designed to fulfill a conservative ideal, she is the only one of his novelistic heroines—light or dark—who is not in some sense an artist. And in contrast to female characters who challenge social and aesthetic boundaries, Phoebe is contained and self-contained, a model of conformity. Despite her contagious cheerfulness, she is "orderly and obedient to common rules" (2:68), and she "shocked no canon of taste; she was admirably in keeping with herself, and never jarred against surrounding circumstances" (2:80).

The closest that Phoebe comes to the artistic power of Hawthorne's other heroines is in exercising a "homely witchcraft" (2:72), but while the others' artistry is designed to disclose new worlds of experience, Phoebe's domestic abilities purge the space around her of anything unpleasant or problematical. Although her room in the Pyncheon house was once a "chamber of very great and varied experience" and a "scene of human life"—births, deaths, and the "joy of bridal nights" that "had throbbed itself away here"—Phoebe transforms it into a "maiden's bed-chamber" that has been "purified of all former evil and sorrow by her sweet breath and happy thoughts" (2:72). In contrast to Hawthorne's own deeply psychological art and to the power he attributed to Sophia and to his other heroines, Phoebe is reluctant to probe the depths of the mind. She tells Holgrave that she cannot see Clifford's thoughts, although sometimes when he is cheerful, "when the sun shines into his mind," she dares "peep" in, "just as far as the light reaches, but no farther. It is holy ground where the shadow falls!" (2:178).

Hawthorne seems to have recognized the anomaly of Phoebe's character, as well as the difficulty of building a novel around her, because in several places he suggests that there is more to Phoebe than meets the eye—more, in effect, than his own language expresses. Although her behavior seems consistent throughout, Phoebe does apparently change over the course of the novel. She becomes "less girlish," but "more a woman." Hawthorne, in fact, goes on to describe her in terms usually reserved for dark women such as Ligeia or Isabel Glendinning: "Her eyes looked larger, and darker, and deeper; so deep, at some silent moments, that they seemed like Artesian wells, down, down, into the infinite" (2:175). But if he seemed on the verge of revealing a dark lady in disguise, he quickly remembered his intentions. Other descriptions of Phoebe are much tamer. Nonetheless, Hawthorne uses Phoebe, as he had used Hester, to test the "reading" ability of his male characters. When Holgrave, who prides himself on great insight into human character, fancies "that he could look through Phoebe, and all around her, and could read her off like a page of a child's story-book," Hawthorne is quick to criticize his protagonist's self-confident reading. "But these transparent natures are often deceptive in their depth," he says; "those pebbles at the bottom of the fountain are farther from us than we think" (2:182).

Clifford, too, "reads" Phoebe in this superficial manner. "He read Phoebe, as he would a sweet and simple story; he listened to her, as if she were a verse of household poetry, which God, in requital of his bleak and dismal lot, had permitted some angel, that most pitied him, to warble through the house" (2:142). Hawthorne does not comment so pointedly upon Clifford's shallowness as he does upon Holgrave's, but his characterization of Phoebe's status in Clifford's "story" suggests a misreading of her character—the substitution of fantasy for reality. "She was not an actual fact for him," Hawthorne notes, "but the interpretation of all that he had lacked on earth, brought warmly home to his conception; so that this mere symbol or lifelike picture had almost the comfort of reality" (2:142). As a "mere symbol" or "lifelike picture" who is no "actual fact," Phoebe is another of those female art objects who fulfill the superficial wishes of the male imagination. In thus describing her, Hawthorne is clearly touching upon issues he had treated before and would deal with again. Aylmer, Giovanni Guasconti, the townspeople in *The Scarlet Letter*—all are such "readerly" readers of women's characters. Preferring projection to understanding, they either do not let women express themselves or misinterpret what women say. But Hawthorne clearly wishes not only to dissociate this heroine from the type of experience his other heroines embodied, but also to free her from the power of the male imagination and male language that transformed Hester Prynne, for example, into a devitalized art object. He does so most vividly during the scene in which Holgrave reads Phoebe his story about Alice Pyncheon—a narrative that bears little resemblance to the "child's story-book" or "household poetry" that Holgrave and Clifford ordinarily identify with her.

Although many of her characteristics—pride, strength of will, artistic talent—associate her with Hawthorne's most powerful heroines, within *The House of the Seven Gables* Alice Pyncheon has such a minor role and is so obviously overshadowed by Phoebe that it may seem inappropriate to discuss her at all. She appears in the novel's present time only as a ghost whose music periodically haunts the house. In fact, Alice is most important for her absence; she is a kind of Muse whose creative spirit has left the house. The harpsichord that she brought back from Europe is "like a coffin" that contains a "vast deal of dead music, stifled for want of air," because it has not been touched since she died (2:73). In addition, her story is deeply embedded within the novel—doubly framed so to speak as a story within a story within a story. Holgrave has written the story based on a "wild, chimney-corner legend" (2:197), so Alice's experience is thrice-removed from actuality, and (since she is Phoebe's great-great-grand-aunt) set four generations in the past. Holgrave's narrative does, in a sense, give Alice a presence in the novel, but her resurrection occurs under strict controls. Although she seems on the verge of breaking out of the embedded story that contains her and, rather like Ligeia, entering the novel proper by "becoming" Phoebe, Holgrave short-circuits that metamorphic process. Although Edwin H. Cady cites Clifford as Hawthorne's example of the Christian gentleman, Holgrave actually internalizes and acts out the conflict men experienced in nineteenth-century America between the aggressive, domineering ideology of Jacksonian heroism and the comparatively selfless ideal of Christian gentility.[15] Nowhere is that conflict more apparent than in the telling of Alice's story.

That narrative is an only slightly displaced story; Holgrave and Phoebe obviously have their counterparts in Matthew Maule and Alice Pyncheon. Whether he recognizes it or not, Holgrave reads the story to Phoebe as a courtship strategy designed to sketch out a potential relationship for the two of them.[16] Maule, like Holgrave himself, is one of Hawthorne's typically mesmerical artists, a seductive artist who haunts and dominates the mind. He is "fabled" to possess a "strange power of getting into people's dreams, and regulating matters there according to his own fancy, pretty much like the stage-manager of a theatre" (2:189). Alice, unlike Phoebe, is also an artist. Educated in Italy, she has returned to America hoping to instill some beauty where "nothing beautiful had ever been developed" (2:192), but as she appears in Holgrave's story she seems the kind of female statue we have observed in other works. "If ever there was a lady born, and set apart from the world's vulgar mass by a certain gentle and cold stateliness," he says, "it was this very Alice Pyncheon" (2:201). Although Maule seems to possess the power to reach Alice, he uses his artistic power to control and repress her, not to help her realize herself. With sadistic relish he vows to prove his spirit superior to hers. Even though Alice accepts the challenge, feeling confident of a "power—combined of beauty, high, unsullied purity, and the preservative force of womanhood—that could make her sphere impenetrable" (2:203), she is quickly transformed into a statue. She falls utterly victim to Maule's mesmerical power, so desensitized that she cannot hear her father's pleas to awaken or feel his touch (2:205). In hypnotizing Alice, Maule becomes a type of Pygmalion, creating a living art object wholly subservient to his will. Maliciously, he enjoys his power over her, humiliating her whenever possible by making her laugh or cry or dance wildly in public. His power is implicitly sexual, as "all the dignity of life was lost" and she "felt herself too much abased, and longed to change natures with some worm!" (2:209).

But in fact, as Nina Baym has argued, Maule's power is desexualizing, designed to deny Alice a sexual identity or life of her own. "His power is of the meanest, at once arousing and denying Alice" (*Shape*, 160). Baym, in fact, compares Maule's treatment of Alice to Victorian pornography: "the worst that Maule does is, apparently, what he does *not* do; having aroused sexual desire and admiration in Alice, he cruelly fails to satisfy her." "Alice has been punished by Maule for being attracted to him, and in *this* respect Hawthorne's story is quite different from normal Victorian pornography, where the subjected woman is one who dislikes her tormenter" ("Thwarted Nature," 68–69). Under his control, Alice "would have deemed it sin to marry" (2:209), but Maule makes her wait upon his bride on their wedding night—in effect letting her see what he will not let her have. Alice dies from this denial at least as much as from the ailment she contracts on her walk home from the honeymoon.

Holgrave's narrative is a fascinating variation on the story Hawthorne told in "The Birth-mark" and "Rappaccini's Daughter": a story of woman's victimization and death at the hands of a male artist. In the context in which it appears, however, the narrative is more important for its effect on its female listener than for its content. Like Poe's "Mad Trist" in "The Fall of the House of Usher," Holgrave's story has such a hypnotic power that it effectively transforms its reader into a character. In the act of reading, Holgrave becomes Maule; in the act of being read to, Phoebe becomes Alice. Aesthetic distance from even this doubly framed tale dissolves, as both characters achieve a frightening "writerly" relation to the text.

In a letter to Sophia from Brook Farm, Hawthorne had expressed his fear of such mesmerical power being exercised on her: "it seems to me that the sacredness of an individual is violated by it; there would be an intrusion into thy holy of holies—and the intruder would not be thy husband!" (15:588). As we have seen, moreover, this fear is often realized in the fiction through the misuse of artistic power—the seductive, or mesmerizing power of art. Hawthorne's fear of mesmerism bears directly, it seems to me, on his own relationship to his fictional characters. He was haunted by a vision of himself as an artist at the mercy of forces within himself that he could not control, and in his fiction he most often associated those powerfully creative forces with women characters. Beatrice, Hester, Zenobia, Miriam, Sophia—all have the power to transfix the male imagination and cause an irresistible "gush" of creative energy. Because Hawthorne's male characters fear the loss of control that such an open, or passive, response to women requires, they usually contain the process. They objectify women in art, or they destroy the works of art with which women are identified. That, of course, is exactly what Holgrave does in *The House of the Seven Gables*.

Narration (of a story about a man's hypnotic control of a woman) is itself hypnotic—experienced as penetrating and controlling a woman's mind and body. As Phoebe "leaned slightly towards him, and seemed almost to regulate her breath by his" (2:211), Holgrave becomes aware that his power over her is "as dangerous, and perhaps as disastrous, as that which the carpenter of his legend had acquired and exercised over the ill-fated Alice" (2:212). Most important, he can hardly keep himself from exercising this combined erotic and artistic power. The creative process itself creates a creator who proceeds to take advantage of an unresisting woman reader. "His glance, as he fastened it on the young girl, grew involuntarily more concentrated; in his attitude, there was the consciousness of power, investing his hardly mature figure with a dignity that did not belong to its physical manifestation" (2:211). Hawthorne's language is confusing in this passage, but if I read it correctly, he means that the erotic attraction which Holgrave's narration has revealed in himself is counteracted by an equally powerful reluctance ("dignity") that will not allow him to continue his seduction. That reluctance seems to emerge from his consciousness of his own "hardly mature figure"—as if he is not ready for the sort of relationship toward which this moment could lead. In discovering himself as an artist—as a writer and then as a narrator—Holgrove stands revealed to himself as a lover-violator of the woman who has become the ideal "reader" of his story, that one heart and mind of a sympathy so perfect that she actually regulates her breathing by his. Although he recognizes that, if he indulged the one wish, he could "complete his mastery over Phoebe's yet free and virgin spirit" (2:212), like Hawthorne in his letter to Sophia a decade earlier, he resists temptation. He refuses to be seduced by the seductive power of his art, refuses to be the aggressive, seductive male that his narrative and Phoebe's response to it have created. He vows to burn the manuscript, forsaking his writing, it turns out, to marry the girl to whom he dares not read it.

The embedded story of Alice Pyncheon and the chapters framing its narration reveal Hawthorne's dilemma as an artist and as the creator of female characters whom he identified with the deepest creative impulse. However attractive she may have appeared in the immediate aftermath of *The Scarlet Letter,* Hawthorne obviously recognized that a relationship between Holgrave and Phoebe, despite encouraging Holgrave's resistance to the seductive power of art, created problems for the kind of fiction he wanted to write. On the other hand, this recognition does not automatically support the contention of such critics as Frederick Crews, who argues that Holgrave compromises himself and his art in marrying Phoebe and that Hawthorne himself sets "Phoebe-ism as the steep ransom from obsession."[17] If we can indeed read the ending autobiographically, then Holgrave's marriage to Phoebe and their removal to the gingerbread house does not necessarily mean the end of creativity. Hawthorne himself had certainly discovered that marriage and the removal to an Edenic rural retreat at the Old Manse opened up new possibilities for his writing. Furthermore, he wanted to read *The House of the Seven Gables* to Sophia, he told James Fields, not to give her another headache, but in order to "know better what to think of it" (16:382). Two weeks later he could report that the novel had "met with extraordinary success" with Sophia (16:386), and he would later tell his sister Louisa with obvious pleasure that he had received many "adoring" letters from "young ladies" in response to the novel (16:433). In other words, writing and relationship were not suddenly incompatible for Hawthorne. Rather, relationship encouraged a different, more "feminine" kind of writing: less selfish and self-centered, more attuned to reader response, more aware of the reciprocal possibilities in the writer-reader relationship.[18] Holgrave's refusal to seduce Phoebe through art anticipates Coverdale and Kenyon, who surrender even more power to women. Both *The Blithedale Romance* and *The Marble Faun,* in fact, feature a female character who would not only read a story like Holgrave's, but probably write one of her own.

CHAPTER SEVEN

The Blithedale Romance *and* The Marble Faun

Dazzling Male Discourse

Hawthorne addresses the aesthetic issues he associated with male-female relationships more directly in *The Blithedale Romance* and *The Marble Faun* simply because his most important female characters, Zenobia and Miriam Schaefer, are artists. He goes furthest in *The Marble Faun* in exploring the qualities of a female or feminine poetics; indeed, Miriam is the most prolific woman artist to be found in the fiction of Poe, Melville, or Hawthorne. She is as important, moreover, for her mode of creativity as for the content of her paintings, because Hawthorne deliberately identifies her with his own artistry and pointedly offers her as a model for Kenyon. Miriam dazzles the sculptor's imagination, inspires and critiques his art, and challenges his aesthetic as well as moral values. A literary rather than a graphic artist, Zenobia has a less obvious effect on Coverdale's art than Miriam does on Kenyon's, although her effect on Coverdale's imagination is even more profound. Most important, as a first-person male narrative, *The Blithedale Romance* offers the best example we shall see of the way a woman's presence and voice challenge masculine literary forms and disrupt or dazzle male discourse. The novel may bear a male signature, but the novel and its male narrator reflect tensions between feminine—indeed feminist—and masculine values.

From the beginning of *The Blithedale Romance,* when Coverdale summarizes the history of the Veiled Lady, to his concluding revelation of the secret he has concealed for most of the novel—his love for Priscilla—

women are shrouded in mystery. Although critics generally emphasize the allegorical opposition of light and dark women in the novel, to Coverdale both Priscilla and Zenobia are Veiled Ladies.[1] Whether or not Allan and Barbara Lefcowitz are right in arguing that Priscilla is a reformed prostitute, it is important to recognize the lengths to which Hawthorne goes to confuse and link the two women.[2] She and Zenobia are symbolic as well as biological sisters, and Coverdale stands in much the same relation to each of them. He readily transforms each woman into a player on his own "mental stage" at the same time that he actively resists a full revelation of their puzzling characters.

As an artist, a "Minor Poet, beginning life with strenuous aspirations, which die out with his youthful fervor" (3:2–3), Coverdale hopes to "produce something that shall really deserve to be called poetry—true, strong, natural, and sweet" (3:14). With her previous knowledge of Coverdale's work—she has learned some of his poems "by heart" (3:14)—Zenobia persistently criticizes his artistic efforts. She possesses the experience and personal energy to inspire him to write that new kind of poetry and to become a different kind of man. As Nina Baym argues, "Coverdale's intention of tapping the soul's reservoir of energy, of contacting its passionate, creative, active principle requires a representation in the romance of that underlying principle. Zenobia, who unites sex, art, and nature in one image, is that symbol."[3] Specifically, she subjects Coverdale to a series of potentially instructive experiences; she supervises his education, limited though it finally is, in the nature of women and the complexities of art. As both object and subject, Zenobia resists what Mary Suzanne Schriber calls the "limitations of conventions, the limitations Coverdale continually attempts to force upon her in order to bring her within the sphere of his understanding."[4] Hawthorne termed her a "high-spirited Woman, bruising herself against the narrow limitations of her sex" (3:2)—simultaneously identifying her creative power and foreshadowing her fate.

Even as a living art object, Zenobia challenges Coverdale's imagination. Associated with openness, fluidity, and extraordinary energy, she has "bloom, health, and vigor"; when "really in earnest," she is "all alive, to her finger-tips" (3:16) and has "free, careless, generous modes of expression" (3:17). She is the sort of woman who, in Barthes' term, "dazzles" the lover's discourse. Her dynamic quality, her changing mood and appearance, evidences a protean character that refuses to stay within the bounds of Coverdale's language. "Zenobia had a rich, though varying color," he observes. "It was, most of the while, a flame, and anon a sudden paleness. Her eyes glowed, so that their light sometimes flashed upward to me, as when the sun throws a dazzle from some bright object on the ground. Her gestures were free, and strikingly impressive. The whole woman was alive with a passionate intensity, which I now perceived to be the phase in which her beauty culminated" (3:102). Far from being a stereotype, Zenobia resists containment by type or by language; her presence always implies more than Coverdale or Hawthorne can denote.

Coverdale's attitude toward Zenobia, therefore, is understandably anxious. Her ready intimacy easily penetrates his "inward regions"; as a protean character who dazzles and blinds him, she threatens his narrative control. But like other of Hawthorne's reserved males, Coverdale is irresistibly attracted to such a free and "generous" woman. Like Hawthorne with Sophia, he feels some necessity to communicate with a woman who can make his heart "gush out" with "warmth and freedom." Zenobia provokes thoughts and feelings that this "frosty bachelor" (3:9) cannot repress. Where Hawthorne relished Sophia's power to evoke truths that his own words could not "clothe," Coverdale cannot seem to resist imagining Zenobia naked. An innocently facetious remark about donning the "garb of Eden" "irresistibly brought up a picture of that fine, perfectly developed figure, in Eve's earliest garment" (3:17). The language that Hawthorne attributes to his first-person narrator, of course, perfectly expresses his ambivalence; he clothes Zenobia in a euphemistic verbal "garment" even as he means to describe her without an actual one.[5]

As much as anything else, Zenobia's power as an object is indicated by the defensive strategies Coverdale brings to bear upon her. He would prefer to repress his "naked" thoughts of her altogether, for they have the "effect of creating images which, though pure, are hardly felt to be quite decorous, when born of a thought that passes between man and woman" (3:17). From the first, Zenobia challenges Coverdale's ability to "clothe" his thoughts in language, and she certainly offers him an opportunity to put his own relationship to woman on a new footing. With her aura of archetypal womanhood, the "influence breathing out of her, such as we might suppose to come from Eve," she represents everything that has been "refined away out of the feminine system" (3:17), and she possesses a sexual nature as rich as Hester Prynne's before her "sad transformation."[6] Besides Eve, however, Zenobia appears to Coverdale like Pandora, "fresh from Vulcan's workshop, and full of the celestial warmth by dint of which he had tempered and moulded her" (3:24). In that comparison, Coverdale perfectly expresses the problem he will face for much of the novel. Conforming Zenobia to type allows him to contain her frightening power, but the figure he chooses—Pandora—symbolizes resistance to containment and the power to break out of "moulds."

Like Hawthorne's other heroines, Zenobia is an artist, as well as an art object, and in that role, too, she is associated with imaginative openness and energy. She possesses an enchanting power, as Coverdale alleges during his feverish illness, to transform him into "something like a mesmerical clairvoyant." Her mere presence causes him to fantasize. He speculates about her history, each time imagining her as one to whom the "gates of mystery" (3:47) have been opened. He associates her with depth of mind and with the revelation of secret truths. "She bent her head towards me," he reports, "and let me look into her eyes, as if challenging me to drop a plummet-line down into the depths of her consciousness" (3:47–48). The image obviously has sexual connotations, but Hawthorne also stresses Zenobia's challenge to Coverdale to enter her *consciousness*—to listen to her story and, like Beatrice Rappaccini, to let her define herself.

Unlike Hester, who expresses her subversive thoughts largely through the symbolic medium of the scarlet letter, Zenobia is given a much stronger voice within Coverdale's narrative. Although she writes stories, Coverdale notes that they "never half did justice to her intellect" (3:44). The reason is not a lack of creative talent but the limitations of the written word. Zenobia's power requires more immediate and emotional expression; like Ann Hutchinson or the Quaker woman Catharine, she "was made (among a thousand other things that she might have been) for a stump-oratress" (3:44). She herself recognizes that "the pen is not for woman," because her "power is too natural and immediate. It is with the living voice, alone, that she can compel the world to recognize the light of her intellect and the depth of her heart!" (3:120). As much as Melville with Isabel's music, Hawthorne seeks to embody in Zenobia's character a creative power that transcends the limits of his own chosen medium, a power not less than, but much greater than his own or his narrator's, a power generated from her perception of "difference." "Listen to a woman speak at a public gathering," says Hélène Cixous. "She doesn't 'speak,' she throws her trembling body forward; she lets go of herself, she flies; all of her passes into her voice, and it's with her body that she vitally supports the 'logic' of her speech."[7] Cixous could be paraphrasing Hawthorne's description of Zenobia's oratorical power, also generated from the body and the heart—a case, in Cixous's phrase, of "writing in the feminine." Appropriately, Zenobia's most important literary contribution to the novel is a feminocentric legend, a tale of female victimization, the legend of the Veiled Lady.

I shall have more to say about the content and the effect of Zenobia's legend later; equally important is her remarkable mode of narrating it. The process that Coverdale describes fulfills the ideal Hawthorne had defined in such narratives as "The Haunted Mind" and "Fancy's Show Box"—a story that flows according to its own momentum, that writes itself in the very act of "gushing" out of the artist's "inward regions." His diction stresses an absence of mediation and thus the achievement of a "passive sensibility." Zenobia tells the story "wildly and rapidly," Coverdale notes, "hesitating at no extravagance, and dashing at absurdities" that he himself is "too timorous to repeat." Just as his imagination had been dazzled by her appearance, he marvels at the "varied emphasis of her inimitable voice, and the pictorial illustration of her mobile face," and most suggestively at "the freshest aroma of the thoughts, as they came bubbling out of her mind" (3:107). As artist and art object, Zenobia seems to transcend all available linguistic and literary forms and to achieve, at least in the manner of her discourse, the ideal kind of "gushing out" that Hawthorne had defined in his love letter.

Coverdale, however, is less than anxious to "drop a plummet-line" into the "depths" of Zenobia's "consciousness" or to let her character and voice "bubble" out too freely into his narrative. The alternative to surrendering imaginative and narrative control to such a woman is, as we have seen, suppressing the woman's creative power by containing it in the forms of art. Like Giovanni Guasconti, Coverdale tries to repress the thoughts that Zenobia evokes; his squeamishness is especially evident when he imagines her as a potential subject for art. Even as he admits that Zenobia would make a perfect model for a painter or sculptor, if not for a "minor poet," he views those media as specially devitalizing. The "cold decorum of the marble," he thinks, "would consist with the utmost scantiness of drapery, so that the eye might chastely be gladdened with her material perfection, in its entirety" (3:44). Even though he still imagines Zenobia virtually naked, or at least "scantily" clothed, that vision is tolerable only when her "material perfection"—her naked body—has been confined within the "cold decorum" of the marble.[8]

Hawthorne, however, does not let his hero solve his imaginative problem so easily, for Zenobia promises to retain such vitality even as a statue that the poet will find little solace in so viewing her. Her body, her "full bust," makes the statue Coverdale has imagined so provocative that he feels compelled to "close [his] eyes, as if it were not quite the privilege of modesty to gaze at her" (3:44). Despite the decorously objectified form in which Coverdale tries to imagine her, throughout the novel Zenobia threatens to break out of any mold in which his imagination tries to confine her.

Besides her impressive oratorical talent, Zenobia has more power than any Hawthorne heroine before Miriam Schaefer to influence the behavior of those around her. She is a kind of sculptress within the narrative, conforming other characters to her own designs. Despite Coverdale's personal timidity, Hawthorne seems to be attempting with Zenobia a portrait of a lady who possesses unique life-enhancing powers. He gives her a "magical" ability to revive faded flowers, and she rapidly melts Priscilla's coldness with a single touch. Indeed, so "vivid a look of joy flushed up beneath those fingers, that it seemed as if the sad and wan Priscilla had been snatched away, and another kind of creature substituted in her place" (3:35). Although we should not press the similarity too far, Zenobia's relationship to Priscilla resembles Hester's to Pearl. Transforming Priscilla into a younger version of herself, she uses her as a kind of living work of art whose mystery—like the "hieroglyphic" that Pearl becomes—must be interpreted. At the same time, of course, Zenobia does abuse her power. At the end of her legend, for example, she startles the company by throwing a piece of gauze over Priscilla, through the hypnotic power of her own art returning her sister to her bondage as Westervelt's Veiled Lady. Later she helps make her own story come true, when she conspires with Hollingsworth to return Priscilla to Boston and to Westervelt's power.

Zenobia's effect on Priscilla clearly causes problems for Coverdale. As he watches the transformation, he applauds Zenobia's transfiguring power but also calls it "deviltry," because, in dressing Priscilla as a maid of the May by ornamenting her with flowers, she includes a "weed of evil odor and ugly aspect." To Coverdale, the presence of the weed simply "destroyed the effect of all the rest"; he cannot tolerate anything that confuses his notion of Priscilla as the "very picture of the New England spring" (3:59). Yet, like Beatrice Rappaccini, Zenobia effectively demands that Coverdale encounter a woman in her fully human nature; she subverts his inclination to idealize. As Priscilla gradually becomes a woman, she becomes more attractive and, to Coverdale, more troubling As he sees "Nature shaping out a woman before our very eyes," he feels a "more reverential sense of the mystery of a woman's soul and frame" (3:72–73). Despite his reliance on first-person narration in *The Blithedale Romance,* Hawthorne achieves a unique perspective on his hero, largely through the challenges that Zenobia poses. As he did less dramatically in *The Scarlet Letter,* he seeks to teach his male protagonist and his readers about women by surrendering the narrative in several places to Zenobia.

The most important example occurs in the scene at Eliot's pulpit, immediately following the triumph of her legend. When she vows to lift up her own voice "in behalf of woman's wider liberty," she notices that Coverdale smiles. With a "flash of anger in her eyes," she proceeds to lecture him about the plight of women: "That smile, permit me to say, makes me suspicious of a low tone of feeling, and shallow thought. It is my belief—yes, and my prophecy, should I die before it happens— that, when my sex shall achieve its rights, there will be ten eloquent women, where there is now one eloquent man. Thus far, no woman in the world has ever once spoken out her whole heart and her whole mind. The mistrust and disapproval of the vast bulk of society throttles us, as with two gigantic hands at our throats! We mumble a few weak words, and leave a thousand better ones unsaid" (3:120). Zenobia's "prophecy" is considerably stronger than that attributed to Hester Prynne, and her claim that no woman has yet spoken from her "whole heart" recalls Beatrice Rappaccini's effort to speak "from the depths of the heart outward." Her indictment of Coverdale, moreover, is the most direct of the many challenges she poses to his imagination and thought. The measure of his ability to "read" her message will be in what he says and does during the rest of the novel.

For the most part, Coverdale struggles to disengage himself from the problems that Zenobia, as well as Hollingsworth and Priscilla, poses. He leaves Blithedale as a wounded and rejected lover who now stands, he perceives, on "other terms than before, not only with Hollingsworth, but with Zenobia and Priscilla" (3:138). As he leaves, moreover, Zenobia pointedly suggests that he is failing the test as her sympathizer. She admits that she has thought of making him her "confidant" but has decided that he is "too young" for a "Father Confessor" (3:141). When he offers to be her counsellor instead, she says that he has forfeited that privilege by just now resuming "the whole series of social conventionalisms" implicit in his leavetaking. She requires an "angel or a madman" to "speak the fitting word," and when she decides that the latter "would be the likeliest of the two," she dismisses the "minor Poet" with a simple "Farewell!" (3:142). In effect, she recognizes Coverdale's preference for being a spectator rather than a sympathizer.

Coverdale, of course, finds even spectating an anxious business. He may have disengaged himself from the three people who trouble him, but he is still at the mercy of his own haunted mind. "The train of thoughts which, for months past, had worn a track through my mind, and to escape which was one of my chief objects in leaving Blithedale," he says, "kept treading remorselessly to-and-fro, in their old footsteps, while slumber left me impotent to regulate them" (3:153). As we would expect, his imaginative impotence involves the troubling relationship among Hollingsworth, Zenobia, and Priscilla. He has, he believes, successfully "consummated" his escape from these "goblins of flesh and blood"; now, in the city, he experiences a "positive despair, to find the same figures arraying themselves before [him], and presenting their old problem in a shape that made it more insoluble than ever" (3:157).

In fact, in the city all three characters seem even more menacing than they had at Blithedale. He dreams one night of Hollingsworth and Zenobia bending over his bed to "exchange a kiss of passion" and of Priscilla melting away when she beholds the lovers. Claire Sprague sees this dream as an example of wish-fulfillment, demonstrating the "sexual overtones of Miles's response to Zenobia and Hollingsworth."[9] But Coverdale has also clearly projected his own anxiety about sexual experience onto Priscilla; although he tries as much as possible to dissociate her from Zenobia (Priscilla's dream image melts away rather than observe the scene of passion), the very next day he discovers the two of them living next door. Hawthorne obviously wants him to confront them together—so much so that Coverdale finally gives up any hope of regulating the "train" of his own thoughts. "Let it all come!" he says.

"As for me, I would look on, as it seemed my part to do, understanding, if my intellect could fathom the meaning and the moral, and, at all events, reverently and sadly" (3:157).

When he finally discovers courage enough to visit their apartment, Coverdale finds Zenobia transfigured into a living work of art—but still embodying the "old problem." Rather than the hothouse flower she had worn in the country, she wears a "flower exquisitely imitated in jeweller's work, and imparting the last touch that transformed Zenobia into a work of art" (3:164). In this case, however, the jewelled flower is not one of the objectifying artistic forms we have encountered in other works; it is a freely chosen art object through which Zenobia can express her complex character. It allows her more freedom of self-expression than Hester's externally imposed scarlet A, although it poses a similar challenge to the male imagination that suddenly must interpret it.[10]

Though Zenobia makes no effort to entice him, Coverdale is both dazzled and frightened by the sensuous appearance of her person and room. The chamber seems the "fulfilment of every fantasy of an imagination, revelling in various methods of costly self-indulgence and splendid ease" (3:164), and, as such, violates his sense of decorum. As he describes it in retrospect, he regrets his inability to respond sympathetically to Zenobia. "It cost me, I acknowledge, a bitter sense of shame, to perceive in myself a positive effort to bear up against the effect which Zenobia sought to impose on me. I reasoned against her, in my secret mind, and strove so to keep my footing" (3:164). His confusion at the time, he recognizes, was a deliberate effort to deform and thus distance himself from her character. With remarkable insight, he admits, "I malevolently beheld the true character of the woman." Stringing words together, he runs a verbal gamut of positive and negative qualities, reflecting his own calculated movement from attraction to repulsion: "passionate, luxurious, lacking simplicity, not deeply refined, incapable of pure and perfect taste" (3:165). Yet, even in verbally objectifying Zenobia as a "bad" woman, Coverdale finds himself unable to sustain such verbal assault. He recognizes his own duplicity—his doubleness—by observing himself with Zenobia in a full-length mirror. And as he admits, "she was too powerful for all my opposing struggles" (3:165). He is clearly divided by those thoughts and feelings which Zenobia provokes and by this encounter with a mirrored image of himself-with-Zenobia. He must split himself in two and enter his "secret mind" in order to achieve a characteristic distance from that part of himself that threatens to exceed his "reasoned" control. But, like other protagonists we have seen, he finds his imagination at the mercy of a fluid, protean image of woman that he cannot define or categorize. He cannot tell whether this image of Zenobia, or that which he had seen at Blithedale, is her "truest attitude," because, he recognizes, Zenobia's image as other is ultimately under her control. Reclaiming Pygmalion's power, this Galatea insists on creating herself. In both of her "attitudes," Coverdale admits, "there was something like the illusion which a great actress flings around her" (3:165).

As important as anything else in this scene is Hawthorne's continued reliance on Zenobia, not only as living art object, but as critic of Coverdale's imaginative limitations. His is a "poor and meagre nature," she says, "that is capable of but one set of forms, and must convert all the past into a dream, merely because the present happens to be unlike it" (3:165). And Coverdale immediately proves her right by insisting ingenuously that what he sees and imagines is not real. "I determined to make proof if there were any spell that would exorcise her out of the part which she seemed to be acting," he says. "She should be compelled to give me a glimpse of something true; some nature, some passion, no matter whether right or wrong, provided it were real" (3:165).

Coverdale apparently gets the response he seeks. Criticizing Hollingsworth, he provokes a violent rebuke from Zenobia, whose "eyes darted lightning" and "cheeks flushed; the vividness of her expression was like the effect of a powerful light, flaming up suddenly within her" (3:166). In causing Zenobia to defend Hollingsworth in this manner, Coverdale has actually helped himself solve his "old problem." Reassuring himself of Zenobia's love for Hollingsworth, he can free himself from her "spell." Immediately, in fact, he inquires about Priscilla; having consigned Zenobia to Hollingsworth, he can think of Priscilla for himself.

Observing Priscilla from his room, he had been impressed by her uncharacteristic finery; when he actually meets her, she seems more than ever "like a figure in a dream," a "wonderful creature" who perfectly fulfills the fantasy he has created for her (3:168, 169). She is virtually disembodied, a feminine ideal that can be memorialized in imagination. "She was now dressed in pure white," he notes, "set off with some kind of gauzy fabric, which—as I bring up her figure in my memory, with a faint gleam on her shadowy hair, and her dark eyes bent shyly on mine, through all the vanished years—seems to be floating about her like a mist" (3:169). Like the young Theodore of Zenobia's Veiled Lady fable, Coverdale obviously veils all but the most ephemeral fantasy about Priscilla. Although in actuality she has been dressed up by Zenobia for the role she has reassumed in Westervelt's show, in Coverdale's mind she has clearly melted out of any dream that includes Zenobia.

Besides being a "parody of melodramatic literature," as Schriber argues, Zenobia's narrative about the Veiled Lady is an obvious commentary on Coverdale's relationship to Priscilla.[11] Illustrating the instructive power she wields within the novel, she recounts a tale of radical ambivalence in male attitudes toward women. Hester was able to embroider the scarlet letter and thus alter its meaning; Zenobia has at least a short narrative of her own and an opportunity to educate Coverdale and the others about the dangers of a vision that veils more of women than it discovers. For Theodore and his companions, the Veiled Lady is a figment of their collective imagination. What they imagine, it turns out, is a woman who is at once attractive and repulsive and thus embodies the most radically opposed views of women—*Frau Welt,* the woman who is both angelic and demonic. "Some upheld, that the veil covered the most beautiful countenance in the world," Zenobia notes; "others—and certainly with more reason, considering the sex of the Veiled Lady—that the face was the most hideous and horrible, and that this was her sole motive for hiding it. It was the face of a corpse; it was the head of a skeleton; it was a monstrous visage, with snaky locks, like Medusa's, and one great red eye in the centre of the forehead" (3:109–10). As much as Giovanni Guasconti, then, Theodore faces a test of faith when he vows to discover the mystery of the Veiled Lady. To do so, he must lift the veil—but not before kissing her lips as a pledge of his "pure and generous purpose" (3:113). Frightened of what she might be, Theodore fails the test of faith. He refuses to kiss the lady sight unseen. Instead, he lifts the veil, and thus only momentarily glimpses the "pale, lovely face, beneath" (3:114). As surely as Priscilla, the Veiled Lady has melted away. Like Giovanni, Theodore fails to liberate a woman from a mysterious bondage and thus suffers appropriate retribution: "to pine, forever and ever, for another sight of that dim, mournful face—which might have been his life-long household, fireside joy" (3:114). A pointed

criticism of male stereotyping of women, Zenobia's narrative dramatizes Coverdale's failure of imagination, his wish to enclose and veil
a woman's character. Although he prides himself on being the only
mortal who "really cares" for Priscilla, he admits that he cares less for
"her realities" than for the "fancy-work with which [he has] idly
decked her out!" (3:100). He prizes those "mysterious qualities which
make her seem diaphanous with spiritual light" (3:129). As surely as
Theodore, he thereby destines himself for a future in which he "pines"
for the "dim, mournful face" he has imagined.

As an interpolated narrative, Zenobia's legend recalls Holgrave's
story of Alice Pyncheon; indeed, both are parables of a woman's victimization by men. But in this case, of course, a woman creates and
tells the story, so dazzling her male listener that he incorporates what
amounts to a feminist critique—a story pointedly critical of himself—
into his narrative.

Furthermore, when Coverdale attends the mesmerism exhibition at
the Lyceum, he comes close to acting out Theodore's experience with
the Veiled Lady, as if matching himself to the character of Zenobia's
tale. He views the mesmerist as an artist for whom human character is
"but soft wax in his hands." Earlier he had remarked upon Priscilla's
"pleasant weakness" (3:74) and had called her "impressible as wax"
(3:78), so his diction here subtly identifies him with the mesmerist.
Most important, he stresses the sexual or seductive power that the
mesmerist enjoys over his young female subject—his power to turn her
passion for a lover, with his kiss "still burning on her lips," into "icy
indifference" (3:198). Hawthorne had expressed the fear that the mesmerist might violate Sophia's "holy of holies" and had vowed not to
use such power. Coverdale would go a step further, using mesmerical
attraction to freeze rather than enflame passion. But his speculations
are consistent with the sort of fantastical relationship he covets in his
memories of Priscilla. Even at the end of the novel, she remains a
Veiled Lady; it is Hollingsworth, after all, who releases her from her
bondage to Westervelt—Hollingsworth, not Coverdale, who steps
through the frame of the work of art, if so Westervelt's exhibition of
Priscilla can be called, to dissolve the threat it poses to her.

Coverdale returns to Blithedale two nights later, he says, because of a
"yearning interest to learn the upshot of [his] story" (3:205). He is still
troubled by his "old problem," still at the mercy of his own haunted
mind, and he compares his emotions to "mysterious growths, springing

suddenly from no root or seed, and growing nobody can tell how or wherefore" (3:205). In retrospect, he seems to recognize his irresistible involvement in the "passions, the errors, and the misfortunes" of the three characters into whose exclusive circle he steps "at a peril that [he] could not estimate" (3:206). When he comes upon the men and women of Blithedale, he finds them elaborately costumed and enjoying what seems to him to be an illicit or satanic rite. The result is a surrealistic carnival that challenges all formal categories of thought. Women in various guises—the goddess Diana, a "vivacious little gypsy," Moll Pitcher, the "renowned old witch of Lynn" (3:210)—seem to dominate the scene. All together, the characters compose a closed circle of energy in which Coverdale appears a "profane intruder" (3:211). Even observation is a challenge, as the scene devolves into formlessness: "whirling round so swiftly, so madly, and so merrily, in time and tune with the Satanic music, . . . their separate incongruities were blended all together; and they became a kind of entanglement that went nigh to turn one's brain, with merely looking at it" (3:210). Instead of approaching the others, Coverdale flees. "I was like a mad poet," he says, picking up the very image Zenobia had mentioned when he left, "hunted by chimaeras" (3:211).

When he comes upon the other principal characters at Eliot's pulpit, Coverdale recognizes that everything that has kept his heart and imagination "idly feverish" has reached a climax (3:215). Most important, Zenobia's stature in the community and in the novel has diminished greatly. Her attitude remains "free and noble" and her "eyes were on fire," but she appears like a "dethroned" queen who is "on trial for her life, or perchance condemned, already" (3:213). Like Hester in the final pages of *The Scarlet Letter,* she is becoming more and more an object, largely because of her unsympathetic treatment by the other characters: the blood has drained from her face and she now looks to Coverdale "like marble" (3:213). Like Hester, she has suffered a kind of petrification within a community which seems increasingly dominated by men, and Hawthorne emphasizes their blindness to the meaning of her life.

Many critics have complained about Zenobia's ignominious death in *The Blithedale Romance,* viewing it as incompatible with her previous strength and determination, and there is much to be said for the judgment that Hawthorne simply could not tolerate such a powerful character, even though he had created her. But while Zenobia's character dies, she does not exit the narrative quite as gently as her suicide might suggest.[12] As both object and subject, as image and voice, she has a dynamic life after death. The test of her residual power is her effect on Coverdale's imagination and on his narrative.

When she left Coverdale at Eliot's pulpit after her rupture with Hollingsworth, her hand had felt as "cold as a veritable piece of snow" (3:227). In death, her body locked in one position by rigor mortis, she has assumed a posture of "terrible inflexibility," a "marble image of a death-agony" (3:235). But even in this condition, Zenobia retains considerable vitality for Coverdale's imagination.[13] Although limited to this single attitude, she at least assumes an energetic one—a posture of rebellion, "as if she struggled against Providence in never-ending hostility," her hands "clenched in immitigable defiance" (3:235). Indeed, Zenobia's hostile appearance has burned itself indelibly into Coverdale's imagination. His initial desire to subject her to the "cold decorum" of marble has had a paradoxical effect, and even his impulse to close his eyes in her presence will avail him little; his imagination is finally impotent to regulate, much less contain, Zenobia's presence. While Coverdale ends his narrative with a declaration of love for Priscilla, he admits that Zenobia's memory haunts him more. "For more than twelve long years I have borne it in my memory," he admits, "and could now reproduce it as freshly as if it were still before my eyes" (3:235).

Coverdale's climactic confession of his love for Priscilla appears to displace Zenobia in his narrative and in his emotional life—just as Priscilla has supplanted her in Hollingsworth's affection. But Coverdale's own words belie the very conclusion he hints at. His admission to being haunted by Zenobia's death mask echoes a statement he had made when he introduced her. Zenobia's character "impressed itself on me so distinctly," he admitted, "that I can now summon her up like a ghost, a little wanner than the life, but otherwise identical with it" (3:15). As an object, in other words, Zenobia is as challenging to his imagination as ever.

More important is Zenobia's influence on Coverdale's narrative. Before she left him for the final time, she had chided him for his tendency to turn everything "into a ballad," challenging him to write "lines of fire" instead of "glittering icicles" (3:223, 224). Coverdale's final effort to explain her death does an injustice to her defiant posture, as he conforms her behavior to the sentimental stereotype of a popular ballad: "she deemed it well and decorous to die as so many village-maidens have, wronged in their first-love, and seeking peace in the bosom of the old, familiar stream—so familiar that they could not dread it—where, in childhood, they used to bathe their little feet" (3:236). In thus adapting her story to a pre-established form, Coverdale has made a choice in favor of "glittering icicles" instead of "lines of fire." On the other hand, in response to Westervelt's callous remarks at Zenobia's funeral, Coverdale manages an impassioned eulogy that demonstrates her influence on his thinking. Instead of turning her death into a ballad, he sees in it a general lesson about women's status. "It was a woful thought," he says, "that a woman of Zenobia's diversified capacity should have fancied herself irretrievably defeated on the broad battlefield of life, and with no refuge, save to fall on her own sword, merely because Love had gone against her. It is nonsense, and a miserable wrong—the result, like so many others, of masculine egotism—that the success or failure of woman's existence should be made to depend wholly on the affections, and on one species of affection; while man has such a multitude of other chances, that this seems but an incident" (3:241). His statement virtually echoes what Zenobia had said earlier in the novel, when she asked how a woman could be happy "after discovering that fate has assigned her but one single event, which she must contrive to make the substance of her whole life? A man has his choice of innumerable events" (3:60). That is, as a subject and spokeswoman for a feminist ideal, Zenobia still retains a voice in Coverdale's narrative. He may love Priscilla, as he alleges, but he writes like Zenobia—"like a woman."

Miriam Schaefer in *The Marble Faun* (1860) bears obvious similarities to Zenobia. Although she does not speak as explicitly for women, she is a more active and successful artist—in many respects, the most successful artist in Hawthorne's fiction. Indeed, in the contrasts among his major characters, especially that between Miriam and Kenyon, *The Marble Faun* shows Hawthorne coming most directly to terms with conflicts in his attitudes toward art.[14] And despite an ending similar to that in *The Blithedale Romance*—the hero's declaration of love for a Pale Maiden—Miriam dominates much of the novel and consistently challenges Kenyon's imagination.[15] So often does Hawthorne associate her with historical, mythical, and Biblical women

(Jael, Judith, Cleopatra, Eve, Rachel, Beatrice Cenci) that she becomes an archetypal composite of the most beautiful, provocative, and potentially dangerous women in the "history" of the male imagination. The effect, however, is not to objectify her character or force her into a projected stereotype; it is tantamount to an admission that male language is inadequate to the task of expressing what a woman is—that it can only approximate her dynamic character by giving her multiple identities. She is "sprite-like in her most ordinary manifestations" (4:23), and she appears through most of the work as a magical creation of the various rumors that swirl around her: "She resembled one of those images of light, which conjurors evoke and cause to shine before us, in apparent tangibility, only an arm's length beyond our grasp" (4:21).

At the same time, Miriam possesses a strength of character and will, a desire to define and create herself, at least equal to Zenobia's or Hester Prynne's. Even though as a child she had been betrothed to an old marchese—another Chillingworth, in view of their "disproportioned ages" (4:430)—she has rebelled against such an arranged marriage. Although Judith Fryer says that Miriam has been "caught up in and pursued by a corrupt patriarchal order," Hawthorne is careful to note that her self-reliant spirit has descended matrilineally.[16] There was "something in Miriam's blood, in her mixed race, in her recollections of her mother—some characteristic, finally, in her own nature—which had given her freedom of thought, and force of will, and made this prearranged connection odious to her" (4:430).

In addition to emphasizing her protean nature and self-reliance, Hawthorne also stresses Miriam's cultural and moral complexity. In an image that recalls his dual characterization of Sophia, he notes that Miriam is an "impressible and impulsive creature, as unlike herself, in different moods, as if a melancholy maiden and a glad one were both bound within the girdle about her waist, and kept in magic thraldom by the brooch that clasped it" (4:83). With her suggestion of secret experience in some mysterious past and her knowledge of the Roman underground, she is eager to introduce Hilda and Kenyon to her city. She guides them through the catacombs at the beginning of the novel, directs Hilda on a labyrinthine route to the Cenci home near the end, brings Kenyon to the ruins on the Campagna, and leads him through the street carnival during his search for Hilda. Indeed, something like Melville's Isabel, Miriam seems to embody all those "dark caverns, into which all men must descend, if they would know anything beneath the surface and illusive pleasures of existence" (4:262). Especially for Kenyon, Miriam plays a tutelary role even greater than Zenobia's for Coverdale.

As an artist within the work of art, a "romance artist par excellence," in Joel Porte's words, and particularly as director of the final scenes of *The Marble Faun,* Miriam performs her most significant role.[17] Just as she more successfully resists the tradition of arranged marriage, she exercises more artistic freedom than Hester Prynne, and given the power she wields over Kenyon's imagination—a power to direct his actions and inspire him temporarily to sculpt—she seems more powerful than even Zenobia. Her own paintings consistently represent a world of darkness and shadow, illuminated solely by her own haunted mind. Even in the innocent domestic scenes that she paints, she depicts herself as an estranged figure with an "expression of deep sadness" (4:46). She seems to recognize that in the realm of conventional art, she will always occupy a place off-center. Her more profound visions (Jael, Judith, Salome) unabashedly represent murderous women who seek vengeance against men. She calls such images "ugly phantoms that stole out of my mind; not things that I created, but things that haunt me" (4:45), thus linking herself directly to Hawthorne's most creative characters and to Hawthorne himself. Miriam even makes her paintings come true in the world of the novel. She gains revenge upon the model who persecutes her by convincing Donatello, a work of art she has brought to life—another male Galatea—to kill him.

Most important, however, is Miriam's self-portrait. With more freedom than Hester or Zenobia, she is able to create an art object that expresses herself—and also fulfills the ideal that Hawthorne has established for an artistic vision that haunts the mind. The portrait is of a "beautiful woman, such as one sees only two or three, if even so many, in all a lifetime; so beautiful, that she seemed to get into your consciousness and memory, and could never afterwards be shut out, but haunted your dreams, for pleasure or for pain; holding your inner realm as a conquered territory, though without deigning to make herself at home there" (4:47–48). Although Hawthorne emphasizes the effect of Miriam's portrait on the viewer's imagination more than what it expresses about her, he accords the painting extraordinary aggressive power. He describes a perfect example of the kind of art object, in

Barthes' term, that "dazzles" the imagination and demands an open-minded, writerly response.[18] Like Melville's chair-portrait or Isabel's music, Miriam's aesthetic image has a spontaneous, mesmerizing life of its own that resists objectification. Recalling Hawthorne's wish for Sophia to penetrate his own "inward regions," the painting insinuates itself into the viewer's consciousness and conquers his imagination.

Besides its profoundly attractive appearance and the "dark eyes, into which you might look as deeply as your glance would go," Miriam's painted self wears a sad expression, "as if some evil had befallen it" (4:48, 49). A prophetic picture of beauty submerged in evil, a vision of her own "secret soul," the painting is as significant for its mode of creation as for its content. At her best, Miriam is a visionary artist, like Isabel in *Pierre,* who achieves an open, "conversational" relationship with her medium and materials. She surrenders control of her "pen" to the phantoms that steal out of her haunted mind. As such, she serves as a potential model for the other characters.

In marked contrast, Hilda is essentially a copyist; she has "ceased to consider herself as an original artist" (4:56). Like Lucy in *Pierre* she idealizes her subjects, reifying them into the "spirit and essence of [a] picture" (4:58). "If a picture had darkened into an indistinct shadow, through time and neglect, or had been injured by cleaning, or re-touched by some profane hand, she seemed to possess the faculty of seeing it in its pristine glory" (4:58–59). With such a purifying vision, Hilda does more than copy and restore; she censors and reforms—a sharp contrast to the revelations that emerge from the depths, so to speak, of Miriam's canvas. "Accuracy was not the phrase" for Hilda's copies, Hawthorne observes; they are "evanescent and ethereal" through her "divine touch" (4:58). Seeing the world through Hilda's art is like "looking at humanity with angel's eyes" (4:55).

As an artist Kenyon is cast squarely between the two women. At times he is remarkably sensitive to the "hidden order" of his own character, but he usually reasserts a rational control over the creative process and so refuses to give his own "ugly phantoms" an aesthetic life. As he had with Zenobia in *The Blithedale Romance,* Hawthorne allows Miriam to voice the most severe criticisms of Kenyon's artistry. As his aesthetic conscience, she accuses the sculptor of turning "feverish men into cool, quiet marble" (4:119).[19] Later, she even wishes that he would exercise such a "cooling" effect on her. "You can do nothing for me," she tells him when he asks if he can help her, "unless you petrify me into a marble companion for your Cleopatra there; and I am not of her sisterhood, I do assure you" (4:129). Despite her almost compulsive efforts at self-expression, even Miriam feels tempted to allow her haunted nature to be objectified and so, in a manner, redeemed through the medium of Kenyon's devitalizing art. In the same breath, of course, she recognizes the inherent resistance of her own dynamic character to such a dehumanizing process.

Kenyon's most successful creations, the Cleopatra and the bust of Donatello, occur largely by accident when he relinquishes strict control over the creative process. As Millicent Bell observes, he is "unable to accomplish satisfactory results until he surrenders to the nonrational forces of his nature and becomes a 'medium.'"[20] It is especially significant that these two sculptures are Kenyon's most successful; modelled after Miriam and Donatello, they reveal his sensitivity to the complex experience the two characters represent. In forming the bust of Donatello, he "gave up all pre-conceptions about the character of his subject, and let his hands work, uncontrolled, with the clay, somewhat as a spiritual medium, while holding a pen, yields it to an unseen guidance other than that of her own will" (4:271). Even Hawthorne's use of the feminine pronoun suggests an association of such an unmediated process with women. Kenyon has achieved the same state of "passive sensibility," what Ehrenzweig calls a "passive watchfulness," in sculpting the statue of Cleopatra. As the figure of a woman, the statue recalls Drowne's carving of the Portuguese lady and clearly suggests, it seems to me, Kenyon's effort to express his response to Miriam. A near perfect embodiment of the sculptor's ambivalence toward women, the statue is also an interesting composite of values that are often mutually exclusive. Both "implacable as a stone, and cruel as fire" (4:127), Cleopatra stands in "marvellous repose," yet reveals a "great, smouldering furnace, deep down in [her] heart" (4:126). At the very least, the statue represents a dynamic tension between energy and form; that is, as much as Miriam's own self-portrait, the passion of Kenyon's creative response to Miriam has discovered a form that enhances rather than diminishes her powerful character. Momentarily, by empowering his creativity "in the feminine," Kenyon achieves a feminized masculine art—feminized not by a woman's weakness, but by her strength.

Examples of Kenyon's potential, the bust and the statue represent an aesthetic ideal he only rarely achieves. In contrast to the Cleopatra, there is the "small, beautifully shaped hand, most delicately sculptured in marble" (4:120), the idea for which Kenyon "stole" from Hilda. Not only do Miriam and Hilda create very different kinds of art; they inspire Kenyon to use art in different ways to mediate his relationships to them. Miriam's self-portrait works irresistibly on his consciousness; as a model she causes him to surrender his artistic will to the very deepest creative impulse. With Hilda, on the other hand, Kenyon exercises the full dehumanizing power of his medium. Miriam had accused him of being no more human than one of his statues—"as cold and pitiless as [his] own marble"—and that characterization seems confirmed in this diminutive replica of Hilda's hand. He objectifies the smallest and most "delicate" part of her to stand for the whole, and rather than encouraging a deeply passionate response, that hand keeps him at a distance. Hilda herself is a "partly ideal creature, not to be handled, nor even approached too closely" (4:63), and even her marble replica has a repressive power. Kenyon "dared not even kiss the image that he himself had made" (4:122). It is this Kenyon, moreover, who finally looks to Hilda's hand to lead him out of the moral and psychological quandary that Miriam and Donatello reveal to him during the final scenes of the novel.

Appropriately, it is Miriam, the most successful artist in the work of art, who supervises the conclusion of *The Marble Faun*. At the end of *The Scarlet Letter* Hester seemed wholly dependent upon Dimmesdale for vitality; when he failed her, she assumed the form of cold marble. Similarly, despite her much greater freedom of expression, Zenobia also was objectified into a frozen posture of hostility at the end of *The Blithedale Romance*. But Miriam operates very actively in the final scenes of her novel. She arranges for the separation of Hilda and Kenyon, forcing them, in effect, to enter her dark, surrealistic world of art before they can be reunited. Through her, Hawthorne tries to educate his American characters in the experiences of the "secret soul" before allowing them to return to the sanctuary of their native land. Hilda must enter the Cenci castle and thus approach an understanding of Miriam's own experience, while Kenyon has two important experiences—first on the Campagna and then at the Roman carnival.

As he searches for Hilda in the Roman countryside, Kenyon discovers instead a statue of the Venus de' Medici. The statue has been unearthed by Miriam and Donatello and becomes a tangible reminder of the passionate, sensual art that Kenyon has only rarely created. In its dismantled state, it is a truncated emblem for Kenyon's emotional weaknesses and a more full-bodied surrogate for his "marble" Hilda, but as Baym points out, the "order in which Kenyon puts together the pieces of this shattered work—torso, arms, head—represents the progressive embodiment of the fundamental erotic force, an epitome of the artistic process of creation."[21] As he puts the pieces of the fractured Venus together, he creates a "magical" effect, a perfect, holistic image of "Womanhood," another work of art informed by a kind of sacred fire (4:423, 424). Placing the final piece, the head, on the trunk "immediately lighted up and vivified the whole figure," Hawthorne notes, "endowing it with personality, soul, and intelligence. The beautiful Idea at once asserted its immortality, and converted that heap of forlorn fragments into a whole, as perfect to the mind, if not to the eye, as when the new marble gleamed with snowy lustre" (4:423–24). Resembling Kenyon's Cleopatra much more than Hilda's diminutive hand, the Venus that Miriam and Donatello place in Kenyon's way is designed to test his ability to unite the objectified and fragmented parts of a woman into a perfect whole.

In the end, however, Kenyon cannot assimilate the Venus's energy and become a true Pygmalion because he does not wish to include the statue's sensuality in his image of woman. He is more like Theodore in Zenobia's legend than like the woodcarver Drowne; he allows the Venus to create her creator only momentarily before, like Hawthorne in the Custom House with the scarlet letter, he drops an object too "hot" to handle. He cannot follow Miriam's advice that he respond to the statue's "frightening" aspect, he says, because "Imagination and the love of art have both died out of [him]" (4:427). According to Hawthorne's logic in this scene, because Kenyon does not respond sympathetically to the statue, it immediately decomposes. By the "greater strength of a human affection," Hawthorne notes, "the divine statue seemed to fall asunder again, and become only a heap of worthless fragments" (4:424). On the surface, of course, Kenyon has acted laudably, preferring a "human affection" to aesthetic appreciation. That is, Hawthorne would seem to be criticizing the Pygmalion myth, the inhumanity of such characters as Aylmer, Rappaccini, and Drowne in preferring their own objectified replicas of woman to the real thing. But in fact Hawthorne suggests the opposite. For in *The Marble Faun,* statues with the power to come to life—the Venus, Cleopatra, Miriam herself—seem more human than the "real" Hilda, whom Kenyon has transformed into a statue he dares not kiss.

Having failed, according to my reading, to heed the lesson of the Campagna, Kenyon finds himself in an even more dynamic world of art when he goes to the Roman carnival. Recalling the revelry in *The Blithedale Romance,* the carnival represents another alternative to Kenyon's own sculpture—a living work of art whose "material" is human character. As the carnival swirls around him, in effect he has entered his own haunted mind to confront the "ugly phantoms" that refuse to stay under his control: "Clowns and parti-colored harlequins; orang-outangs; bear-headed, bull-headed, and dog-headed individuals; faces that would have been human, but for their enormous noses; one terrific creature, with a visage right in the centre of his breast; and all other imaginable kinds of monstrosity and exaggeration" (4:446). Like Coverdale, Kenyon feels threatened by these examples of the wild forms that human character can assume. Much as Coverdale is threatened with an arrow through the heart by Zenobia, Kenyon's experience is climaxed when he is "killed" by a "gigantic female figure" who sprays him with lime dust and thus transforms him into one of his own dusty-white statues (4:445, 446). Symbolically, he represents living proof that, as Miriam had asserted, he is as "cold and pitiless" as his own marble.

In the works we have examined, it is usually a woman who is "captured" in the form of a statue, so that her frightening qualities may be rendered harmless while more benign qualities are idealized. In *The Marble Faun,* that process certainly occurs in the case of Hilda's marble hand, but Miriam seems to escape such a fate. The art objects with which she is associated all burn with some inner fire. By the same token, the novel itself originated from the idea of a statue, the Faun of Praxiteles, coming to life, and Hawthorne works an interesting variation on the Pygmalion myth in the experiences of his two male characters, Donatello and Kenyon. Under Miriam's influence, for better or worse, according to one's judgment of his "fall," the Faun comes to have a fully human life, while Kenyon, like Hilda, undergoes the process in reverse. Both characters resist implication in Miriam's experience. Kenyon refuses to be another Donatello and so hardens from within. As an artist he prefers Hilda's marble hand to the Venus's "frightening" vitality; as a man he is himself gradually transformed into a cold and pitiless statue.

Hawthorne had already developed this idea in his early story "The Man of Adamant" (1837). So hard-hearted does Richard Digby become in his self-righteous estrangement from the rest of humanity that

he assumes the form of a "marble statue, wrought by some dark imagined sculptor to express the most repulsive mood that human features
could assume" (II:167). As he does in *The Marble Faun*, Hawthorne
tests his hero's humanity with the image of a young girl, Mary Goffe,
but Digby refuses to consider her anything but sinful and perverse,
thus hardening himself, according to the fable, into a block of stone.
Kenyon, of course, is nowhere near as "adamant" as Digby, although
being "killed" into a statue by a gigantic female figure does suggest
retribution for his insensitivity to women. More important, Kenyon
certainly judges Miriam and Donatello harshly and prefers to know as
little as possible about their experience. He is unruffled by the "feverish dream" of the carnival (4:446), and as soon as the masqueraders
leave his haunted mind, "as dreams and spectres do," he doggedly
pursues his single-minded quest for Hilda (4:447).

But Hawthorne, it seems, refuses to let his hero off so easily. He
places in Kenyon's path a remarkable number of impediments, post-
poning the gratification of reunion with Hilda in favor of a series of
object lessons in responding to other human beings. The final scenes of
The Marble Faun, in fact, offer the best examples in Hawthorne's fiction of his distance from his male protagonists. With Miriam as stage
manager, each scene works at cross purposes with Kenyon's intentions.
Soon after leaving the carnival, for example, he meets Miriam and
Donatello. When he implores them to "give [him] a little light on the
matter which [he has] so much at heart" (4:447), their response re-
bukes his ignorance and insensitivity. "We gave you all the light we
could," Miriam replies. "You are yourself unkind, (though you little
think how much so,) to come between us at this hour" (4:447–48).
His devotion to Hilda, she implies, makes Kenyon incapable of understanding any other relationship. On the other hand, when Kenyon asks
forgiveness, the two lovers make another effort to include him in the
"magic circle" of their experience. They extend their hands "so that
they were a linked circle of three," and this laying on of hands sends a
transfusion of energy, emotion, and vision through the sculptor, as
"many reminiscences and forebodings flash[ed] through their hearts"
(4:448).

Such a kinetic experience—an effort by the lovers to reanimate the
"cold" statue which the sculptor has become—is destined to be short-
circuited. For as the three characters separate, Miriam and Donatello
are arrested, and Kenyon is reunited with Hilda. Although the two
characters do see Miriam one last time in the Pantheon, they never

speak with her again. In declaring their separation from Europe and from art, they dissociate themselves from Miriam and her experience. When they see her for the final time, it is as if she "stood on the other side of a fathomless abyss, and warned them from its verge" (4:461).

Like Zenobia, however, Miriam retains some influence, some presence, in the main characters' imaginative lives. Kenyon, for example, continues to be troubled by her experience. In an earlier conversation with Hilda, he had advocated looking at Miriam and Donatello's "crime" from their point of view. "They are perhaps partners in what we must call awful guilt," he said; "and yet, I will own to you—when I think of the original cause, the motives, the feelings, the sudden concurrence of circumstances thrusting them onward, the urgency of the moment, and the sublime unselfishness on either part—I know not well how to distinguish it from much that the world calls heroism. Might we not render some such verdict as this?—'Worthy of Death, but not unworthy of Love!'" (4:384). Kenyon's efforts to mitigate the two characters' guilt through active sympathy can be likened to Coverdale's euology for Zenobia. His plea for at least a degree of moral relativism also echoes Hester's impassioned avowal that what she and Dimmesdale did "had a consecration of its own." It must be contrasted, however, with the "clear, crystal medium" of Hilda's integrity and her simple answer to his question—"Never!" (4:384). To his credit, Kenyon seems genuinely disturbed by Hilda's moral absolutism, which condemns their friends. He calls her a "terribly severe judge" and wonders how her "tender sympathy could coexist with the remorselessness of a steel blade" (4:384). At this point in the novel, in other words, Kenyon is at least as sympathetic to Miriam's experience as he is to Hilda's character.

Like Zenobia, tempted to make Coverdale her confidant, Miriam seems to recognize the sculptor's sensitivity. On the Campagna, as she tells him about her relationship with the model, she admits that she had thought of telling him sooner—indeed, at the moment he had shown her the bust of Cleopatra. Sensing his coldness, however, she had "thrust" back the impulse (4:433). Her decision seems validated by Kenyon's subsequent conduct; in his gravitation toward Hilda, he is never again as sensitive to Miriam's plight.

In a scene at the very end of the novel that echoes his earlier conversation with Hilda, Kenyon again broaches the idea of moral relativism. He admits being perplexed that Donatello appears "elevated" by sin, and wonders if sin is "merely an element of human education, through which we struggle to a higher and purer state than we could otherwise have attained" (4:460). Hilda is shocked "beyond words" by such an idea, a striking indication of the effect she is likely to have on Kenyon's thinking. This time, however, instead of criticizing Hilda's insensitivity, Kenyon begs her forgiveness for letting his mind wander so "wild and wide" (4:460). He implores her to guide and counsel him—as his "inmost friend"—protecting him from his own wayward thoughts with the "white wisdom" that "clothes" her "as with a celestial garment" (4:460–61). Whatever his earlier sympathy for Miriam, the open-mindedness that produced the Cleopatra and earned her confidence, Kenyon has lost it as surely as "imagination and a love of art" have died out of him.

The novel proper simply draws rapidly to a close. Kenyon has "won gentle Hilda's shy affection," Hawthorne says, although one must suspect, in view of her imminent canonization "as a household Saint, in the light of her husband's fireside" (4:461), that the former sculptor will see little more of her than the dainty hand whose impression he stole in a weak moment. Indeed, a bit earlier in the novel, during a tour of St. Peter's, Kenyon had imagined an ideal "nuptial home" for the two of them in the sanctity of the church. What a "delicious life it would be," he said, "if a colony of people with delicate lungs (or merely with delicate fancies) could take up their abode in this ever-mild and tranquil air! These architectural tombs of the Popes might serve for dwellings, and each brazen sepulchral door-way would become a domestic threshold" (4:369). In an extraordinary fantasy, Kenyon imagines a lover asking his mistress to share his tomb. Perhaps indicating the atmosphere of his own nuptial home, he says fondly, "What a life would be theirs, Hilda, in their marble Eden!" (4:369). Kenyon's vision recalls the "marble image of happiness" that Roger Chillingworth "imposed" upon Hester Prynne when he married her, but it does seem entirely appropriate to his character and his sculptor's penchant for turning "feverish men into cool, quiet marble." In marked contrast to the electric "circle of three" in the carnival scene, Hilda's dainty hand guides Kenyon away from those "characters of fire" and toward a marital tomb, a "marble Eden" where the American Adam and Eve can enjoy a cold and pitiless life.22

The only souvenir of their European experience that Hawthorne mentions is an Etruscan bracelet which Hilda receives from Miriam just before they leave. The bracelet expresses the "sevenfold sepulchral gloom" which Miriam's imagination was "wont to fling over its most sportive flights" (4:462) and thus seems to reproduce sevenfold the meaning of the red carbuncle that Miriam wears on her bosom. While the carbuncle "seemed an emanation of herself, [of] all that was passionate and glowing, in her native disposition" (4:396), the bracelet is a reminder of her creative power: "a symbol of as sad a mystery as any that Miriam had attached to the separate gems" (4:462). The gems of the bracelet thereby fulfill an ideal of symbolic communication that reverberates through Hawthorne's fiction: an ideal in which "words were gems, that would flame with many-coloured light upon the page, and throw thence a tremulous glimmer into the reader's eyes" (4:345). Dazzling male discourse, Hawthorne's women typically encourage men to write or create in the feminine and thereby to produce a dazzling discourse of their own. In this case, of course, as a gift to Hilda and Kenyon, Miriam's bracelet assumes ironic meaning; it is hard to imagine the two characters being "dazzled" by her "many-coloured light."

Like *The House of the Seven Gables*, *The Marble Faun* ends with an impending marriage, but in this case, the objectifying imagery associated with the seemingly positive male-female relationship, as well as the hero's disengagement from art, suggests the suppression of knowledge more than the achievement of the ecstatically self-creative relationship Hawthorne had described in his love letters. Kenyon's marriage to Hilda does not seem to promise a creative surrender like the one Hawthorne described as Sophia's incorporation into his "inward regions" to take over his share of their correspondence and to make his heart "gush out" in "warmth and freedom."

On the other hand, Miriam's fate in *The Marble Faun* is more positive than those of Hawthorne's other heroines. As we have seen, even in death Hester is identified and eclipsed by the scarlet letter now etched durably in the marble of the tombstone she shares with Dimmesdale. Alice Pyncheon is mesmerically transformed into a kind of puppet by Matthew Maule; her musical talent is thereby frozen in the image of the coffin-like harpsichord, and, although liberated at the end of the novel, it discovers no audience among the major characters in the novel. Zenobia, like Hester, is imaged in the rigid posture of a marble statue and finally buried on the hill she might have shared with Hollingsworth. Her death mask, however, barely contains the hostile energy of her expression, and her memory haunts Coverdale's imagination. In *The Marble Faun* Hawthorne has worked an interesting variation on this ending. Although consistently associated with the Roman underground and with things repressed, Miriam remains alive at the end of the novel—above ground, haunting the streets of Rome while she awaits Donatello's release from prison. More successfully than even Zenobia, she has a tangible presence in the Etruscan bracelet that Hilda and Kenyon take back with them to America, but she is not thereby contained by that single object. Although she herself has been separated from her creation, she has not lost her creative ability to express herself through art.

In committing himself to Hilda, of course, Kenyon has allowed an exorcising rather than a creative power to dominate his imaginative life. In sharp contrast to the fire that smoulders in the "furnace" of Cleopatra, or the "characters of fire" in which Hester and Zenobia write, Hilda is like a "taper of virgin wax, burning with a pure and steady flame, and chasing away the evil spirits out of the magic circle of its beams" (4:409). At the end of the novel, Kenyon steps back from the abyss (of moral confusion, further European experience, continued artistic effort) symbolized by Miriam, and so cries out, "I dare not follow you into the unfathomable abysses, whither you are tending" (4:434). In the preface to *The Scarlet Letter* Hawthorne had identified the most exclusive readership imaginable for his novel—"the one heart and mind of perfect sympathy"—recognizing that such intimate communication was essential to his communion with the "divided segment" of his own nature. If, as I have argued, Hawthorne embodied his deepest creative impulse in his strongest female characters, he also destined each of them for a life of frustrated seeking for that perfect reader. More than any of the other heroines, Miriam, wandering the streets of Rome, suggests the pathos of that seeking.

CONCLUSION

Writing in his journal in the spring of 1843, Ralph Waldo Emerson offered his view that the "finest people marry the two sexes in their own person. Hermaphrodite is then the symbol of the finished soul. It was agreed that in every act should appear the married pair: the two elements should mix in every act."[1] A year or so later, Margaret Fuller said much the same thing: "Male and female represent the two sides of the great radical dualism. But, in fact, they are perpetually passing into one another. Fluid hardens to solid, solid rushes to fluid. There is no wholly masculine man, no purely feminine woman."[2] These similar statements by two of the most influential male and female writers of the mid-nineteenth century both express a profound interest in an androgynous ideal, a combination or interpenetration of masculine and feminine characteristics. In quoting them I am not suggesting that Poe, Melville, and Hawthorne had searched for this elusive ideal in their fiction. Nor have I argued that a case can be made for any of the three writers as a feminist. Except for Hawthorne (in selected passages in *The Scarlet Letter* and *The Blithedale Romance*), none of these writers directly addressed women's issues, partly because the conventions of the tale and the romance encouraged the kind of "sacrifice of relation" that Michael Davitt Bell has noted. At the same time, all three writers were seriously interested in questions of gender and the effect gender issues could have on their writing. If not androgynous or feminist, their fiction helps to sustain ideas implicit in the statements by Emerson and Fuller: that gender and gender characteristics were more fluid than solid (to borrow Fuller's suggestive terms), that questions about gender, masculinity as well as femininity, intrigued male as well as female writers.

With few exceptions the fiction of Poe, Melville, and Hawthorne remains male-centered, although none of the three writers seems secure in a conventional masculinity. Their interest in women is usually

narcissistic in the sense of being largely concerned with male experiences *of* women, but, given that obvious limitation and acknowledging
the problems it creates for women readers, the fiction I have examined
does represent serious male efforts to explore the creative possibilities
of relationships to women. More to the point, I hope I have been able
to demonstrate that none of these authors wrote automatically "in the
masculine," inscribing nineteenth-century masculine ideology and
using women to satisfy a desire for power. While they did not often
bring social and political issues about gender to the surface of their
texts, their fiction does suggest considerable unease with prevailing
assumptions about gender differences, especially the radically oppositional ideology that has been labelled the Jacksonian cult of masculinity. If they do not themselves deconstruct that masculine ideology,
they encourage readers to recognize the destructive as well as self-destructive effects of phallocentric discourse by consistently depicting the
failure of male efforts to control women through language, imagery,
and larger artistic forms. And at their best, in *Pierre, The Blithedale
Romance,* and *The Marble Faun,* for example, they explore the possibility of an alternative poetics—a feminized masculine poetics characterized, not by the assertion of male power over women, but by male
identification of power with women or by male surrender of power to
women.

Not surprisingly, such surrenders of power to women or identification of creative power with women produced significant anxiety in
male characters and writers alike and help account for the negative
endings of so many works (from a male as well as female perspective).
In those passages in *The Marble Faun* describing Kenyon's bursts of
creative achievement, each of them inspired by and modelled after
Miriam's "feminine" aesthetics, Hawthorne comes closer than either
Poe or Melville, closer than he himself had in previous works, to representing the achievement of a truly feminized masculine poetics characterized by openness to the most creative depths of the self, a "conversation-like intercourse" with the work of art, and a vitality resistant to
conventional artistic form. Given such successful "gushes" of creativity
in the middle of the narrative, it is fair to wonder why Kenyon does
not sustain such a high level of achievement and why Miriam must be
written out of the narrative and out of Kenyon's thinking at the end of
the book. The same questions can be raised about Melville's *Mardi* or
Pierre, or about Hawthorne's other works. Indeed, even a cursory

glance at the endings of the works we have examined and at what happens to their strong female characters raises serious doubts about the authors' commitment to the feminine aesthetic values I have cited. Isabel, Beatrice Rappaccini, Zenobia—each heroine represents an ideal, yet dies in a way that suggests male hostility toward women and the dangers they symbolize. Such inconsistencies not only make it difficult to determine what attitudes the authors hold toward women, but also complicate readers' responses. Perhaps it is most accurate simply to suggest that the phenomenon I have cited, the feminization of a masculine poetics, creates as much as reflects conflicts about gender in the thinking of these nineteenth-century male writers. The fates of Isabel, Zenobia, and Miriam exemplify an imperfect "feminization" that may be said to characterize most of the works we have examined—an anxiety not only about masculinity but about its feminization. Feminizing their masculine discourse, in other words, could cause as well as cure certain aesthetic headaches for male writers.

Despite obvious anxiety about women and male-female relationships, the fiction of Poe, Melville, and Hawthorne does suggest that masculinity and a masculine poetics were open questions for these writers, rather than unexamined assumptions or tools of oppression. The phallocentric model of male creativity, in which the masculine writer confidently reduces everything to the "reign of the One" or "kills women into art" in order to oppress them, is not a monolith but an extreme that some male writers questioned or rejected. Without abandoning their conception of "difference" or their views of women as "other" than themselves, these three writers did try to free themselves and their fiction from an oppositional view of women. Although all three writers were products of their culture and were certainly influenced by the Jacksonian cult of masculinity, each of them repeatedly undermined male hegemony in his fiction, subverting conventional masculinity by demonstrating its weakness or impotence in the presence of strong women. In the climactic return to life of Ligeia and Madeline Usher, Poe abruptly reverses the flow of power in his narrative along lines of gender as his male characters are reduced to conditions of passivity, objectified in the presence of women who refuse to be repressed. The resistance of dynamic female characters to the static forms of literary typology is a recurrent motif in the fiction of Melville and Hawthorne as well: in the characters of Hautia, Isabel Glendinning, Beatrice Rappaccini, Hester Prynne, Zenobia, and Miriam.

Transcending the denotative power of male language, bursting the bounds of artistic forms, such characters exemplify their creators' fascination with female strength and "feminine" creative power. But Melville and Hawthorne go further than Poe in exploring the possibility of positive rather than negative female power—in trying to empower their own fiction "in the feminine" by incorporating creative female characters who not only resist masculine containment but assert a feminine poetics of their own. The result is a feminized masculine poetics.

Chapter 1. The Feminization of a Masculine Poetics

1. Leslie A. Fiedler, *Love and Death in the American Novel*, rev. ed. (New York: Dell, 1966), 301; Joel Porte, *The Romance in America: Studies in Cooper, Poe, Hawthorne, Melville, and James* (Middletown, Conn.: Wesleyan University Press, 1969), 22. The seminal study of the Fair Maiden and Dark Lady is Frederic I. Carpenter, "Puritans Preferred Blondes: The Heroines of Hawthorne and Melville," *New England Quarterly* 9 (1936): 253–72.

2. William Wasserstrom, *Heiress of All the Ages: Sex and Sentiment in the Genteel Tradition* (Minneapolis: University of Minnesota Press, 1959), 3; Paul John Eakin, *The New England Girl: Cultural Ideals in Hawthorne, Stowe, Howells, and James* (Athens: University of Georgia Press, 1976), 5. Ernest Earnest, *The American Eve in Fact and Fiction, 1775–1914* (Urbana: University of Illinois Press, 1974), measures the disparity between real American women and their fictional counterparts.

3. Judith Fryer, *The Faces of Eve: Women in the Nineteenth-Century American Novel* (New York: Oxford University Press, 1976).

4. Cynthia Griffin Wolff, "A Mirror for Men: Stereotypes of Women in Literature," *Massachusetts Review* 13 (1972): 218.

5. Judith Fetterley, *The Resisting Reader: A Feminist Approach to American Fiction* (Bloomington: Indiana University Press, 1978), xii. Fetterley, too, sees women as "mirrors for men" which "serve to indicate the involutions of the male psyche with which literature is primarily concerned, and their characters and identities shift accordingly. They are projections, not people; and thus coherence of characterization is a concept that often makes sense only when applied to the male characters of a particular work" (28–29).

Annette Kolodny has also examined the ways "power relations," especially those in which males "wield various forms of influence over females," are inscribed in texts. Specifically, in *The Lay of the Land* she analyzes male writers' identification of the land as feminine and their "pastoral longings both to return to and to master the beautiful and bountiful femininity of the new continent" (*The Lay of the Land: Metaphor as Experience and History in American Life and Letters* [Chapel Hill: University of North Carolina Press, 1975], 139).

6. Joyce W. Warren, *The American Narcissus: Individualism and Women in Nineteenth-Century American Fiction* (New Brunswick: Rutgers University Press, 1984), 4, 17.

7. Jane Gallop, *The Daughter's Seduction: Feminism and Psychoanalysis* (Ithaca: Cornell University Press, 1982), 66.

8. Sandra M. Gilbert and Susan Gubar, *The Madwoman in the Attic: The Woman*

Writer and the Nineteenth-Century Literary Imagination (New Haven: Yale University Press, 1979), 7.

9. Susan Gubar, "'The Blank Page' and the Issues of Female Creativity," *Critical Inquiry* 8 (1981): 247, 244.

10. Judith Montgomery, "The American Galatea," *College English* 32 (1971): 890.

11. Leslie Fiedler, "The Male Novel," *Partisan Review* 37 (1970): 74–89.

12. R. D. Laing, *The Divided Self* (1960; reprint, Baltimore: Pelican, 1965), 46.

13. Roland Barthes, *A Lover's Discourse*, trans. Richard Howard (New York: Farrar, Straus, and Giroux, 1978), 34.

14. David G. Pugh, *Sons of Liberty: The Masculine Mind in Nineteenth-Century America* (Westport: Greenwood Press, 1983), xvii. The women's auxiliary to the cult of masculinity, of course, was the "cult of true womanhood." See Barbara Welter, "The Cult of True Womanhood: 1820–1860," *American Quarterly* 18 (1966): 151–74.

15. John William Ward, *Andrew Jackson: Symbol for an Age* (New York: Oxford University Press, 1962), 193.

16. John Demos, "The American Family in Past Time," *American Scholar* 43 (1973–74): 436.

17. Charles E. Rosenberg, "Sexuality, Class and Role in 19th-Century America," *American Quarterly* 25 (1973): 141, 144.

18. Nancy Chodorow, "Family Structure and Feminine Personality," *Women, Culture, and Society,* ed. Michelle Zimbalist Rosaldo and Louise Lamphere (Stanford: Stanford University Press, 1974), 50.

19. Nina Baym, *Woman's Fiction: A Guide to Novels by and about Women in America, 1820–1870* (Ithaca: Cornell University Press, 1978), 11. John G. Cawelti, *Apostles of the Self-Made Man* (Chicago: University of Chicago Press, 1965), 79. See also Ann Douglas, *The Feminization of American Culture* (New York: Alfred A. Knopf, 1977).

20. Edwin H. Cady, *The Gentleman in America: A Literary Study in American Culture* (Syracuse: Syracuse University Press, 1949), 183.

21. As A. E. Newton put it, "Reserve is the grand secret of power everywhere. Be noble, generous, just, self-sacrificing, continent, manly in all things—and no woman worthy of you can help loving you, in the best sense of the word" (Rosenberg, "Sexuality, Class and Role," 139–40).

22. Laing, *Self and Others* (1961; reprint, Baltimore: Pelican, 1971), 82.

23. Anton Ehrenzweig, *The Hidden Order of Art: A Study in the Psychology of Artistic Imagination* (Berkeley: University of California Press, 1967), 84. Cf. Robert M. Adams's description of "romantic openness, in which the mind strains to remain unresolved before the fullness or magnitude of an experience and will not close form because to do so implies exclusion" (*Strains of Discord: Studies in Literary Openness* [Ithaca: Cornell University Press, 1958], 180).

24. Henri F. Ellenberger, *The Discovery of the Unconscious: The History and Evolution of Dynamic Psychiatry* (New York: Basic Books, 1970), 168.

25. Such a state of inspiration is also very similar to what Carl Jung called the "visionary" mode of creativity, although for Jung such inspiration reflected the workings of the collective unconscious: "While his conscious mind stands amazed

and empty before this phenomenon, he is overwhelmed by a flood of thoughts and images which he never intended to create and which his own will could never have brought into being. Yet in spite of himself he is forced to admit that it is his own self speaking, his own inner nature revealing itself and uttering things he would never have entrusted to his tongue" (Carl G. Jung, *The Spirit in Man, Art, and Literature,* trans. R. F. C. Hull [Princeton: Princeton University Press, 1966], 73). Jung associated creativity with femininity and with the anima archetype. "The creative process has a feminine quality, and the creative work arises from unconscious depths—we might say from the realm of the Mothers" (103). This is not to say that any of the authors in this study directly anticipated Jungian theories, but it is certainly true that they, like many other romantic and post-romantic writers, characterized the creative process as similarly dualistic and associated the state of greatest creativity with unconscious forces. For a Jungian analysis of the American romantics (especially Poe), see Martin Bickman, *The Unsounded Centre: Jungian Studies in American Romanticism* (Chapel Hill: University of North Carolina Press, 1980).

26. Michael Davitt Bell, *The Development of American Romance: The Sacrifice of Relation* (Chicago: University of Chicago Press, 1980), 31, 35.

27. Catharine Stimpson, "Ad/d Feminam: Women, Literature, and Society," *Selected Papers from the English Institute, Literature & Society,* ed. Edward W. Said (Baltimore: Johns Hopkins University Press, 1978), 179.

28. Luce Irigary, "When Our Lips Speak Together," trans. Carolyn Burke, *Signs* 6 (1980): 76–77.

29. Gallop, *The Daughter's Seduction,* 78.

30. Mary Jacobus, "The Difference of View," *Women Writing and Writing About Women,* ed. Mary Jacobus (New York: Barnes and Noble, 1979), 16.

31. Peggy Kamuf, "Writing Like a Woman," *Women and Language in Literature and Society,* ed. Sally McConnell-Ginet, Ruth Borker, and Nelly Furman (New York: Praeger, 1980), 284–99. Although she remains skeptical of the likelihood, Hélène Cixous admits that "the fact that a piece of writing is signed with a man's name does not in itself exclude femininity. It's rare, but you can sometimes find femininity in writings signed by men: it does happen" ("Castration or Decapitation?" trans. Annette Kuhn, *Signs* 7 [1981]: 52).

32. Roland Barthes, *The Pleasure of the Text,* trans. Richard Miller (New York: Farrar, Straus and Giroux, 1973), 14.

33. Roland Barthes, *S/Z: An Essay,* trans. Richard Miller (New York: Farrar, Straus and Giroux, 1974), 5.

34. Barthes, *A Lover's Discourse,* 28.

35. Annette Kolodny, "A Map for Rereading: Or, Gender and the Interpretation of Literary Texts," *New Literary History* 11 (1980): 465, 467.

36. Hélène Cixous, "The Laugh of the Medusa," *New French Feminisms: An Anthology,* ed. Elaine Marks and Isabelle de Courtivron (Amherst: University of Massachusetts Press, 1980), 247.

37. Annette Kolodny, "Some Notes on Defining a 'Feminist Literary Criticism,'" *Critical Inquiry* 2 (1975):78. As she goes on to point out, "What we have not fully acknowledged is that the variations among individual women may be as

great as those between women and men—and, in some cases perhaps, the variations may be greater within the same sex than that between two particular writers of different sexes" (79).

38. See Judith Kegan Gardiner, Elly Bulkin, Rena Grasso Patterson, and Annette Kolodny, "An Interchange on Feminist Criticism: On 'Dancing Through the Minefield,'" *Feminist Studies* 8 (1982): 629–75.

39. Kolodny, "Some Notes on Defining a 'Feminist Literary Criticism,'" 92.

Chapter 2. Poe's Fiction

1. See Joseph J. Moldenhauer, "Murder as a Fine Art: Basic Connections between Poe's Aesthetics, Psychology, and Moral Vision," *PMLA* 83 (1968): 297.

2. Martin Bickman argues that "Poe's female figures should strictly not even be called 'projections,' because the word implies that there is enough of an external person to serve as a reflecting screen. Poe's creations usually exist purely on the plane of what he would call 'ideality' and therefore are less distorting to our view of real women than those of other authors who hopelessly confound their own dreams and fears with the inhabitants of this middle earth" (*The Unsounded Centre: Jungian Studies in American Romanticism* [Chapel Hill: University of North Carolina Press, 1980], 60).

3. Richard Wilbur, "The House of Poe," *The Recognition of Edgar Allan Poe,* ed. Eric W. Carlson (Ann Arbor: University of Michigan Press, 1966), 267, 265.

4. Simone de Beauvoir, *The Second Sex,* trans. H. M. Parshley (New York: Alfred A. Knopf, 1952), 180.

5. Quotations are from *The Letters of Edgar Allan Poe,* ed. John Ward Ostrom, 2 vols. (1948; reprint, New York: Gordian Press, 1966) and are cited in the text.

6. According to Floyd Stovall, Poe's "was a passionate love, but it was generally directed towards an ideal which had its nearest material counterpart in himself; that is why his love for others was so ardent at times, and yet so inadequate. Even among the living women of his acquaintance he loved those most passionately who he fancied were most like himself" ("The Women of Poe's Poems and Tales," *Texas Studies in English* 5 [1925]: 208).

7. Quotations from Poe's fiction are from *The Collected Works of Edgar Allan Poe,* ed. Thomas Ollive Mabbott, 3 vols. (Cambridge: Harvard University Press, 1978) and are cited by volume and page in the text. In "Morella" (1835), Poe's narrator reports, "I felt the consuming thirst for the unknown" and would "listen to the music of [Morella's] thrilling voice, until at length its melody was tinged with terror, and I grew pale, and shuddered inwardly at those too unearthly tones—and thus, suddenly, Joy faded into Horror, and the most beautiful became the most hideous" (2:226).

8. G. R. Thompson, *Poe's Fiction: Romantic Irony in the Gothic Tales* (Madison: University of Wisconsin Press, 1973), 90.

9. Daniel Hoffman, *Poe Poe Poe Poe Poe Poe Poe* (Garden City: Doubleday, 1972), 234.

10. Nina Baym, "The Function of Poe's Pictorialism," *South Atlantic Quarterly* 65 (1966): 54, 52.

11. David Ketterer, *The Rationale of Deception in Poe* (Baton Rouge: Louisiana State University Press, 1979), 28, 36.

12. Also see Richard P. Benton, "Is Poe's 'The Assignation' a Hoax?" *Nineteenth-Century Fiction* 18 (1963): 193–97.

13. Edward W. Pitcher, "Poe's 'The Assignation': A Reconsideration," *Poe Studies* 13 (1980): 2.

14. Daniel Hoffman, "I Have Been Faithful to You in My Fashion: The Remarriage of Ligeia's Husband," *Southern Review* 8 (1972): 103.

15. David Halliburton, *Edgar Allan Poe: A Phenomenological View* (Princeton: Princeton University Press, 1973), 202.

16. As Moldenhauer says, "Before Ligeia's own death, the protagonist had consistently described her in the language of the fine arts (particularly sculpture), revealing that her value resides largely in her loveliness as an aesthetic object, and that his 'appreciation' of her is essentially that of the critic" ("Murder as a Fine Art," 291).

17. Michael Davitt Bell, *The Development of American Romance: The Sacrifice of Relation* (Chicago: University of Chicago Press, 1980), 113, 115.

18. Joseph M. Garrison, Jr., "The Irony of 'Ligeia,'" *ESQ: A Journal of the American Renaissance* 60 (Fall 1970): 15, 16. G. R. Thompson also argues that Poe "develops ironic distance between the reader and narrator"; his "real subject is the delusive madness of his narrator" (*Poe's Fiction*, 81, 82).

19. Evan Carton, *The Rhetoric of American Romance: Dialectic and Identity in Emerson, Dickinson, Poe, and Hawthorne* (Baltimore: Johns Hopkins University Press, 1985), 104. Terence J. Matheson argues that the narrator murders both Ligeia and Rowena because they thwart his efforts to dominate them ("The Multiple Murders in 'Ligeia': A New Look at Poe's Narrator," *Canadian Review of American Studies* 13 [1982]: 279–89).

20. Joel Porte, *The Romance in America: Studies in Cooper, Poe, Hawthorne, Melville, and James* (Middletown, Conn.: Wesleyan University Press, 1969), 67.

21. Eric W. Carlson, "Poe's Vision of Man," *Papers on Poe: Essays in Honor of John Ward Ostrom* (Springfield, Ohio: Chantry Music Press, 1972), 17.

22. Eric W. Carlson, "Poe on the Soul of Man" (Baltimore: Edgar Allan Poe Society and the Enoch Pratt Free Library, 1973), 17–18; Colin Martindale, "Archetype and Reality in 'The Fall of the House of Usher,'" *Poe Studies* 5 (1972): 10.

23. Renata R. Mautner Wasserman, "The Self, the Mirror, the Other: 'The Fall of the House of Usher,'" *Poe Studies* 10 no. 2 (1977): 33. Charles Feidelson, *Symbolism and American Literature* (Chicago: University of Chicago Press, 1953), 41.

24. For a similar view, see John S. Hill, "The Dual Hallucination in 'The Fall of the House of Usher,'" in *Twentieth Century Interpretations of Poe's Fiction,* ed. William L. Howarth (Englewood Cliffs: Prentice-Hall, 1971), 55–62. In an important recent article, on the other hand, Cynthia S. Jordan distinguishes Roderick from the narrator. In her view, Roderick is a "new character in Poe's repertoire, an androgynous spokesperson capable of giving voice to female experience and cri-

tiquing male-authored fictions [such as that by the narrator] which mute that experience" ("Poe's Re-Vision: The Recovery of the Second Story," *American Literature* 59 [1987]: 12).

25. Cynthia Jordan argues that, at the end of the story, while the narrator reads the "Mad Trist," Roderick is successful in "freeing himself of the narrator's control and authoring a second story that explicitly reveals the crime perpetrated against femaleness" ("Poe's Re-Vision," 11). While it is true that Roderick recognizes the sounds of Madeline's breaking out of her vault for what they are, Jordan ignores his terrified reaction to her appearance and Madeline's evident design of revenging herself upon him, rather than upon the narrator.

26. See Richard W. Dowell, "The Ironic History of Poe's 'Life in Death': A Literary Skeleton in the Closet," *American Literature* 42 (1971): 478–86.

27. Patrick F. Quinn, *The French Face of Edgar Allan Poe* (1954; reprint, Carbondale: Southern Illinois University Press, 1957), 264.

Chapter 3. Melville's Early Fiction

1. Gene Patterson-Black, "On Herman Melville," *American Novelists Revisited: Essays in Feminist Criticism,* ed. Fritz Fleischmann (Boston: G. K. Hall, 1982), 116, 113; Charles J. Haberstroh, Jr., *Melville and Male Identity* (Rutherford: Fairleigh Dickinson University Press, 1980), 66; Joyce Warren, *The American Narcissus: Individualism and Women in Nineteenth-Century American Fiction* (New Brunswick: Rutgers University Press, 1984), 115; Ann Douglas, *The Feminization of American Culture* (New York: Alfred A. Knopf, 1977), 355, 357. The best study of male friendship in Melville's fiction is Robert K. Martin's recently published *Hero, Captain, and Stranger: Male Friendship, Social Critique, and Literary Form in the Sea Novels of Herman Melville* (Chapel Hill: University of North Carolina Press, 1986). Although this study and Martin's might seem contradictory on the question of Melville's heterosexual and homosexual interests, I think they are actually complementary. Indeed, many of the subversive tendencies that Martin finds in Melville's male friendships I find in his male-female relationships.

2. Henry A. Murray has noted the "large feminine component" in Melville's personality ("Introduction," *Pierre; or, The Ambiguities* [New York: Hendrick's House, 1949], xliii). Sanford Marovitz has recently catalogued the "feminine" males in his writing: Yoomi in *Mardi,* Harry Bolton and Carlo in *Redburn,* Queequeg in *Moby-Dick,* Pierre and Billy Budd ("Ahab's 'Queenly Personality' and Melville's Art," *Melville Society Extracts* 65 [February 1986]: 6–7).

3. Herman Melville, *Billy Budd, Sailor (An Inside Narrative),* ed. Harrison Hayford and Merton M. Sealts, Jr. (Chicago: University of Chicago Press, 1962), 50, 53; Herman Melville, *Moby-Dick,* ed. Harrison Hayford and Hershel Parker (New York: Norton, 1967), 33, 290.

4. *The Writings of Herman Melville,* ed. Harrison Hayford, Hershel Parker, and G. Thomas Tanselle (Evanston: Northwestern University Press and the Newberry Library, 1968-), 9: 155. Citations appear in the text by volume and page number.

5. Warner Berthoff, *The Example of Melville* (Princeton: Princeton University

Press, 1962), 28. Newton Arvin, *Herman Melville* (New York: William Sloane, 1950), 90. Richard Brodhead, *Hawthorne, Melville, and the Novel* (Chicago: University of Chicago Press, 1976), 123, 131. See also Brodhead's *"Mardi:* Creating the Creative," *New Perspectives on Melville,* ed. Faith Pullin (Kent, Ohio: Kent State University Press, 1978), 29–53.

6. *The Letters of Herman Melville,* ed. Merrell R. Davis and William H. Gilman (New Haven: Yale University Press, 1960), 86. Subsequent citations appear in the text.

7. Barbara Meldrum characterizes Melville's fear of such creative epiphanies as "the loss of a sense of identity . . . because the artist feels driven by a power or being beyond himself and so becomes a stranger to himself" ("The Artist in Melville's *Mardi," Studies in the Novel* 1 [1969]: 464).

8. Leon Howard, *Herman Melville: A Biography* (Berkeley: University of California Press, 1951), notes the relationship between Lombardo and Melville (128–29). Melville even referred to *Mardi* as his "Koztanza."

9. I think Joyce Warren is wrong when she says that the protagonist's attitude toward the "mute enchantress" in the Fragment "is the same attitude that characterizes all of Melville's subsequent writing: woman is a beautiful abstraction, a background figure to be looked upon and revered but not interacted with as an individual. And the less she is heard from, the better" (*The American Narcissus,* 116). In my view, Melville's treatment of male-female relationships grows more complex over the course of his career, at least through *Pierre.*

10. For the actual, as well as literary, sources of many of the incidents in *Typee,* see Charles R. Anderson, *Melville in the South Seas* (1939; reprint, New York: Columbia University Press, 1949).

11. Douglas, *The Feminization of American Culture,* 359.

12. Anderson points out that Melville was inaccurate; Marquesan women were more elaborately tattooed than he allows, although they were not completely covered, as were the men (*Melville in the South Seas,* 150–51). This minor inaccuracy suggests that Melville wished to keep women such as Fayaway relatively pure of the sort of physical transformation symbolized by tattooing.

13. Merrell R. Davis, *Melville's "Mardi": A Chartless Voyage* (New Haven: Yale University Press, 1952), 141.

14. As Howard notes, Melville "addressed perhaps more of his book than he realized to the girl who shared his hopes for it, kept his inkwell filled and his paper in order, and prized the hour at the end of the day when he would read the result of his labors aloud to her" (*Herman Melville: A Biography,* 114). Elizabeth, moreover, apparently enjoyed the role of auditor and she seemed to view herself as more than a mere copyist. She even commented to her stepmother (6 June 1848) that she was reluctant to visit Boston because she was afraid to trust Melville to "finish up" the book without her. *The Melville Log,* ed. Jay Leyda, 2 vols. (New York: Gordian Press, 1969), 1:277.

15. Haberstroh, for instance, argues that "the act is the murder of a powerful male of special status, Aleema, just the sort of individual that Melville in his own life so often resorted to depending on. Aleema . . . is chief priest on the island of Amma, as Lemuel Shaw was Chief Justice of Massachusetts. Melville, the acquies-

cent son-in-law, dreams in the pages of his new novel about a murder that would not only free his narrator's potential bride irrevocably from her 'father,' but would also establish his narrator's own total independence from any male but himself, no matter how strong" (*Melville and Male Identity,* 55).

16. Howard, *Herman Melville,* 116. For the best account of the four characters' roles in *Mardi,* see Davis, *Melville's "Mardi,"* 160–92.

17. As Mildred Travis puts it, "Because of the similarity which Taji sees between Hautia and Yillah and by the dazed way in which he confuses the two women, the reader can infer that they are but two expressions of the same person" (*"Mardi:* Melville's Allegory of Love," *Emerson Society Quarterly* 43 [1966]: 92–93).

18. For example, in a famous letter to Duyckinck (3 March 1849) Melville wrote, "I love all men who dive," and he extolled the "whole corps of thought-divers, that have been diving & coming up again with bloodshot eyes since the world began" (*Letters,* 79). In that latter image, of course, Melville also recognized the high cost of "diving."

Chapter 4. Pierre *and Melville's Later Fiction*

1. Joel Porte, *The Romance in America: Studies in Cooper, Poe, Hawthorne, Melville, and James* (Middletown: Wesleyan University Press, 1969), 173–74. For similar readings see Frederic I. Carpenter, "Puritans Preferred Blondes: The Heroines of Melville and Hawthorne," *New England Quarterly* 9 (1936): 253–72; and R. Scott Kellner, "Sex, Toads, and Scorpions: A Study of the Psychological Themes in Melville's *Pierre,*" *Arizona Quarterly* 31 (1975): 5–20.

2. Judith Fryer, *The Faces of Eve: Women in the Nineteenth-Century American Novel* (New York: Oxford University Press, 1976), 54. Joyce Warren simply dismisses both female characters; *Pierre's* "failure," she informs us, "lies in Melville's absolute inability to portray women" (*The American Narcissus: Individualism and Women in Nineteenth-Century American Fiction* [New Brunswick: Rutgers University Press, 1984], 119).

3. Michael Davitt Bell, "The Glendinning Heritage: Melville's Literary Borrowings in *Pierre,*" *Studies in Romanticism* 12 (1973): 753–54. Barbara Nieweg Blansett, on the other hand, points out that the symbolism of Lucy and Isabel "defies a simple interpretation" because Melville "had progressed to the point of realizing that symbols can no more remain static than can life itself" ("'From Dark to Dark': *Mardi,* a Foreshadowing of *Pierre,*" *Southern Quarterly* 1 [1962]: 220).

4. See Hershel Parker, "Why Pierre Went Wrong," *Studies in the Novel* 8 (1976): 7–23.

5. John D. Seelye identifies Isabel's inspiration of Pierre with Hawthorne's "germinous" effect on Melville: "The incestuous basis of the love between Pierre and Isabel hints at the unnaturalness of the attraction Melville seems to have felt for Hawthorne" ("'Ungraspable Phantom': Reflections of Hawthorne in *Pierre* and *The Confidence Man,*" *Studies in the Novel* 1 [1969]: 439).

6. William Ellery Sedgwick, *Herman Melville: The Tragedy of Mind* (New York: Russell and Russell, 1962), 139.

7. Brian Higgins and Hershel Parker trace Melville's attention to psychological process in *Pierre*, especially the "involuntary character of [Pierre's] thought." See "The Flawed Grandeur of *Pierre*," in *New Perspectives on Melville*, ed. Faith Pullin (Kent, Ohio: Kent State University Press, 1978), 162–96. Also see Joan Magretta, "Radical Disunities: Models of Mind and Madness in *Pierre* and *The Idiot*," *Studies in the Novel* 10 (1978): 234–50. Magretta demonstrates Melville's influence by nineteenth-century interests in the limits of reason and the importance of the unconscious as a source of truth.

8. John T. Irwin, *American Hieroglyphics: The Symbol of the Egyptian Hieroglyphics in the American Renaissance* (1980; reprint, Baltimore: Johns Hopkins University Press, 1983), 320.

9. Edgar A. Dryden, "The Entangled Text: Melville's *Pierre* and the Problem of Reading," *Boundary* 7 (1979): 163.

10. Eric J. Sundquist, *Home as Found: Authority and Genealogy in Nineteenth-Century American Literature* (Baltimore: Johns Hopkins University Press, 1979), 175.

11. Ann Douglas, *The Feminization of American Culture* (New York: Alfred A. Knopf, 1977), 355.

12. Ibid., 375.

13. See, for example, Sandra Gilbert and Susan Gubar, *The Madwoman in the Attic: The Woman Writer and the Nineteenth-Century Literary Imagination* (New Haven: Yale University Press, 1979). They argue that, while the "male child's progress toward adulthood is a growth toward both self-assertion and self-articulation," a "development of the *powers* of speech," the "girl child must learn the arts of silence either as herself a silent image invented and defined by the magic looking glass of the male-authored text, or as a silent dancer of her own woes, a dancer who enacts rather than articulates" (43).

14. Charles Feidelson, Jr., *Symbolism and American Literature* (Chicago: University of Chicago Press, 1953), 194.

15. Douglas, *The Feminization of American Culture*, 373. See also Edgar Dryden, who says that Pierre's "maturity is defined by his decision to abandon one form of literary activity in favor of a more profound one" (*Melville's Thematics of Form: The Great Art of Telling the Truth* [Baltimore: Johns Hopkins University Press, 1968], 132).

16. Leon Howard, *Herman Melville: A Biography* (Berkeley: University of California Press, 1951), 114.

17. In a letter to Evert Duyckinck (12 December 1850) Melville commented that "a book in a man's brain is better off than a book bound in calf—at any rate it is safer from criticism" (*Letters*, 117).

18. Several critics have argued that Melville consistently views Pierre with irony. The most ingenious is Raymond J. Nelson, "The Art of Herman Melville: The Author of *Pierre*," *Yale Review* 59 (1969–70): 197–214. Nelson accounts for the novel's often embarrassing prose by arguing that Pierre himself is the narrator-author of the book. Melville thereby parodies the romantic melodramas he so

detested. Also see Robert Milder, "Melville's Intentions in *Pierre*," *Studies in the Novel* 6 (1974): 186–99. Milder argues that Melville was "in command of his material from the very start—in command of his plot, which did not change substantially as he labored on it, and in command of his complex and ironic attitude toward Pierre, which also did not change" (192–93). While I agree that Melville subjects Pierre and his motives to microscopic scrutiny, I do not think that he simply adopts an ironic stance toward his hero. The novel features a constant tension between authorial distance and involvement, objectification and identification.

19. Newton Arvin, *Herman Melville*, (New York: William Sloane, 1950), 231. Karl F. Knight, on the other hand, argues that *Pierre* "probably is bitter, but Melville's technical experiment with his implied author is a remarkable feat, a confirmation of his faith in 'the literary act'" ("The Implied Author in Melville's *Pierre*," *Studies in American Fiction* 7 [1979]: 172).

20. Warner Berthoff, *The Example of Melville* (Princeton: Princeton University Press, 1962), 54.

21. William Bysshe Stein, "Melville's Eros," *Texas Studies in Literature and Language* 3 (1961): 301; W. R. Thompson, "'The Paradise of Bachelors and the Tartarus of Maids': A Reinterpretation," *American Quarterly* 9 (1957): 39.

22. Edwin Haviland Miller, *Melville* (New York: Persea, 1975), 260. For other discussions of the sexual symbolism of the story, see E. H. Eby, "Herman Melville's 'Tartarus of Maids,'" *Modern Language Quarterly* 1 (1940): 95–100; Richard Harter Fogle, *Melville's Shorter Tales* (Norman: University of Oklahoma Press, 1960), 49–54; Egbert S. Oliver, "Melville's Tartarus," *Emerson Society Quarterly* 28 (1962): 23–25; and Alvin Sandberg, "Erotic Patterns in 'The Paradise of Bachelors and the Tartarus of Maids,'" *Literature & Psychology* 18 (1968): 2–8.

23. Richard Chase, *Herman Melville: A Critical Study* (New York: Macmillan, 1949), 163.

24. William B. Dillingham disputes the assignment of sexual meanings to so many objects in the story. Viewing the "great machine" as a symbol of "universal nature," he sees the maids as mankind "caught in the iron grip of universal laws" (*Melville's Short Fiction: 1853–1856* [Athens: University of Georgia Press, 1977], 202–5).

25. Helmbrecht Breinig analyzes the tale as an investigation of aesthetic issues (The Destruction of Fairyland: Melville's 'Piazza' in the Tradition of the American Imagination," *ELH* 35 [1968]: 254–83). Breinig views the story as a "demonstration of Melville's views on the range and limits of the artistic imagination and on the possibilities of art as epistemology" (254). Dillingham reads the tale as Melville's "search for a radiant savior-friend and his ultimate disappointment"; Marianna is Nathaniel Hawthorne, and the story records Melville's "loss of Hawthorne as a vital force in his life" (*Melville's Short Fiction*, 320, 336).

26. Dillingham views the narrator's return to his piazza more positively, arguing that he achieves a "philosophical stance, a way of surviving for an extraordinary mind," a way to "mediate" between the "security and craven comfort that Melville had spoken of with contempt in *Moby-Dick*" and the "perilous sea of freedom" that "ultimately maddens and destroys" (*Melville's Short Fiction*, 337).

Chapter 5. Hawthorne's Letters and Tales

1. *The Letters of Margaret Fuller,* ed. Robert N. Hudspeth, 4 vols. (Ithaca: Cornell University Press, 1983–87), 3:66, 1:198.

2. *The Recognition of Nathaniel Hawthorne,* ed. B. Bernard Cohen (Ann Arbor: University of Michigan Press, 1969), 10.

3. Hawthorne's female characters have most often been discussed for their light-dark symbolism, with debate centering on Hawthorne's attitudes toward these paired opposites. See, for example, Frederic I. Carpenter, "Puritans Preferred Blondes: The Heroines of Melville and Hawthorne," *New England Quarterly* 9 (1936): 262; Philip Rahv, "The Dark Lady of Salem," *Partisan Review* 8 (1941): 367; Morton Cronin, "Hawthorne on Romantic Love and the Status of Women," *PMLA* 69 (1954): 89, 95; Virginia Ogden Birdsall, "Hawthorne's Fair-Haired Maidens: The Fading Light," *PMLA* 75 (1960): 251; Gloria C. Erlich, "Deadly Innocence: Hawthorne's Dark Women," *New England Quarterly* 41 (1968): 179. Judith Fryer places Hawthorne's characters in three of her four categories: Priscilla and Hilda are "American Princesses," Beatrice Rappaccini, Zenobia, and Miriam are "Temptresses," while Zenobia is a "New Woman" (*The Faces of Eve: Women in the Nineteenth-Century American Novel* [New York: Oxford University Press, 1976]).

4. Quotations from Hawthorne's writing are from the Centenary Edition, ed. William Charvat et al. (Columbus: Ohio University Press, 1962–).

5. Nina Baym, "Thwarted Nature: Nathaniel Hawthorne as Feminist," *American Novelists Revisited: Essays in Feminist Criticism* (Boston: G. K. Hall, 1982), 62.

6. Nina Baym, "Hawthorne's Women: The Tyranny of Social Myths," *Centennial Review* 15 (1971): 258. For more extended comments on individual works, see Nina Baym, *The Shape of Hawthorne's Career* (Ithaca, N.Y.: Cornell University Press, 1976).

7. "It is the other *as a whole* who produces in him an aesthetic vision: he praises the other for being perfect, he glorifies himself for having chosen this perfect other; he imagines that the other wants to be loved, as he himself would want to be loved, not for one or another of his qualities, but for *everything,* and this *everything* he bestows upon the other in the form of a blank word, for the Whole cannot be inventoried without being diminished: in *Adorable!* there is no residual quality, but only the *everything* of affect. Yet, at the same time that *adorable* says everything, it also says what is lacking in everything; it seeks to designate that site of the other to which my desire clings *in a special way,* but this site cannot be designated; about it I shall never know anything; my language will always fumble, stammer in order to attempt to express it, but I can never produce anything but a blank word, an empty vocable, which is the zero degree of all the sites where my very special desire for this particular other (and for no other) will form" (Roland Barthes, *A Lover's Discourse,* trans. Richard Howard [New York: Farrar, Straus and Giroux, 1978], 19).

8. Nancy K. Miller, "'I's' in Drag: The Sex of Recollection," *The Eighteenth Century* 22 (1981): 47–57.

9. "Writing in the feminine," says Hélène Cixous, "is passing on what is cut out

by the Symbolic, the voice of the mother, passing on what is most archaic. The most archaic force that touches a body is one that enters by the ear and reaches the most intimate point. This innermost touch always echoes in a woman-text. So the movement, the movement of the text, doesn't trace a straight line. I see it as an outpouring" ("Castration or Decapitation?" trans. Annette Kuhn, *Signs* 7 [1981]: 54).

10. Nathaniel Hawthorne, *The English Notebooks,* ed. Randall Stewart (1941; reprint, New York: Russell and Russell, 1962), 88–89.

11. Simone de Beauvoir, *The Second Sex,* trans. H. M. Parshley (New York: Knopf, 1952). Woman's "first lie" is "that of life itself—life which, though clothed in the most attractive forms, is always infested by the ferments of age and death . . . It is upon woman's body—this body that is destined for him that man really encounters the deterioration of the flesh" (180–81).

12. Rita Gollin, *Nathaniel Hawthorne and the Truth of Dreams* (Baton Rouge: Louisiana State University Press, 1979), 45, 74. Also see Joseph C. Pattison, "Point of View in Hawthorne," *PMLA* 82 (1967): 363–69. Pattison argues that "Hawthorne is the artist as conscious dreamer, often of dreams that turn into nightmares and bare the tragic realities of human existence" (363).

13. Nathaniel Hawthorne, "Mrs. Hutchinson," *Tales and Sketches,* ed. Roy Harvey Pearce (New York: Library of America, 1982), 23.

14. For an account of Hawthorne's productivity at the Old Manse, see John J. McDonald, "The Old Manse Period Canon," *Nathaniel Hawthorne Journal 1972,* ed. C. E. Frazer Clark, Jr. (Washington: NCR/Microcard Editions, 1973), 13–39. McDonald speculates that Hawthorne wrote "The Birth-mark" in January 1843, "Drowne's Wooden Image" and "The Artist of the Beautiful" between February and May, 1844, and "Rappaccini's Daughter" in October and November of the same year (19).

15. John Crowley calls Hawthorne's publication of twenty-one new tales and sketches between July, 1842, and April, 1845, "an accomplishment equalling the most productive of his earlier years" ("Historical Commentary," Centenary Edition [10: 500]).

16. Judith Fetterley, *The Resisting Reader: A Feminist Approach to American Fiction* (Bloomington: Indiana University Press, 1978), 22–23, 24. Nina Baym cites "Hawthorne's sense that there is a close but unhealthy relationship between artistic and sexual power. Art is an expression of deformed sexuality, for its obsessive fantasy is that of doing harm to a woman. Sometimes Hawthorne represents this deformity as his own oddity, sometimes as his culture's curse, and sometimes as the nature of men" ("Thwarted Nature," 67–68). See also Jules Zanger, "Speaking of the Unspeakable: Hawthorne's 'The Birthmark,'" *Modern Philology* 80 (1983): 364–71.

17. Robert D. Arner notes that Aylmer's story "exactly reverses Pygmalion's, for it ends where the legend began, with a perfect but lifeless idol" ("The Legend of Pygmalion in 'The Birthmark,'" *American Transcendental Quarterly* 14 [1972]: 169–70).

18. As Michael Davitt Bell says, Owen "protects himself from his own impulses through idealistic rationalization," but he is in fact "terrified by reality and es-

pecially by sex; he manages to escape into art and there express his repressed and guilty fantasies in the sublimated, rationalized form of artistic 'beauty'" (*The Development of American Romance: The Sacrifice of Relation* [Chicago: University of Chicago Press, 1980], 138).

19. Hyatt Waggoner, *Hawthorne: A Critical Study,* rev. ed. (Cambridge: Harvard University Press, 1963), 123.

20. Roy Male, *Hawthorne's Tragic Vision* (New York: Norton, 1957), 54.

21. Richard Brenzo, "Beatrice Rappaccini: A Victim of Male Love and Horror," *American Literature* 48 (1976): 157. Kenneth Dauber explains such "swings" between extremes by arguing that the story is "two works simultaneously presented": the story of an innocent girl "destroyed by a faithless love," and the story of a "dangerous woman enticing an innocent boy" (*Rediscovering Hawthorne* [Princeton: Princeton University Press, 1977], 30–31).

22. Frederick Crews emphasizes Beatrice's sexuality, arguing that both she and Giovanni use her "poisonousness as a kind of *double entendre* for what they cannot discuss or even contemplate without fear" (*The Sins of the Fathers: Hawthorne's Psychological Themes* [New York: Oxford University Press, 1966], 119).

23. R. D. Laing, *The Divided Self* (1960; reprint, Baltimore: Pelican, 1965), 52.

Chapter 6. The Scarlet Letter *and* The House of the Seven Gables

1. Michael J. Colacurcio speculates that the two young ladies have been "nurtured on a soft but steady diet of gift books and other ladies' magazines" (*The Province of Piety: Moral History in Hawthorne's Early Tales* [Cambridge: Harvard University Press, 1984], 79).

2. Mark M. Hennelly, Jr., argues that "Hawthorne ironically condemns his prying and perverted Artist-Narrator." The girls' "personal integrity," he says, is "assaulted" by the "illegitimate medium of the Narrator's probing black art" (" 'Alice Doane's Appeal': Hawthorne's Case Against the Artist," *Studies in American Fiction* 6 [1978]: 125, 129).

3. Judith Fryer, *The Faces of Eve: Women in the Nineteenth-Century American Novel* (New York: Oxford University Press, 1976) 78; Joyce W. Warren, *The American Narcissus: Individualism and Women in Nineteenth-Century American Fiction* (New Brunswick: Rutgers University Press, 1984), 192; Carolyn Heilbrun, *Toward a Recognition of Androgyny* (New York: Harper & Row, 1973), 63.

4. I disagree in this respect with Louise K. Barnett, who emphasizes Hawthorne's "confidence in the resources of language to communicate meaning." "That truthful speech occurs so seldom in the novel cannot be attributed to the faulty instrumentality of language but to the nature of the society which language reflects" ("Speech and Society in *The Scarlet Letter,*" *ESQ: A Journal of the American Renaissance* 29 [1983]: 16, 19). Barnett's essay is very perceptive, but I think she places too little emphasis on the *speakers* in the novel (and on their motives).

5. Charles Feidelson, *Symbolism and American Literature* (Chicago: University of Chicago Press, 1953), 9, 10. John T. Irwin examines Hawthorne's use of "multiple

perspectives" as a "major structural element" in the novel: "Hawthorne evokes the relativity of truth to one's perspective through images of objects whose significance radically alters with the changing light" (*American Hieroglyphics: The Symbol of the Egyptian Hieroglyphics in the American Renaissance* [1980; reprint, Baltimore: Johns Hopkins University Press, 1983], 239–43). Also see Millicent Bell's reading of the novel as an "essay in semiology," "The Obliquity of Signs: The Scarlet Letter," *Massachusetts Review* 23 (1982): 9–26.

6. Eric J. Sundquist, *Home as Found: Authority and Genealogy in Nineteenth-Century American Literature* (Baltimore: Johns Hopkins University Press, 1979), 113.

7. Joel Porte calls Pearl a "complex symbolic representation of the sources and attributes of the romance itself—an embodiment of that bond of sex and creativity linking the artist Hester and her lover, the would-be romancer Dimmesdale" (*The Romance in America: Studies in Cooper, Poe, Hawthorne, Melville, and James* [Middletown: Wesleyan University Press, 1969], 106).

8. Terence Martin, "Dimmesdale's Ultimate Sermon," *Arizona Quarterly* 27 (1971): 235.

9. Michel Small, "Hawthorne's *The Scarlet Letter:* Arthur Dimmesdale's Manipulation of Language," *American Imago* 37 (1980): 117, 118.

10. Barnett points out, however, that Dimmesdale's confession is ambiguous. Shifting from the first to the third person in referring to the "one" among them who also bore the scarlet letter, he makes plausible the interpretations of those who see his behavior "not as a deathbed confession of personal culpability but as an emblematic tableau, a last exemplum dramatically rendered by the dying pastor for the benefit of his flock" ("Speech and Society," 21). Dimmesdale, in short, may present himself as a type of sinfulness, but not as a sinner.

11. Terence Martin has noted Hawthorne's joke at the townspeople's expense, evidence of their poor reading ability: "The community has pinned the initial of [Hester's] lover on her breast, then wondered for seven years who he might be" (*Nathaniel Hawthorne,* rev. ed. [New York: Twayne, 1983], 120). And as John T. Irwin comments, "So convincing has Dimmesdale been in the role of the godly minister that he has lost the credibility needed to reveal his own sinfulness" (*American Hieroglyphics,* 253).

12. Ernest Sandeen also views Dimmesdale's effect on the townspeople as ironic. "For the reader knows, as the people cannot, that the creative energy which produced the sermon and sustained Dimmesdale in the pulpit had its source in the lovers' meeting in the forest" ("*The Scarlet Letter* as a Love Story," *PMLA* 77 [1962]: 432).

13. Michael Davitt Bell points out that while both Hester and the scarlet letter "are revived, in the book, as in their first bloom," by the end of the novel "the letter is again on its way to decay and Hester is a corpse" (*The Development of American Romance: The Sacrifice of Relation* [Chicago: University of Chicago Press, 1980], 181). Roy Male, on the other hand, views the heraldic wording of Hawthorne's conclusion as a reiteration of the "symbol into which the whole meaning of the book has been distilled" and thus more positively than I do. He sees in the final word of the novel—"gules"—the "perfect word with which to

conclude the book. It means 'scarlet,' of course, but it originates from the Latin *gula,* meaning 'throat.' Here condensed in one word is the Tongue of Flame; here, joining the language patterns of vision and eloquence, is the perfect capstone for Hawthorne's symbolic structure" (*Hawthorne's Tragic Vision* [New York: Norton, 1957], 117, 118).

14. Quoted in William Charvat, "Introduction," *Centenary Edition,* 2:xvi.

15. Edwin H. Cady, *The Gentleman in America: A Literary Study in American Culture* (Syracuse: Syracuse University Press, 1949), 56.

16. Kenneth Dauber calls it "courtship through story of the kind that won Hawthorne the heart of Sophia Peabody" (*Rediscovering Hawthorne* [Princeton: Princeton University Press, 1977], 142).

17. Frederick Crews reasons that Phoebe possesses the power to purge Holgrave of all inner conflict, but that to "become free of anxiety is to lose all reason for creativity" (*The Sins of the Fathers: Hawthorne's Psychological Themes* [New York: Oxford University Press, 1966], 192). Eric Sundquist, on the other hand, points out that, while Holgrave may forego his seduction of Phoebe through Alice's story, by the end of the novel he has "fulfilled his revenge and taken virtual possession of the Pyncheon property and its owners"—including Phoebe (*Home as Found,* 133). In my view, however, Hawthorne makes it very clear that Holgrave's relationship to Phoebe is not at all possessive.

18. The best analysis of Hawthorne's sensitivity to his readers is Michael T. Gilmore, "The Artist and the Marketplace in *The House of the Seven Gables,*" *ELH* 48 (1981): 172–89. Gilmore argues that Hawthorne's desire to write a salable book conflicted with his desire to be a "private teller of truth" (182); unable to resolve the dilemma, he contrived a happy ending but, in the process, identified himself with the con man, Jaffrey Pyncheon, "the character whom he hated most in all his fiction" (187).

Chapter 7. The Blithedale Romance *and* The Marble Faun

1. Joel Porte, for example, views Zenobia and Priscilla as "opposed personalities," representatives of "sexual truth" and "sentimental deception," respectively, and argues that every "major male character in the book is obliged in some sense to make a choice between the two women" (*The Romance in America: Studies in Cooper, Poe, Hawthorne, Melville, and James* [Middletown, Conn.: Wesleyan University Press, 1969], 133).

2. See Allan and Barbara Lefcowitz, "Some Rents in the Veil: New Light on Priscilla and Zenobia in *The Blithedale Romance,*" *Nineteenth-Century Fiction* 21 (1966): 263–75. To Judith Fryer, Priscilla has "no identity of her own" and is in all respects a "depressing and devastating portrait of woman in the nineteenth century" (*The Faces of Eve: Women in the Nineteenth-Century American Novel* [New York: Oxford University Press, 1976], 93).

3. Nina Baym, *The Shape of Hawthorne's Career* (Ithaca, N.Y.: Cornell University Press, 1976), 190.

4. Mary Schriber, "Justice to Zenobia," *New England Quarterly* 55 (1982): 68.

Some critics believe that Coverdale has his revenge. John Harmon McElroy and Edward L. McDonald even convict him of murdering Zenobia because she repeatedly scorned his love-making; see "The Coverdale Romance," *Studies in the Novel* 14 (1982): 1–16. Beverly Hume agrees but emphasizes the narrative strategies Coverdale employs to confess and conceal his crime, "Restructuring the Case against Hawthorne's Coverdale," *Nineteenth-Century Fiction* 40 (1986): 387–99. While I find the case against Coverdale compelling, I am more interested in the effect Zenobia or her memory has on Coverdale's imagination and his narrative—in the way Hawthorne "feminizes" Coverdale's narrative by incorporating Zenobia's presence and story.

5. Not surprisingly, Coverdale's sexual attraction for Zenobia has received much emphasis. Donald Ross views the central plot of the novel as Coverdale's "discovery and subsequent repression of his sexual desire for Zenobia" ("Dreams and Sexual Repression in *The Blithedale Romance*," *PMLA* 86 [1971]: 1014). See also Frederick Crews for an analysis of Coverdale's "erotic furtiveness" (*The Sins of the Fathers: Hawthorne's Psychological Themes* [New York: Oxford University Press, 1966], 205).

6. Gustaaf Van Cromphout considers Zenobia a "rudimentary incarnation of the androgynous ideal," although he goes on to argue that Hawthorne's treatment of her "betrays his lack of sympathy with feminist aspirations" ("*Blithedale* and the Androgyne Myth: Another Look at Zenobia," *ESQ* 18 [1972]: 142, 144).

7. Hélène Cixous, "The Laugh of the Medusa," *New French Feminisms: An Anthology,* ed. Elaine Marks and Isabelle de Courtivron (Amherst: University of Massachusetts Press, 1980), 251.

8. Ross comments that "Coverdale disguises a socially unacceptable phenomenon, fleshly nudity, behind an acceptable image, the statue, thereby alleviating the tension of his desire for Zenobia" ("Dreams and Sexual Repression," 1014).

9. Claire Sprague, "Dream and Disguise in *The Blithedale Romance*," *PMLA* 84 (1969): 596.

10. Kenneth Dauber has also compared Zenobia's flower to Hester's letter, arguing that, unlike the letter, "which takes Hester outside herself," Zenobia's flower "is Zenobia. It enacts her without expanding her" (*Rediscovering Hawthorne* [Princeton: Princeton University Press, 1977], 189).

11. Schriber, "Justice to Zenobia," 69.

12. Schriber questions the common view that Zenobia commits suicide, attributing that conclusion to Coverdale's limited imagination. Even if the death *is* a suicide, she maintains, the motive might well be despair at "woman's lot" rather than unrequited love ("Justice to Zenobia," 76). In fact, Hawthorne's long notebook entry on the incident that suggested this scene (the drowning of a Miss Hunt) offers a clue to motivation. "I suppose one friend would have saved her," he speculated; "but she died for want of sympathy—a severe penalty for having cultivated and refined herself out of the sphere of her natural connections" (8:266). Hawthorne's explanation need not suggest unrequited love nor imply that women, anymore than men, can be happy only in relationship; it might easily suggest the failure of others to offer the "sympathy" that every individual needs.

13. Zenobia's effect on Coverdale's imagination is no less dazzling than Miss

Hunt's on Hawthorne's. Recounting the discovery of the drowned woman's body on 9 July 1845 (his third anniversary), he emphasizes its horrible rigidity, which, he says, is beyond words: "it is impossible to express the effect of it; it seemed as if she would keep the same posture in the grave, and that her skeleton would keep it too, and that when she rose at the day of Judgment, it would be in the same attitude" (8: 264).

14. For discussions of Hawthorne's use of the artistic background of Rome, see Paul Brodtkorb, Jr., "Art Allegory in *The Marble Faun*," *PMLA* 77 (1962): 254–67; Gary J. Scrimgeour, "*The Marble Faun:* Hawthorne's Fairy Land," *American Literature* 36 (1964): 271–87; Spencer Hall, "Beatrice Cenci: Symbol and Vision in *The Marble Faun*," *Nineteenth-Century Fiction* 25 (1970): 85–95; and especially Rita K. Gollin, "Painting and Character in *The Marble Faun*," *ESQ* 21 (1975): 1–10.

15. Nina Baym sees Miriam as "another representative of passion, creativity, and spontaneity" that "must be accepted if man is to do her justice and grow to his own fullest expression," and she attributes Kenyon's collapse as an artist to his estrangement from Miriam's experience (*The Shape of Hawthorne's Career*, 236).

16. Fryer, *The Faces of Eve*, 66.

17. Porte, *The Romance in America*, 139.

18. Robert Brooke discusses the way this and other works of art described in the novel frustrate easy interpretation. "Many of the discussions of art objects in the romance develop through the counterpointing of several characters' perceptions of an object, all arising from different perspectives" ("Artistic Communication and the Heroines' Art in Hawthorne's *The Marble Faun*," *ESQ* 29 [1983]: 82). In Brooke's view, Hawthorne thereby questions the communicative power of art.

19. Jonathan Auerbach observes that Hawthorne divides aesthetic media in the novel along gender lines: sculpture "provides a cold, masculine medium," whereas painting is a "warmer, softer, feminine medium" ("Executing the Model: Painting, Sculpture, and Romance-Writing in Hawthorne's *The Marble Faun*," *ELH* 47 [1980]: 106, 107).

20. Millicent Bell, *Hawthorne's View of the Artist* (New York: State University of New York Press, 1962), 168.

21. Baym, *The Shape of Hawthorne's Career*, 245.

22. Kenyon's vision of a marital tomb unwittingly echoes a wish Hilda had expressed earlier. Contemplating a picture by Guercino at St. Peter's of a maiden's body in the "jaws of the sepulchre" (4: 352), Hilda wishes, "by some miracle of faith, so to rise above her present despondency, that she might look down upon what she was, just as Petronilla in the picture looked at her own corpse" (4: 353). Clearly, Kenyon will help make her wish come true.

Conclusion

1. *Emerson in His Journals*, ed. Joel Porte (Cambridge: Harvard University Press, 1982), 304.

2. Margaret Fuller, *Woman in the Nineteenth-Century* (New York: Norton, 1971), 115–16.

INDEX